BEIJING
FROM
BELOW

BEIJING FROM BELOW

*Stories of Marginal Lives
in the Capital's Center*

HARRIET EVANS

Duke University Press   *Durham and London*   2020

© 2020 Duke University Press
All rights reserved
Printed and bound by CPI Group (UK) Ltd, Croydon, CR0 4YY
Designed by Drew Sisk
Typeset in Portrait Text by Westchester Publishing Services

Library of Congress Cataloging-in-Publication Data
Names: Evans, Harriet, author.
Title: Beijing from below : stories of marginal lives in the capital's center /
Harriet Evans.
Description: Durham : Duke University Press, 2020. | Includes bibliographical
references and index.
Identifiers: LCCN 2019041829 (print)
LCCN 2019041830 (ebook)
ISBN 9781478006879 (hardcover)
ISBN 9781478008156 (paperback)
ISBN 9781478009184 (ebook)
Subjects: LCSH: Urban poor—China—Beijing—Social conditions. | Marginality,
Social—China—Beijing. | Urbanization—China—Beijing. | Economic development—
China—Beijing. | Neighborhoods—China—Beijing—History—21st century. |
Beijing (China)—Social conditions—21st century. | Beijing (China)—Economic
conditions—21st century.
Classification: LCC HT384.C62 . B455225 2020 (print)
LCC HT384. C62 (ebook) | DDC 305.5/690951156—dc23
LC record available at https://lccn.loc.gov/2019041829
LC ebook record available at https://lccn.loc.gov/2019041830

Cover art: *Chai*, the "awful mark" of demolition. Dashalar, Beijing, China, 2010.
Photograph by Harriet Evans.

For the people of Dashalar,
with affectionate gratitude for all they taught me,
and in fond memory of Zhao Tielin (1949–2009)

CONTENTS

Figures

Maps

By the time I was completing this book in early 2018, the circumstances of most of those I had known since 2007 had changed, and Dashalar no longer resembled the neighborhood with which I was familiar. I therefore decided to use the past tense in narrating my friends' stories.

The full value of the characters for *Dashalar* is *Dashanlan*. Tourist websites tend to use *Dashilar* or *Da Zha Lan*. In previous publications I have used *Dashalanr*, but here I prefer *Dashalar* as a compromise between the phonetic value of the characters and local oral usage.

Dazayuan is variously translated as "compound courtyard," "big messy courtyard," "big, mixed courtyard," "tenements," or "slums." I use Wu Liangyong's "big cluttered courtyard," from his *Rehabilitating the Old City of Beijing*, out of respect for an architect who designed a model for the conversion of Beijing's dazayuan into modernized structures that retained a feel of the traditional courtyard.

All those who appear in this book wanted me to use their real names. However, I have preserved their anonymity due to the ongoing political sensitivity around the state's program of urban regeneration. The pseudonyms I have created combine characters from local people's names, some phonetic or semantic element from their "real" name, and the term of address I used with them. The only exception is Jia Yong, whose identity I have decided to retain, given his prominence as a local businessman and photographer.

All direct quotations as transcribed from my recordings or based on my field notes appear in quotation marks or indented paragraphs.

The chapter headings are mostly named after the head of the household in question. This includes chapter 2, named after the eldest woman of the household. Even though in local cultural custom, her gender meant that she could not be acknowledged as "household head" (*jiazhang*), she enjoyed a local reputation as the key figure maintaining the unity of her family.

Unless noted otherwise, translations from archival and recorded materials are my own. XWDG is my abbreviation for Xuanwu qu dangan (Xuanwu District Archives).

In the early summer of 2004, I had long conversations with Beijing anthropologist friends about the difficulties of conveying to young students a sense of the extraordinary intensity, pace, and reach of the changes engulfing Beijing in recent decades. I began to toy with the idea of developing a new research project tracing the transformation of a single district. One friend then introduced me to Zhao Tielin, who since 1997 had been compiling a photographic record of the everyday lives of the long-term residents—"typical old Beijingers"—of Dashalar, a small popular neighborhood just south of Tian'anmen Square that I had visited once in the 1970s but about which I knew virtually nothing. Zhao was one of a kind: loud, full of laughter, a heavy smoker and drinker, always on the side of the down-and-out. He took me to meet several of his friends in Dashalar whom he described as typical "old Beijingers"—born in, grew up in, or married into the neighborhood.

Mostly only minimally educated, Zhao's Dashalar friends were living a hand-to-mouth existence, picking up menial, short-term jobs where they could. Some were unemployed and earned money as unlicensed pedicab cyclists; others, particularly the women, worked long hours as cleaners in local restaurants, or as domestic help. They lived in crowded rooms in the "big cluttered courtyards" (*dazayuan*)—former brothels, native-place associations, and mansions that since the 1920s, and particularly the 1950s, had been divided up and filled in with single-room dwellings to accommodate the capital's growing population.[1] By 2004, it seemed that the extraordinary transformation of Beijing in the previous two decades or so had virtually passed them by. They all had electricity and television but no washing facilities or hot water and only a small stove burner that served as their kitchen, sometimes placed in the common space of the courtyard and shared with neighbors. Few of them knew much about life outside the capital. One, the son of a Hui man who was a mobile street vendor of meat (lamb), had been sent to the Great Northern Wilderness as a sent-down youth in 1967. There he was stripped of his urban registration. Without the connections to enable him to return to Beijing, he spent three decades in a small, desperately poor village in the northeast, where he married a local woman, before finally managing to return to Beijing with his wife in the early 1990s. The wife of one local man visited Hong Kong as part of a group tour in 2010; most of those I knew, however, had rarely if ever left Beijing. Only one of those I met had made good and, as a well-established local restaurateur and photographer, had ample resources to be able to travel, both in China and abroad.

Zhao and I hit it off, and although at the time I had no clear idea about what might come of my visit to the neighborhood, Zhao welcomed me as his "collaborator" when introducing me to his local friends. Over more than five years, together with his research assistant, Huang Mingfang, we made numerous visits to those I first encountered in 2004 and to many more. Mingfang and I continued to visit them after Zhao passed away in 2009. Slowly, as I got to know them better, I became clearer about the themes that would underpin my research project.

My work on the project was suddenly interrupted by a near-fatal illness in early 2015, postponing completion of the book. However, once I returned to it in late 2016, it was as if, imperceptibly, unconsciously, all sorts of ideas had worked themselves out, making the final stages of writing much easier and more pleasurable than I had anticipated. Moreover, the Dashalar I was familiar with had been almost entirely gentrified, marking a physical, spatial, and social closure to the research interests inspiring this volume. In all, the timing of the completion of this book has come at a fitting moment.

The people of Dashalar who made this book possible welcomed me into their homes repeatedly between 2007 and 2014, patiently putting up with my faltering attempts to understand their jokes and anecdotes. Over time, I developed a growing awareness of the immense privilege they gave me, enabling me to share aspects of lives and experiences to which few researchers, Chinese or not, have had access. Their generosity in this gave me unanticipated and wonderful opportunities to reflect on how people strive to live decent, considerate, and ethical lives in everyday conditions of scarcity, social discrimination, and extreme hardship. This is something I shall always treasure, so I first want to acknowledge their place in my life as well as in this book.

For the initial opportunity to conduct this research, I owe a huge debt of gratitude to the late Zhao Tielin, a courageous photographer who was committed to recording the everyday lives of some of China's most deprived people, including those he introduced to me in Dashalar. Zhao's capacity to listen and empathize gave me my first real lessons in oral history. His death in 2009 brought an end to his intention to publish his photographic history of everyday life in Dashalar. *Beijing from Below* is not a substitute for what would have been his, but it does affectionately and gratefully honor his memory. I also owe warm thanks to Zhao's research assistant, Huang Mingfang, who continued to accompany me on my neighborhood visits after Zhao passed away.

The British Academy and the Universities' China Committee in London funded short research trips at the beginning of this project. Funds from the University of Westminster's Department of Modern Languages and Cultures in part funded others. Generous grants from coREACH and the Leverhulme Trust encouraged me to think about Dashalar locals' responses to the heritage reinvention of "old Beijing."

Many people helped me over the years I was working on this project. In the first place, I thank Shen Yuan and Jing Jun for introducing me to Zhao Tielin. Zhou Xun inducted me into the complexities and pleasures of archival research in the early stages of my research and accompanied me on some of my early visits to Dashalar residents. She also helped with some of the transcriptions of my first recordings. Invitations to discuss my ongoing research at seminars and workshops gave me welcome opportunities to think through questions of methodology and theory: Simon Gunn at the University of Leicester, Maria Jaschok at Oxford University, Laura Bear at the LSE, Paul Basu and Beverley Butler at UCL, Jeffrey Wasserstrom at UC Irvine, Stevan Harrell and Gonçalo Santos at the Max Planck Institute, Janet Carsten at the University of Edinburgh, Susanna Brandstätter at Cologne University, Rebecca Karl at NYU, Gail Hershatter at UC Santa Cruz, and Liu Jieyu at SOAS. Correspondence and conversations with Judith Farquhar, Erik Mueggler, Steve Smith, and Yan Yunxiang shed light on many issues. Zhang Lisheng and Luo Pan provided invaluable help by keeping me up to date with developments in Dashalar since I was last there in 2017. Conversations with friends and colleagues—especially Felicity Edholm, Stephan Feuchtwang, Raj Pandey, Peter Guangpei Ran, Mike Rowlands, and Sanjay Seth—were as stimulating as they were pleasurable. Chris Berry inspired the title of the book. Rebecca Karl and Gail Hershatter read the entire manuscript and pushed me to tighten up various arguments and ideas. Any remaining gaps and imperfections are my own responsibility.

Work completing this book was interrupted in early 2015 by a near-fatal illness, after which it took me some time to get down to unfinished business. I thank my brothers Richard and Mark; my sister-in-law, Sarah Jane; and my ex-partner, John, for traveling to Hong Kong from distant places during the first critical stages of my illness. I also thank my stepson, Hans, for helping to circulate email correspondence to keep friends far and wide informed about my progress. There are also many other dear people whose support gave me the confidence to be able to emerge from my illness to complete this book. I regret that I cannot name you all due to limits on word length, but you know who you are. I thank you all.

While I was in the hospital in Hong Kong, I had the good fortune to be treated by Dr. Yiu Wah Fan, whose skill and humanity enabled me, my family, and close friends who were with me in Hong Kong to pull through the first challenging stages of my illness. More recently, I also owe heartfelt gratitude to SF Studios and to Sebastian Hicks in particular for helping me recover a sense of fitness and well-being as I was finishing this book and for identifying the synergies between my attempts to find a new physical balance in my life and my efforts to complete this project.

I thank Grant Dommen's team at Snappy Snaps near my home in Kentish Town, Camden, for patiently digitizing numerous versions of maps for me before I decided on my final selection for this book. I particularly thank Ken Wissoker, Joshua Tranen, and Jessica Ryan for their efficient and speedy support in bringing this book to the light of day. It has been a great pleasure to work with them.

But most of all, the emotional resilience and loving support of three people—my daughters, Bec and Gabe, and my former PhD student, Guangpei—gave me the determination to see this project through.

The spectacular speed and extent of the post-Mao transformation of Beijing's landscape is a familiar theme in commentary on China's global "rise." Beijing's architectural icons—the CCTV tower, the Opera House, Galaxy SOHO Beijing, the National Art Museum of China, and more—share a global visual language structuring a vision of the capital as the stunning pinnacle of China's global might. This vision is accompanied by a flourishing nostalgia industry producing huge quantities of soft-focus photographs of picturesque courtyards, authentic "old Beijing" objects, reprints of old maps, and stories of "old Beijing" customs, all lamenting the loss of Beijing's winding lanes and alleys—the *hutong*—to shopping malls and gated compounds catering to the property-owning middle class and the ex-pat elite.

Ignoring activist and media commentators' exposure of urban residents' difficulties in having to relocate from familiar neighborhoods to new periurban apartment blocks, and silencing lawyers who attempt to support urban residents' resistance to demolition of their homes, Beijing's new brand marshals its spaces alongside the teleological rhythms of progress orchestrated by the urban planners and property speculators.[1] In late 2017, a brutal effect of this process was the forcible eviction from the capital of large numbers of migrants—those whose labor has produced Beijing's spectacular transformation.[2]

Behind such oppositional descriptions of Beijing's transformation not much is known about the vast numbers of working-class Beijing inhabitants whose lives have been turned upside down by this process. While research on Beijing and Shanghai in the 1920s and the Republican era has produced rich descriptions of the lives of the urban poor, it is only recently that studies of urban change in communist China have begun to address the lives of the urban underclass.[3] During the Mao era, restrictions on conducting fieldwork and accessing archival materials, combined with an overriding media, academic, and official emphasis on the revolutionary transformations of working-class life under the state "work unit" (*danwei*) system, effectively prevented acknowledgment of the existence of an urban underclass. The dominant wisdom of the time was that the urban working class was entirely absorbed into the work unit system. A notable exception was Janet Weitzner

Salaff's prescient analysis of household-based urban residents' committees, in which she argued that in comparison with the danwei-based organization of urban residents, urban dwellers such as housewives, unemployed youth, and retired workers were organized under the residents' committees in the neighborhoods in which they lived.[4] The consequent limitations on such urban residents' daily interaction with others, in contrast with workers and professionals formally employed in the danwei system, meant that they were not so effectively integrated into small and controllable groups. Without structural social ties that could compete with their bonds of kinship, their basic loyalty was to the family.

Throughout the 1950s, vast construction projects were launched throughout the capital, involving massive demolition and the relocation of local neighborhood populations.[5] Some of these, particularly those associated with the conflict between the conservationists and the Chinese Communist Party's new leadership in the decision to locate the new government in the former heart of the old city, are well known.[6] The "Ten Great Buildings" constructed between 1958 and 1959 were huge projects involving massive investment, large-scale demolition of old buildings, and the relocation of their residents.

Among those most immediately affected by the disruption caused by these projects were the urban poor living along the sides of Tian'anmen Square before it acquired its current shape. Vast numbers of impoverished Beijing residents who had survived the effects of war, hunger, and destitution in the 1930s and 1940s now found themselves at the mercy of the new government in its bid to transform their neighborhoods into monumental celebrations of the victories of the Chinese Communist Party under its leader. The flagship pair of the "Ten Great Buildings" was the massive Great Hall of the People and the Museum of History, facing each other on the east-west axis of Tian'anmen Square.

The contrast between Tian'anmen Square's forgotten foundations of demolition and dislocation and its emerging presence as the center of a global power compelled my attention when I visited Dashalar, a small and dilapidated neighborhood just southwest of Tian'anmen Square, in 2004. I was taken there by Zhao Tielin, a Beijing photographer who since 1997 had been compiling a photographic record of everyday life in this poor neighborhood. I recall the visual shock of seeing Mao's mausoleum in the near distance, just a stone's throw north of Dashalar. Although I did not know it at the time, the disturbing architectural, spatial, and social juxtaposition between the ramshackle poverty of the neighborhood and the monumental austerity and symbolic might of Mao's mausoleum and Tian'anmen Square anticipated the story of contrasts of power and poverty in the history of "old Beijing" that my research would bear witness to.

This book moves away from the big picture of Beijing's transformation to focus on a specific neighborhood and its disadvantaged residents, the capital's subalterns—the underclass—at the bottom of the social hierarchy, the unemployed and semiemployed outside the formal organizational structures of the work unit system, living hand to mouth on the fringes of the law as street vendors or unlicensed pedicab cyclists. In 2004, most of those who appear here still lived in the crowded courtyards—the *dazayuan*, or "big cluttered courtyards"—where they were brought up or into which they married.[7] Other local residents had already moved to the far outskirts of the city, some taking advantage of the local government's early offer of incentives to those willing to move.[8] Most of the children of those I knew were no longer living in the neighborhood.

The stories narrated in this book share memories of hardship, family fragmentation, struggles and strategies for family survival, sadness, anger and loss, cooperation, loyalty, violence, sickness and death, and occasional pleasure. Together, they span several decades, going back to the 1920s, but their main temporal focus is on the years of the People's Republic (PRC) since the 1950s. Their individual stories converge in common experiences of precarity, scarcity, determination, and resilience, folded into a sense of ethical living. They reveal conditions of deprivation long before the polarizing socioeconomic effects of China's embrace of global capitalism. Indeed, the evidence they give of significant socioeconomic differences among the urban population unsettles the view that there was relatively little urban economic differentiation during the Mao era, and that everyone ate out of the same "iron rice bowl." They imply that the common assumption that socioeconomic differentiation in China is a product of the marketization of the economy, in contrast with the "egalitarianism" of the Mao years, is too simplistic a rendering of a much more complex picture of the 1950s through the 1970s.[9] An oral history of daily life in a disadvantaged neighborhood in Beijing since the early years of the Mao era offers a more nuanced view of history. It does not, as I discuss below, offer an "alternative" and "more truthful" account of Beijing's transformation, but it does give an indication of how history is necessarily multiple.

This book emerged from a desire to understand how nonelite, working-class people in Beijing have accommodated the relentless pace and scale of change in their everyday lives in recent decades. How has the transformation of family and neighborhood, implemented through successive political campaigns, altered their sense of home, belonging, and neighborhood? What memories of childhood and growing up do they hold on to when the physical and social spaces of those memories have been destroyed? How do they transmit those memories to their children when the material evidence sustaining them has disappeared? And what do these memories tell us about the capital's revolutionary transformation?

As my research progressed, I realized that it was only by getting to know local people over time that I could hope to answer these questions. A standard oral historical approach consisting of recorded interviews and life histories was not going to work. The people I knew were not accustomed to verbally reflecting on their lives, and the social and physical circumstances of their daily lives, living in very crowded conditions with lots of noise and people coming and going, made it impossible to imagine being able to record individuals' reflections without extensive interruptions. The result, in this book, is a series of sketches of local lives, which tell a largely subaltern story of Beijing's recent history. In directing a new lens to the social and cultural history of China's capital over the past half century or so, these sketches invite us to think about that history in hitherto unexplored ways.

Memory, the Subaltern, and History

> In their rememberings are their truths.
> The precise fact or precise date is of small consequence.
> —STUDS TERKEL, *HARD TIMES*

Memory is a crucial theme in this book, as it is in any oral history. Memories are articulated by their narrators in specific circumstances and for specific purposes. Far from telling the "truth" of the past, the shifts and occlusions of memory suggest a constant and selective reworking of the past to make sense of the present. Moreover, memories and their associated narratives do not stay still; they may point to a single event but describe it through different dates, places, and people, muddling temporal and spatial boundaries, corresponding with and/or contradicting the main time lines of hegemonic chronology. As Gail Hershatter put it, "Every memory is also a creation—not necessarily a whole-cloth invention (although there are also those), but a product of the confluence of past events and present circumstances" and always revised by or refracted through others' accounts of the same past.[10] The memories contained in individuals' oral narratives may also be reproduced as crucial elements of their narrators' sense of identity, of being a full person in the world. This is particularly the case when for their narrators those memories are all that are left of the only world they knew.

The state's program of "demolition and relocation" (*chaiqian*) launched around Dashalar since the early 2000s has been a process of physical, spatial, and social erasure of local lives such as those I describe in this book. Between 1990 and 2004, some half a million households were relocated in Beijing under a radical development strategy premised on a causal link between demolition of old housing and the creation of demand for new commodity housing.[11] In an evident process of gentrification, this strategy initially targeted other wealthier neighborhoods of "old Beijing." But as chaiqian approached Dashalar, younger residents began to move out. By 2014, some 60 to 70 percent of the people living in Dashalar were from outside Beijing. By 2017, even fewer long-term local residents were still there. Within the space of less than ten years, chaiqian, combined with the arrival of "outsiders" (*waidiren*), had completely transformed the social, spatial, and physical feel of the neighborhood. Capturing the memories of those who still lived there throughout this period was thus crucial to be able to record the importance of place in shaping local lives long after the physical traces of that place had disappeared.

Most of the memories contributing to the stories I narrate in this book are those of middle-aged and older people. This was the result in part of my interest in tapping into memories of change in the neighborhood since the early years of the PRC. It was also because few of the offspring of my acquaintances in Dashalar continued to live there. Given the opportunity through work or marriage, most young people I knew of had left the neighborhood, returning only for family celebrations. I was thus unable to discover much about young people's responses to their elders' tales of past hardship. Indeed, my impression—corroborated by their elders' comments—was that few wanted to hear their elders' stories of woe; maybe they'd heard them too often, and/or had other priorities shaped by their own existential needs.

The stories of neighborhood life in this book reveal memories and experiences that are necessarily singular, shaped by the specific circumstances of family life and personal history. But while they are personal accounts, they are simultaneously social, because they intersect with multiple sources, associated with the various groups with which the individual interacts.[12] Moreover, as "a form of knowledge that is appropriated as a truth for that person and transmitted as such," the individual memory transcends the boundaries of personal experience and becomes enmeshed in a collective, though not necessarily public, memory of neighborhood, place, and space.[13] Even so, there is no necessary congruence between memory as "individual truth" and the larger group, let alone between individual memory/truth and its public presence.[14] Indeed, the individual stories I narrate in this book are not publicly accessible.

My acquaintances' individual stories reveal powerful, intersecting memories of hardship and precarity, yet it is only through the kind of attention a book like this gives them that they can become materials of history.

Long ago, in *A Shared Authority*, the social and urban historian Michael Frisch argued that oral history is "a powerful tool for discovering, exploring and evaluating the nature of the process of historical memory—how people make sense of the past, how they connect individual experience and its social context and how the past becomes part of the present, and how people use it to interpret their lives and the world around them."[15] It is particularly powerful for bringing to light the forgotten, overlooked, ignored, or repressed subjects of history—those at the margins of society and only tenuously associated with the hegemonic institutions of power, those to whom we could loosely refer as the subalterns of history. Without revisiting the debate about the classic question concerning the accessibility of the subaltern to the historian, I nevertheless want to affirm that the subaltern is always constitutive of history, even if in modes of expression—in traces—that are neither apparent in dominant historiographical narratives nor totally accessible to the researcher.[16] Juxtaposing the subaltern oral narrative and history "writ large" gives us the opportunity to analyze the tensions and overlaps between the two, through marking the key moments, events, and temporalities of subaltern experiences distinguishing them from those of the elite. My analysis then is not primarily shaped by a hermeneutical impulse to fill in a gap in the historical record; nor does it follow—indeed, it cannot—the subaltern experience on its own terms, defined by a subaltern subjectivity. However, the terms of subaltern experiences are never entirely immune to the normalizing discursive effects of big history. Attending to the subaltern's disturbance of hegemonic power, as narrated in big history, invites us to reflect on how the system of power is challenged from within by agents who refuse to succumb to its controls. Thus, far from seeing the subaltern as beyond and inaccessible to possibilities of representation by the researcher, I prefer to think of subalternity as a discernible trace *within* the dominant system yet resistant to complete appropriation by it. In Gyan Prakash's words, "Subalternity erupts within the system of dominance, but only as an intimation, as a trace of that which eludes the dominant discourse. It is this partial, incomplete, distorted existence that separates the subaltern from the elite. This means that the subaltern poses counterhegemonic possibilities not as inviolable otherness from the outside but from *within* the functioning of power, forcing contradictions and dislocations in the dominant discourse."[17]

The lives of the subaltern subjects of my study, as anywhere, are powerfully shaped by the shifting forces of politics and the political economy, apparent in common experiences of social and economic disadvantage, and in shared terms of identification as members of the social "underclass" (*shehui diceng*), disdained and neglected by the elite.[18] In the specific history of twentieth-century China, which they both inherit *and* constitute, their shared experiences range from fatalistic resignation to angry resentment against a state system that they see as trapping them in conditions of everyday precarity. They only occasionally make direct reference to the state—"them up there" (*shangmian*) is the standard term used—and rarely narrate their own histories within the temporal frameworks of official discourse. While the party-state has been and continues to be the hegemonic force shaping their material and social conditions of existence, the separation between their terms and temporalities and those of dominant discourse makes language and temporality an important site where the relationship between the urban poor and the elite is played out. Seen in this light, the stories of my Dashalar narrators offer important insights into the entanglements between subaltern lives and state power.

The Official Archive, Oral Narrative, and Ethnographic Knowledge

This book is the result of a combination of different methods: of archival research, oral history, and the ethnographically based practices of anthropology, which together grant rich insights into more than six decades of everyday life in Dashalar. My ethnographic understanding of the places and people my subaltern narrators describe grounds their stories in the spatial, social, affective, sensory, and ethical dimensions of lives that neither the archive nor words alone can convey. Their stories enrich the archival detail about local neighborhood life—such as occupations and incomes, conditions of health and hygiene, educational levels, food shortages, and housing. In turn, this kind of archival detail sheds helpful light on the oral testimony and its references to space, place, time, event, and feeling. Let me explain what I mean here by discussing how I understand the relationship between my acquaintances' narratives, my long-term familiarity with their neighborhood, and the archive.

At first glance, the chronological and thematic organization of the local Xuanwu District archives (which contribute most of the archival material I draw on in this book) closely corresponds with the main contours and rhythms of China's dominant, official history, with what Hershatter calls "campaign time."[19] A 1990s introductory survey on Chinese archives suggested that they "reflect the changes in social life since 1949."[20] Far from "reflecting" changes in social life, however, the publicly available materials in the Xuanwu District archives reveal the party-state's attempts to order its subjects according to a grid of legibility designed by the central authorities to underwrite their claims to implement progressive policy.

Nowhere are these claims more apparent than in the selection of and gaps in the archival materials available to the researcher. Made publicly available by the district government in 1980, the gaps clearly correspond with the political sensitivities of the government, which was keen to avoid difficult issues. Hence, there is little evidence about the effects on either the district or the neighborhood of the Three Antis (Sanfan) and Five Antis (Wufan) campaigns of 1951–52 to eradicate corruption, embezzlement, and waste in urban enterprises and bureaucracy.[21] Given the large number of entrepreneurs operating in the neighborhood around the time of Liberation and immediately afterward, one could reasonably anticipate that these campaigns were not inactive in Xuanwu District. Nor are there references to the policies to nationalize private enterprise (*gongsi heying*), which a number of my acquaintances mentioned as a key moment in their memories of the 1950s. While there were not inconsiderable references to the collective canteen experiment in the early stages of the Great Leap Forward (1958–59), and to difficulties kindergartens faced in finding enough food for their children, there was little indication of the overall extent of the shortages affecting local neighborhood families during the famine years. There was a total absence of reference to the destructive violence of the Red Guards in the district during the early Cultural Revolution. Such gaps and absences make these archives no more than a highly fragmented record of local social and economic life.[22]

Alongside such gaps, detailed attention to names, addresses, dates of birth, gender, and ethnicity appears in local social surveys on issues such as housing, substantiating the existence of the human subjects to which the survey data refer. Yet the ideological and disciplinary interests apparent in the selection, organization, and language of the archive generally abstract the subaltern subject as an unwelcome statistic, pejoratively described under the generic term "social problems" (*shehui wenti*). Under this category, fractious workers employed on low wages in small local factories appear as irrational irritants, "antisocial" elements, thorns in the side of the local government and requiring disciplinary measures as a condition of integration into the system.

Nevertheless, these materials contain much detailed and painstakingly written information—handwritten, and replete with crossings-out and ink smudges—about housing conditions, wages, rations, conditions of work, children's nutritional health, clothing, and so on, that adds important data to our understanding of neighborhood life in Dashalar. A tone of despair emerges in a brief letter written in March 1973 by the Street Revolutionary Committee of

8

Dashalar, pleading with the Xuanwu District Revolutionary Committee for funds to repair a primary school's toilets and build a flushing toilet *inside* the school's courtyard. The same letter also pointed out that the night soil collectors did not regularly clean out the toilets, increasing children's exposure to potentially serious hygiene and health problems.[23] Another document written by the Xuanwu District Committee for the Movement of Patriotic Hygiene (Xuanwu qu aiguo weisheng yundong weiyuanhui) noted the improvements in local people's attention to litter in Dashalar, where past tendencies to dump litter and leave coal anywhere had led to environmental hazards in the form of big heaps of coal and rubbish.[24] The same committee also recorded the numbers of households in Dashalar in which poison had been put down to kill rats, along with the numbers of rats that had been killed.[25] Detailed monthly handwritten tables recorded the numbers of children in each of Xuanwu District's nurseries and kindergartens affected by different kinds of illness or health issues, including lung complaints, colds, and digestive problems.[26] Occasional references to individuals who had a "stubborn attitude," who "did not observe work discipline" and went around saying "bad things," depicted individuals' use of language and behavior in ways that could easily have described some of the people I knew in Dashalar. For example, in early 1961, a former prostitute, age forty-six, whose husband was a drug addict, and who complained about the cotton and grain rations, was recorded as saying, "What the hell can you make with two inches of cloth? I might as well come to work naked . . . or with a cloth over my front and a bare bum." When her leader criticized her for her attitude by reporting her to the head of her small work group, she retorted, "You are a small pig so I suggest if you have anything to report then go to the big pig."[27] I laughed out loud as I read this: it corresponded so closely with the character of one of my Dashalar acquaintances, also a former prostitute, whose story I narrate in chapter 4. This report was one of a series of documents about problems that arose during the "communist wind" (*gongchan feng*) of the Great Leap Forward. It referred to the financial pressures created by 10 percent of the 3,416 workers in the thirteen factories in Dashalar commune, who were "old, infirm and sick, disabled or had onerous domestic responsibilities"—in other words categories of people who could well have resembled the older family members of those I introduce in this book.[28]

All such data, and more, including the number of beds each dazayuan household had and the number of households where three generations had to share the same bed, offer important archival evidence of the messy poverty and lack of hygiene of the neighborhood, particularly at the height of the famine between 1959 and 1961. During these years, there were numerous documents submitted by the Women's Federation and the Dashalar People's Commune about food shortages in nurseries, malnutrition, and local people's attempts to supplement their meager rations by searching for wild plants in the suburbs. A short September 1959 document from a local branch of the Women's Federation praised a kindergarten in a Dashalar hutong for improving itself by changing its political outlook and "relying on the masses." But the initial summary of the problems the kindergarten had faced before this was devastating. It described an environment of chaos and filth, with untrained nursery personnel dealing with the toddlers as if they were "herding sheep," no one discussing what they were doing, personnel completely uninterested in their work, dirty bowls and dishes all over the place, and no attention to kids' sicknesses.[29]

These examples reveal the official record of the fractures in the state's attempts to administer its subjects within its own standardized categories of legibility. James Scott, in his *Seeing Like a State*, argued that across different ideological persuasions, the modern state's schemes to implement social engineering programs to improve the lives of its peoples—whether in the form of modernist urban planning or Soviet collectivization, to name but two examples—failed, largely because they ignored local, practical knowledge (métis) and regarded their subjects as "far more stupid and incompetent than they really were." However, as Scott argued, the informalities of local practices are essential to maintenance of the center's plans. The plan can thus never work according to its own logic because of the inevitability of divergent local practices. While nearly all of the documents noted above, as official records of the state, contain formulaic repetition of official policy rhetoric, they also give detailed attention to "the particular, situated, and contextual attributes of the local population" that constantly interfere with the center's plans.[30] The archival examples above belong to moments of the past predating the memories of most of my Dashalar friends, but the insights into local life they reveal repeatedly surfaced in locals' conversations with me about the government's long-term neglect of the dilapidated congestion of the neighborhood. In this sense, far from entirely excluding the subaltern residents of Dashalar, this archival evidence illuminates and substantiates their narratives.

My long-term familiarity with Dashalar and its residents offered me a spatial, material, and sensory knowledge of the neighborhood that brought to life the detail of the written archive. Observing how people used the spaces of their dazayuan and nearby lanes, witnessing shouting matches between neighbors and the local patrol officers, or coping with the stench of local public toilets all constituted situated practices that set a real-life scene for understanding archival and oral references to overcrowded housing, complaints about the poor condition of public services, and local residents' obstinate refusal to bow down to the dictates of the state. Alongside the individual oral narrative, my familiarity with the neighborhood and its people has permitted a kind of intertextual reading of the relationship between the archive and lived experience that reveals the state's attempts—and its limited ability—to absorb the subaltern within its own disciplinary project.[31]

Paul Thompson, whose work established him as one of the pioneers of the use of life stories and oral history in social science research, wrote that "oral evidence, by transforming the 'objects' of study into 'subjects,' makes for a history which is not just richer, more vivid and heart-rending, but truer."[32] According to this line of thinking, and with reference to China's recent history, local experiences narrated by subjects themselves that diverge from official claims may emerge as the source of the "true" history of China's revolution and the collective repository of evidence exposing the lies of the party-state. This may well apply, for example, to the oral evidence about the great famine in China.[33] Yet the relationship between the oral/local and the official/archival is much less clear than such an oppositional argument suggests. To elucidate this relationship demands disentangling various issues, such as fissures in state interests, whose "truth" counts as more truthful, and connections between campaign and neighborhood time.

It is also necessary to point out that the Xuanwu District archives do not reveal a single unified voice conveying the local authority of an all-powerful single-party state. On the contrary, they reveal the struggles of the different branches of the district government—the poorest of Beijing's municipal districts—to find ways to cope with impossible conditions of crowding and scarcity. On the one hand, these struggles could take the form of submission to higher levels of government for assistance and support, as I have noted above. On the other, they could correspond with tense exchanges between the Dashalar neighborhood committee and the Xuanwu District party secretary. It is even possible to read potential conflicts of interest into some of the relevant archival evidence. For example, the repeated appearance within a few weeks of more or less the same letter urging a response from the higher authorities to neighborhood concerns about lack of funding may be read as evidence of various issues, including the authorities' negligence, overwork, and lack of human resources, and silence as a response to not knowing how to deal with the enormous pressures on resources at the time. The archival detail thus reveals tensions and divisions within state interests as well as fluctuating connections between neighborhood and official concerns.

The key events structuring Dashalar locals' recollections may on the surface have had little to do with the main events of campaign time, as recorded in the archives. Their memories were articulated in a language that rarely echoed either the terms or the temporalities of official discourse. Although its main institutions are only a stone's throw away from their neighborhood, the central party-state barely figured in local people's narratives. Leaders' names occasionally featured, but the "state" appeared only in the vague form of a higher authority—"them up there" (*shangmian,* literally "above")—or in the personified form of local government officials and their henchmen—the police and patrol officers.

However, silence about the party-state in local people's narratives should not be romanticized as resistance to party-state authority.[34] On the one hand, it could, of course, be interpreted as the enactment of agency in the form of a diluted kind of everyday subversion, apparent in deliberate exclusion or feigned ignorance of the authorities' policies, indicative of a recalcitrant detachment from the terms of dominance. It could be seen as a kind of "hidden transcript" giving silent voice to resentment against state power.[35] On the other hand, the entanglements between neighborhood lives and state interests over time just as importantly traced shifting contours of complicity with and fatalistic acceptance of officialdom. Most importantly, however, to read into their silence a distance from the state is to ignore the government's constitutive influence over long decades on the lives of those to whom the archival record implicitly refers. The political interests privileged in the archival record have been major factors shaping local residents' conditions of existence ever since 1949. The individual oral narrative and the official archival record therefore need to be read as distinctive, mutually constitutive, and contradictory parts of a multiply layered history that incorporates both, not simply revealing the truth of the one against the other but also shedding light on both and their conflictive interaction over time.

My attempt, then, in this book, is to try to make sense of Dashalar residents' singular memories and experiences of their pasts to trouble a historical narrative from which they have been absented. Their testimonies and their lives give evidence of an understanding of time and event that departs from the progressive vision of history that dominates the historiography of the PRC. My aim is to interrogate what historical knowledge is, to explore subaltern lives as a strategy of "thinking at the limit" of history, as the great postcolonial cultural studies thinker Stuart Hall put it, through engaging with the stories of individuals who do not appear as agents in the archive or in mainstream history, and by asking how narrating their stories contributes to a fuller, more complex understanding of the past evoking different possibilities and truths.[36]

This oral history of Dashalar does not give evidence of the disastrous effects of a particular campaign or policy, nor does it focus on identifying how local people subverted political authority. Calamity, precarity, suffering, subversion, and resistance all have their part to play in local neighborhood knowledge of China's recent past. Attention to the temporalities structuring local residents' memories of the past, to how their everyday lives and ordinary experiences and understandings, including ethical understandings, have been shaped by the places they inhabit, and to how their social, economic, and cultural activities have at the same time been inseparable from the formation of those spaces offers glimpses of subaltern experiences of change and the fissures between the policies directing change and their implementation at neighborhood level.[37] The temporalities and spatialized memories and accounts of my Dashalar acquaintances invariably diverge from those of dominant historiography, and for their narrators, they certainly do reveal their truth of the past. Yet in the broader terms of historiography, they do not have the prerogative to a single "truthful" ownership of the past. Rather, they complicate our understanding of that past in ways that the institutional and political powers sustaining dominant historiography occlude. They compel a view of history that is multiple.

Methodological Choices

I had to make difficult choices in researching and writing this book. I was aware of the sensitive nature of the project from the outset when I started my research with Zhao Tielin. Across the country, the government's chaiqian strategy had long generated extensive criticism and protest, within China and abroad.[38] Following criticisms of the heavy-handed methods used to implement this policy, official pronouncements began to emerge about the need to reduce the use of coercive methods. Nevertheless, local protests continued, and the individuals involved were routinely harshly treated.

Official accounts of the state's plans to transform Dashalar and its immediate environs were explicit in referring to the difficulties involved, due to the neighborhood's long history of congestion, poverty, and social disadvantage.[39] Demolition of adjacent neighborhoods was accompanied by a high level of state surveillance, and local journalists were routinely prevented from taking photographs.[40] "Interpersonal relationships" (renji guanxi) in the crowded alleys of Dashalar were—and remain—complex and fraught, and Zhao cautioned me to adopt a careful approach to what I said, where, and to whom, so as not to encourage local rivalries and tensions. To begin with, the people I met politely treated me as Zhao's collaborator, and if initially curious about why I, a foreigner, was interested in their lives, they soon seemed relatively unconcerned about my status as a foreign researcher. All were aware that they were to feature in Zhao's intended publication about Dashalar, and they welcomed his project to "tell the truth" of their lives.[41] After his death, they saw me as his successor and were encouraging and supportive of my research. One claimed me as her "friend" who was putting her center stage in writing about her life. She also started sharing details with me about her intimate life in ways that were very different to how she had been accustomed to talk in Zhao's presence. Financial expectations followed in some cases, inflecting my research in ways I had not anticipated. I had to confront the realization that I was seen—at least by some—as a wealthy foreigner whose presence offered the opportunity to make life a bit easier. To be so clearly confronted with the imbalance in the relationship between privileged researcher and disadvantaged "informants" made me feel intensely discomforted.[42] However, my growing familiarity with individuals' family and personal circumstances sometimes revealed a generosity of spirit that went far beyond the etiquette of hospitality expected of attitudes toward the foreigner. In some instances, I had to observe activities and listen to conversations about matters that were the source of shame and humiliation to those involved. In trying to find a narrative path through the complex needs, aspirations, and emotions of the people whose stories I tell here, I have tried to be as respectful as I can of what they shared with me, omitting some things when I know that to publicize them would cause unease and a sense of shame, if not anger. The fact that my local friends will not be able to read this book seems poor excuse for including references that I know they would rather exclude.[43]

Ou Ning's documentary film *Meishi jie* offered important insights into the potential difficulties caused for local people who protested against the authorities' plans. The film focused on the early stages of transformation of the neighborhood, when the famous Meishi Street, along the north-south axis, was being widened, involving extensive demolition of houses and shops. The film's record of the forcible demolition of a house, along with many media reports about local people's responses to forcible relocation in neighboring districts, paints a clear picture of the disciplinary methods the state's law enforcement agencies used in order to impose their chaiqian plans.[44] Over the years there have also been various reports about local people's responses to forcible relocation in neighboring districts. On one occasion, a local journalist told me about the example of a woman in an adjacent district, who refused to leave her dazayuan as required in the local chaiqian plans. After weeks of holding out in what the media increasingly called an example of the *dingzi hu* (nail house), she was eventually left with no alternative when the emergency services all turned up together to evict her: the police to order her out; the fire brigade in case she set fire to her house rather than leave; the ambulance in case she attempted to commit suicide; and the lawyer to keep a record of the proceedings.[45]

The people I knew in Dashalar were not involved in any organized attempt to thwart the state's plans; during the years of my research there, there was little evidence of local interest in overt protest, in contrast with Qin Shao's revelations about Shanghai and media reports about local protest in other areas of Beijing.[46] Nevertheless, given the sensitivity of local chaiqian in Dashalar, and following Zhao Tielin's advice, I had to be cautious about how and with whom I talked about the neighborhood's recent transformation. I decided not to approach the local neighborhood committee offices, since to do so would have called direct attention to my presence and could have potentially jeopardized my relationship with local people, as well as complicate things for them. Some of my friends were quite nervous about how my relationship with them might attract the attention of local authorities. It is possible that nothing untoward would have happened had I attempted to contact the local neighborhood committee. Nevertheless, given my position as a foreign researcher, I decided not to do so, to avoid scrutiny of my work and of my acquaintances. While my decision to limit my research in the local archives to the district level leaves omissions from my account of local neighborhood life, the district archives' inclusion of many neighborhood committee documents was more than adequate for my purposes, given my primary focus on local people's perspectives.

People in Dashalar were routinely cynical about local lawyers' efforts to represent people who wanted to resist government eviction and demolition orders. Their cynicism was eventually borne out by the experience of the only individual I met who decided to go to court to assert his rights over his courtyard home. This was an elderly man, already in his eighties, who as a former opera singer had been sent to Xinjiang in the anti-rightist movement of 1957. On his return to Beijing in the 1990s he had taken up residence in a small courtyard house not too far from Dashalar that had belonged to his ancestral family. One of his neighbors was a lawyer who decided to take on the local government when it issued a demolition order. Needless to say, without leasehold papers proving the elderly man's family's ownership of the property, the court ruling was upheld.

Fig. I.1 Old courtyard on borders of Dashalar due for demolition, 2011.

In carrying out this project I have borrowed mainly from history and anthropology. Much as I approach the archival and personal account as different dimensions of a shared past, so I use the methodological techniques of the oral historian and the anthropologist to enrich each other's findings. Few of the personal narratives I relate here derive from the standard life story interview. Rather, the stories I narrate are compilations drawn from many conversations held in local restaurants and the homes of my acquaintances. Spending time with them in repeated visits over many years gave me the opportunity to observe their comings and goings, witness family quarrels, heartache, and reunions, and to acquire some understanding of their neighborhood relationships. If my understanding of the temporalities—time frames—their memories revealed emerged in large part from their narratives, my understanding of the importance of place in their lives—how their everyday activities and relationships over time gave meaning to that place, and how, in turn, the physical spaces of that place shaped their choices, activities, and relationships—emerged more from observation.

Going through my field notes and listening to the transcripts of my recorded conversations with Dashalar people has yielded rich material, flashes of wisdom, and a powerful sense of ethics. It has also provided evidence of my own changing relationship with local people. One cliché about long-term ethnographically based research is that it grants the researcher the opportunity to develop increasingly trusting relationships with her research subjects. This by no means happened with everyone during my research in Dashalar. Even toward the end of my research there and in conversations with those I knew best, there were evident silences and gaps, about people, events, and periods about which, for whatever reason, my interlocutors chose not to talk or maybe simply didn't remember. Some topics remained difficult to broach. Few talked about the Cultural Revolution, and only two mentioned the events of May and June 1989, despite their spatial proximity to Tian'anmen Square. I repeatedly reminded myself that here, as elsewhere in China, no public space or place of commemoration of these events and their victims is allowed.[47] Without access to events or places of public catharsis, local families' losses and hardship had long been contained behind the walls of their dazayuan homes, occasionally erupting in angry assertions of their rights to be treated as proper people, or internalized in abject states of depression, as I describe in the chapters that follow.

Structures, Stories, and Themes

It took me a long time to find a satisfactory narrative structure for my material. If from a sociological perspective my acquaintances in Dashalar mostly belonged to the same class category, their narratives revealed considerable differences not only in family circumstance but also in how they negotiated a livable life in conditions of precarity and scarcity. These differences were revealed not only in their material conditions of existence but also in their interests, cultural references, and use of language. I therefore wanted to use as much direct quotation from their narratives as possible, in order to give the reader some of the flavor of these differences. After considering different possibilities, I eventually decided to devote each chapter to the story of a particular family. Building on this, the "solution" I finally came up with was inspired by Susan Mann's wonderful work *The Talented Women of the Zhang Family*. While I had long admired this book, its focus on elite households and literary texts did not make it an obvious choice for me to consult in my attempts to find an appropriate structure for my work. But conversations with fellow historians convinced me to look afresh at Mann's revisionist application of the historiographical approach of the great Han historian Sima Qian, who viewed his task as a historian as a way of bringing to life "people from the past with their feelings, words, and deeds intact."[48] Once I decided to investigate this as a possibility, it became increasingly attractive as a way of incorporating my analysis with my interlocutors' memories in a way that could respect the singularity of the narrative style each of them used. Accordingly, the main chapters of *Beijing from Below* combine descriptive narrative with direct quotations from the transcripts and my field notes. The interludes that follow each of the main chapters offer brief analytical discussions of the main themes that emerge from the previous family story.

The main body of the book, then, consists of stories of local lives, put together on the basis of numerous conversations, some recorded, some not, held over many years. All of them, in different ways, center on Dashalar, as a place and symbol of belonging and marginalization. Chapter 1 traces the history of Dashalar's "reconstruction" over the past half century or so to set the spatial, material, and sensory scene for the memories and experiences I narrate in subsequent chapters. Each subsequent chapter is devoted to a single family, mainly narrated by one or two members. The sequence of the family stories combines attention to chronology, in order to convey a sense of the shifts over time in everyday family life in the neighborhood, with local people's self-positioning in relation to the state and market. I start with the oldest people I knew, who had lived in the neighborhood the longest. Then, given that most of my interlocutors were born between the late 1950s and early 1960s, I follow up with a sequencing based on people's view of their relationship to the state and the market. The last two chapters move from those for whom the state, implicitly or explicitly, signified as a negative and even oppressive entity to those in a position to benefit from it, finishing with the only born and bred local individual I knew who had unequivocally benefited from both the Mao era privileging of the industrial working class, *and* from the marketization of the economy since.

Each main chapter contains many direct quotations, of varying lengths. The result is that some chapters contain much more direct narrative than others. I have many recordings and detailed field notes for all the stories I relate in these chapters. However, my decision in some of them to reproduce sometimes lengthy quotations is based in part on the decipherability of my recordings and the verbatim precision of my notes, but more importantly on my desire to convey a sense of how the people in question talked about their lives, and how their narrative style offered clues about how they related to their worlds and concerns—in other words, to their subjective sense of being a person in specific and changing circumstances.

Again, following Susan Mann, my decisions about structure and narrative in these main chapters are my attempt to bring people to life in their own terms.[49] The discussion in the intervening interludes conveys my summaries of what I see as the main topics, historical, conceptual, and theoretical, that emerge from the chapter in question. Chapter 2 leads to a discussion about an elderly woman's agency in turning the bitterness of her past into a source of moral strength acknowledged by her family and near neighbors, and her son's abject self-recrimination for failing to live up to the moral standards associated with being a supportive son and husband. Some of these themes resurface in chapter 3, but the strategy of survival developed by its main character, Zhao Yong, was to transcend the mundane material issues of everyday life by talking about "big" political and universal issues. The strong and impressive woman character in chapter 4 presents us with a paradox of an independent-minded woman, well able to depend on her own resources to sustain her own and her daughter's livelihood, but who at the same time saw dependence on a man as key to her own and her daughter's material and emotional security. Chapter 5 tells the story of the only migrant family I knew in the neighborhood, and the daunting obstacles to survival faced by those even more disadvantaged than the local residents. Tracing a couple's determination to make enough money to support their children's education, and particularly their son's, this chapter exposes the devastating existential despair for parents when their son does not to live up to their expectations of his filial support. The couple in chapter 6, in considerable contrast, reveals a family history that, despite one individual's physical disability and terrible trauma experienced during the Cultural Revolution, generated access to cultural capital and material conditions of modest comfort, as compared with those of the families in the earlier chapters. Chapter 7 tells the story of the only local person I knew who benefitted both from the status of his parents during the Mao era as stably remunerated industrial workers, and from his own personal talent in exploring his social and political connections to his own entrepreneurial advantage. Each story highlights themes particular to that family's experience and touches on themes shared—in different ways—by others. In each I address the particular modality of agency exemplified by the individuals in question, to build up an argument about agency and recognition that departs from the emancipatory liberal ethos associating individual autonomy with subversion of the dominant order.

In the concluding chapter, I return to develop some of the key conceptual and theoretical issues raised in this introduction, but with reference to the main themes elucidated by the main chapters. I structure these in a sequence of arguments, starting with questions concerning what Dasha-lar people's stories reveal about memory, temporality, and place, weaving themes about gender and family into experiences of precarity and oppression, and linking them into what I understand as the modalities of my acquaintances' enactment of agency and their ethical claims for recognition as social subjects. Taken together as subaltern narratives of real, living people whose experiences are integral to Beijing's recent past, they demonstrate that history is multiple and multilayered and cannot be reduced to a single truth or temporality.

I

Dashalar

Most of the people I knew in Dashalar were born and grew up there or nearby, or had lived there since getting married and having children. The dazayuan and the nearby lanes where they lived were where they—particularly the elderly and unemployed—spent most of their time. Their dazayuan homes and the immediate vicinity were thus focal centers of sociality, informal employment, and social identification. In physical, spatial, social, and cultural terms, the neighborhood of Dashalar was, literally, the place bounding the everyday lives and social relationships of my acquaintances. At the same time, acted out in the material and social spaces of the neighborhood, my acquaintances' everyday lives constituted Dashalar as a particular place with its characteristic sounds, sights, and smells.

Over the decades spanned by the narratives of my neighborhood friends, Dashalar suffered from virtual stagnation—meaning "no progressive change"—characterized by overcrowding, minimal sanitation, scarcity, and hardship, from the early years of the Mao era to the present: through the state allocation of housing and employment, near destitution during the Great Leap Forward and the terrible famine that followed (1958–61), the extremes of Red Guard violence in the early years of the Cultural Revolution (1966–69), on into the 1980s, with its faltering steps toward the market economy, and then into Beijing's full-scale engagement with global capital. While the archival record indicates repeated attempts to improve conditions of life and employment in the neighborhood, particularly in the 1950s, throughout the Mao era they came to very little, as I indicate below.

After the 1990s, and particularly since China's ascendance to global center-stage status with the Olympics of 2008, the pace of change around Dashalar accelerated, with the conspicuous polarization of wealth and poverty under policies of state-supported privatization, and an increasing awareness on the part of local residents of their disadvantage in the stakes of market competition.[1] Far from corresponding with the official narrative of rupture—the great "turning point"—between the Mao and post-Mao reform periods, local residents' experiences reveal material and spatial conditions of existence that were barely altered, let alone transformed, by either revolutionary or reform regimes, spanning both the Mao and post-Mao eras.[2] Indeed, the crowded and chaotic living conditions in the neighborhood throughout the 1950s and 1960s were only marginally better than those of Beijing in the 1920s, described by David Strand.[3] Into the 1990s and 2000s, local residents acknowledged considerable improvements in their diet but without much accompanying sense of material or existential security. As one of my friends put it in July 2009, "We may have a bit more to eat, but we are not at ease [xinli bu'an]." Housing continued to be as cramped as before, and most dazayuan had only cold water, not infrequently from a shared faucet. Some people shared cooking facilities with other households. Without even basic sanitation or heating, their living conditions had barely changed since their childhoods. When change did arrive in the hutong near the homes of those I knew, it was shocking in its pace and intensity: it occurred not gradually through progressive improvements but drastically and suddenly under the program of urban demolition, relocation, and regeneration as it gathered speed in the neighborhood in the years leading up to the 2008 Olympics.[4]

In what follows, I take the reader back through time to situate the Dashalar of today within the recent history of government attempts to transform it.

A Brief Visit to Dashalar

Dashalar is a small neighborhood of about 1.26 square kilometers just outside the former inner-city walls, southwest of Qianmen.[5]

Its main street runs east to west and is intersected by Meishi Street on the north-south axis. Historically part of the outer city, and locally known as "South City" (Nan cheng), it is also often referred as the "eight big lanes" (ba da hutong).[6]

A stone's throw from the Forbidden City at the north end of Tian'anmen Square, between the late Qing and early Republican eras (roughly between the 1870s and the 1930s), Dashalar was known for its opera singers, teahouses, and prostitutes; it was where court personnel went to indulge their pleasures, where aspiring literati stayed as they prepared for the imperial examinations, and where many Han officials lived, barred from living in the inner city by the Manchu government's segregationist laws.[7] It was also a place where itinerant merchants from outside the capital crossed paths with beggars and the down-and-out hoping to make a living from the vibrant melee of people traversing the neighborhood.

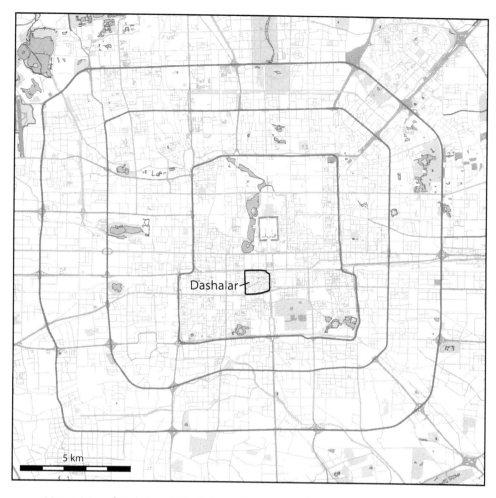

Map 1.1 Map of Dashalar within Beijing's three ring roads.

Dashalar has long been one of central Beijing's most densely populated and poorest neighborhoods, with a mixed and mobile population of Han, Manchu, and Muslim people. The report on Beijing's "urban corners" in 2005 noted that it had a population of 57,551, with a density of 45,000 people per square kilometer, more than double that of other inner-city areas, with many families living in rooms of less than ten square meters.[8] The same report also noted that some 90 percent of the 2,950 courtyards (*dazayuan*) in the ten single-story communities (*shequ*) of Dashalar were categorized as "dilapidated

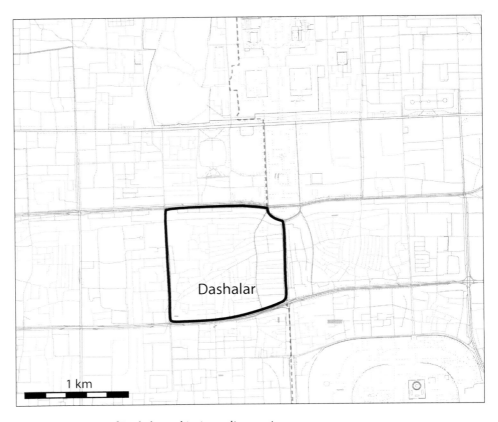

Map 1.2 Map of Dashalar and its immediate environs.

housing" (*weijiu fangwu*).[9] 30 percent of the local population was classified as "masses in difficulties" (*kunnan qunzhong*).[10] Nearly a fifth of the population was a "migrant population" (*liudong renkou*).[11]

In recent years the main streets of Dashalar have had a complete makeover. Tourist websites now brand it as the epitome of "old Beijing"—a "commercial city with 600 years of history."[12]

The first-time visitor to Dashalar today would encounter a range of delights, from the old-style feel of its refurbished artisan shops to the competitive prices of its merchandise to its "traditional" architecture and the neat, clean spaces of its pedestrian walkways. Lining the two sides of Dashalar's main street—now named Dashalar Commercial Street (Shangye jie)—are famous stores with names that date back to commercial establishments first set up a century or more ago.[13]

Fig. 1.1 Dashalar's commercial heritage reinvention as "old Beijing," 2007.

Their gray brick facades recall the somber style of the late Qing, early Republican era, when the neighborhood was home to popular theaters and opera houses, artisan shops, native place association lodges (*huiguan*), brothels, and numerous small eateries.[14] Some of the shops are massive, announced by pillars, porticos, magnificent balustrades, ornamental balconies, and big character signs painted in gold displaying their names above the doorway. The street also offers leisure activities, such as the local opera for which the neighborhood used to be famous. In contrast with the expensive boutique concept of other gentrified neighborhoods of "old Beijing," catering to the urban and foreign elites, such as Nanluogu xiang, Dashalar's Commercial Street exudes a decidedly down-market feel. Bona fide artisan specialists are difficult to find. In their place, what are described as "authentic old Beijing" artisan wares— silk, cloth shoes, knives, combs, tea, and Chinese medicine—sell at prices that announce their quality as "cheap goods and fakes."[15] Many local people made similarly disdainful remarks about the fake artisan goods on sale in the neighborhood. Open shop fronts invite shoppers in to sift through display

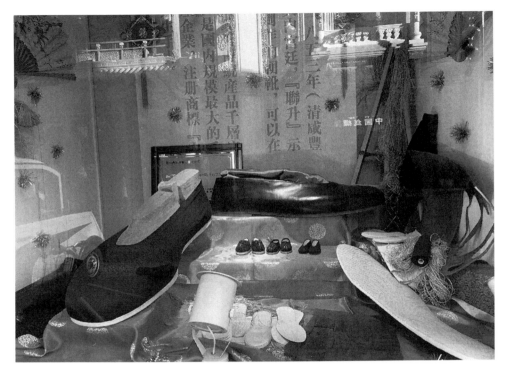

Fig. 1.2 Recent window display of Nei Lian Sheng, 2018. Courtesy of Luo Pan.

compartments packed with colorful cosmetic bags, back scratchers, key rings, soft toy pandas, beads and fans, and much more. Tourists used to stop to have their photograph taken in front of statues of cloth-capped, long-gowned "old Beijing" men sitting at a low table playing chess.[16] The famous shoe shop Nei Lian Sheng displays a giant "old Beijing" black cotton-soled shoe in one of its windows. The entrance to Da Guan Hall (Da Guan Lou), the first commercial cinema in Beijing, reveals a wide sweeping staircase lined with photographs of film stars of the pre-Liberation years.[17]

At night, the dull gray hues of the daytime street give way to bright reds and yellows emanating from the street lamps and the red lanterns hanging in front of the main shops. There are no cars, bikes, or rickshaws, nor are there any of the small street stalls or eateries for which the neighborhood used to be famous and which used to spill out onto the lanes until they were prohibited in the lead-up to the Olympics in 2008. But there is constant noise: of shop assistants shouting out their wares to passersby, the hubbub of the crowds strolling in the street, loud music, and recorded announcements about discounted items blaring out from the shop interiors. The street teems with commercial vitality, celebrating sights and sounds associated with Beijing's popular cultural heritage.

The eastern end of Commercial Street opens onto Beijing's famous Qianmen dajie long known as the capital's main commercial artery running south from Tian'anmen Square. This traditionally used to be a bustling thoroughfare of travelers, rickshaw pullers, merchants with pack animals, and itinerant vendors coming into the city from the south to ply their trade. During the Mao years it continued to be one of the capital's main popular shopping streets, selling everything from food, household goods, clothes, Beijing opera, and martial arts items to the small singing birds and doves older men used to keep in bamboo birdcages. But by 2008, after several years of reconstruction work, it had been transformed into an austere stretch of gray-fronted shops sporting global brands and catering to consumer tastes that had nothing to do with the popular traditions of Dashalar. The two- and three-story buildings lining the entire length of the street display names that would be familiar to any visitor from the world's big cities: H&M, Apple, Zara, Louis Vuitton, and more. Jewelry, watches, precious stones, expensive furs, and fine teas are also in abundance. As if to assert its distance from the contaminating effects of popular practices associated with Beijing's "South City," in early 2010, a large rectangular sign standing between the eastern end of Commercial Street and where it opened on to Qianmen dajie displayed diagrams of prohibited items and activities in the newly opened street: guns, knives, juggling, skateboarding, ball games, bicycling, loud music, camping, dogs, and beggars.

Instead of its former bustle of bicycles, buses, and people, Qianmen dajie reemerged in its post-Olympics form as an almost clinically clean wide pedestrian shopping area, with uniform, Republican era–style features on the shop fronts, and large white lanterns hanging in front.[18]

Along its center, a Republican-era tram (*dangdang che*) runs south to Yongdingmen Gate for twenty yuan a ride. A few famous restaurants remind the visitor of the street's former days of glory in the 1930s, in particular the Peking duck restaurant, the Quan Ju De, now a vast complex occupying the equivalent of one block along the side of the street.[19] Passing under an imposing and elaborately decorated blue-and-gold-painted entrance arch, customers approach the restaurant up a slight incline paved with traditional cobblestones, and have to queue to acquire a numbered ticket before waiting up to an hour or more to be seated among the crowded tables. Yet further east, behind the facades of the main street, tidily paved walkways open onto small plazas, where expensive boutique-style shops beckon to the well-heeled customer seeking

Fig. 1.3 Street sign with prohibitions on activities in the refurbished Qianmen dajie, 2008.

more exclusive brands than those available on the main street, and tasteful coffee bars are set out with tables, chairs, and parasols. Here the visitor has access to any number of Western-style lavatories, set in fragrantly refreshing designer interiors where attendants wait to sweep the floor and wipe the lavatory seats immediately after usage.

At the other, western end, Commercial Street opens onto Meishi Street, on the north-south axis. Over the road, to the west of this, is a large wrought-iron arch announcing Guanyinsi jie (Street of the Bodhisattva Temple), otherwise known as Dashalar's West Street (Xi jie).

The temple, situated at a fork in the street some two hundred meters further west, was ransacked by the Red Guards in the mid-1960s during the campaign to attack the Four Olds, and its ruins have long been boarded up.[20] All that could be seen of it over the years I was conducting research in the neighborhood was part of a former wall and a dilapidated moss-covered roof, but it was still referred to by locals as an important meeting place.[21]

Like Commercial Street, the facades of West Street are now tidy and gray, and no pedicabs, bikes, or cars interfere with its pedestrians.

Fig. 1.4 Refurbished Qianmen dajie with white street lanterns, 2008.

It has many small restaurants, including one that features in the *Rough Guide*, and is well known for its "old Beijing" dishes. There are a few small, down-market hotels, including some that charge by the bed rather than the room. A single-story bar kitted out with wooden benches and tables, English-language menus, and world music fronts a hostel catering to international backpackers. But the feel of West Street cannot compete with Commercial Street. Its small shops have unassuming glass fronts, and few make any claims to historical fame. Rather, they sell badly made imitations of designer bags, umbrellas that fall apart almost as soon as they are opened, cheap shoes and clothes, bangles and ornaments, and cigarettes and alcohol. As the streetlamps light up in the evening, the mood of the street becomes more vibrant, but there is little of the popular tourist excitement of Commercial Street, and it is a world apart from the global emblems of Qianmen dajie, only a stone's throw away.

Going Back in Time

When I first visited Dashalar together with Zhao Tielin in the late summer of 2004, the neighborhood was extremely dilapidated. People looked shabby and poor; the shop fronts were tatty, with wares spilling out randomly onto

Fig. 1.5 Wrought-iron archway at entrance to Guanyin Temple (West) Street, Dashalar, 2007.

Fig. 1.6 Roofs of the Guanyin Temple, Dashalar, 2007.

Fig. 1.7 Beautified facades of Dashalar's West Street, late 2009.

the pedestrian areas in front. There was little indication of the popular consumerism of global brands that was to engulf the neighborhood after 2008.
The area around the eastern section of Dashalar and Qianmen dajie was partly
cordoned off by vast billboards, corrugated iron sheets, and bamboo scaffolding covered in turquoise-blue colored netting. Nevertheless, Zhao knew his
way around, and there were enough gaps between the billboards where, if
there were no guards on the lookout, the pedestrian could get through. Caution was needed to find a way around the endless piles of rubble and rubbish.
Even greater caution was needed inside the half-demolished courtyards. Many
buildings were padlocked shut, and the big white-painted character—*chai*, the
"awful mark"—was an omnipresent reminder of the process of chaiqian that
had already transformed most other old neighborhoods of central Beijing.[22]
The walls of some buildings displayed the murals that made the now interna-
tionally known artist Zhang Dali a local cause célèbre—huge black profiles of
dehumanized bald heads, sometimes with doves flying off into the distance,
and his AK-47 logo.[23]

Evacuation orders were stuck on doors, some giving only two months' no-
tice; other notices appeared urging inhabitants who were reluctant to move,

Fig. 1.8 Chai, the "awful mark" of demolition, 2010.

to "say farewell to dangerous housing" (*gaobie weifang*), and to benefit from the bonuses offered on top of the compensation for voluntary relocation. One half-demolished single-story courtyard gave a sad glimpse into the everyday life of its former occupants—big water jars inside the main entrance, posters of Republican era Shanghai calendar girls fluttering from the open rafters, and a discarded guitar and a pram. Save for the reconstructed wooden exterior of what Zhao told me used to be a tea house, there was little material evidence, at this stage, of any attempt to rebuild rather than demolish existing structures. Nor were there many signs apart from the rather crude, cartoon-like images on the billboards, that this neighborhood epitomized the rich commercial traditions of "old Beijing." On the contrary: the small eateries and artisan shops for which the neighborhood had once been famous were not in much evidence.

As I have already noted, most of the people I knew in Dashalar lived in the small lanes and alleys off West Street, in the crowded conditions of shared courtyards they had occupied for several decades. Some of these dazayuan were once the spacious and elegant courtyards (*siheyuan*) of Beijing's famous architectural history, and, during the Qing dynasty, were occupied by officials, aristocrats, and courtiers. Since the late nineteenth century, however, population growth and a constant flow of impoverished people from rural areas and small towns transformed the physical and social features of the courtyard compound. While those that retained their original features were occupied largely by elite families, most were subdivided and "critically ghettoized into slum-like tenements . . . a cramped, raucous, and filthy space that sheltered multiple families struggling at the margin of subsistence living."[24] This process accelerated through the early decades of the twentieth century as the dynastic system was overthrown and China became embroiled in war, invasion, and chaos. Refugees and outsiders who flooded into the capital took over the already dilapidated courtyard compounds, further subdividing their interior spaces and filling them in with small, brick structures and makeshift rooms, each occupied by a different household. These congested and dilapidated buildings remained home to the capital's subalterns well into the early years of the People's Republic, when the vast numbers of dispossessed peasants and demobilized soldiers who converged on the capital needed to be housed.[25]

Several households generally lived in one dazayuan throughout the Mao years, but as Dashalar locals' stories and the archives reveal, such living arrangements were far from stable. In times of extreme pressure and crisis, such as the so-called "three years of disaster" (1959–61), when poor peasants flooded Beijing from the countryside in search of basic survival, families already pressed for space were required to vacate or subdivide a room to create space for other occupants.[26] Since the 1980s, and particularly in the past two decades, many of the internal rooms of these courtyards have been rented out to "outsiders" (waidiren), labor migrants from other parts of China—who now run many if not most of the local neighborhood shops and restaurants. Many already narrow unpaved alleys became even narrower as tiny, makeshift, shacklike dwellings or "hutments" of not more than one or two square meters were added onto the exterior walls of the dazayuan.

Inside the dazayuan one would find a path leading from the main wooden doorway on the hutong along a narrow, rammed earth or sparsely tiled passageway, which in wet weather filled up with puddles. Lining the passageway would be an apparently chaotic profusion of objects, virtually obscuring from view the doorways to the individual dwellings. Larger items would be propped up along the walls of the passageways—bicycles, old wheels, old doors, window frames, discarded water barrels, and mops; enamel washing basins, brightly colored hot water flasks, ceramic food bowls, old toys, old boxes, tool handles, and old books and newspapers would be stacked on randomly ordered shelves and dressers. Order seemed to appear only on the

Fig. 1.9 Hutong in Dashalar, 2011.

washing lines weighed down with drying clothes and linen, stretched across windows and doors. Carefully watered potted plants occasionally announced the main door of a household.

By mid-2005, the eastern section of the neighborhood, including Dashalar Commercial Street, was completely cordoned off from pedestrian access, as work on the reconstruction of Qianmen dajie got under way. Gigantic cranes and trucks moved in, and huge billboards and screens covered with digital images hailed the street's imminent rebirth as a heritage-style consumer paradise for international tourism, where the architectural and artisan traditions of "old Beijing" jostled tantalizingly with global design and high-end retail. No traffic was yet allowed to pass north or south through the neighborhood.

However, despite the evidence of the neighborhood's demolition, Guanyin Temple Street still throbbed with noise and bustle: pedicab cyclists shouting to pedestrians to get out of the way as they steered a path through the tiny lanes, angry street brawls amplified by the shouts of unsolicited advice from the crowds of onlookers, restaurateurs booming out "old Beijing"–style

Fig. 1.10 Inside a dazayuan, 2011.

cries to attract passersby, and street vendors selling anything from fruit to household goods. It was also a place of smells, from the warm fragrance of tripe stew steaming in enormous woks in front of restaurants to the incense burning on the stalls of vendors selling Buddhist trinkets to the stench of the public lavatories.

Between 2005 and the winter of 2008, neither the main part of Guanyin Temple Street nor the maze of small alleyways behind it appeared to indicate much change, apart from cosmetic improvements to shop fronts. At its eastern end, however, as it ran into Meishi Street, it was clear that more ambitious plans were afoot. Ou Ning's 2006 documentary film *Meishi jie* is testimony to the coercive mechanisms the local law enforcement agents and construction companies were prepared to use to demolish buildings that interrupted their plans for regeneration.[27] However, as work on the reconstruction of Qianmen dajie was nearing completion in time for the Olympics in August 2008, it was clear that the refurbishment of Dashalar's West Street was going to be put on hold.[28]

Fig. 1.11 New "old Beijing" in construction behind old-style protective walls, 2007.

Street excavation and housing and shop renovations of the main part of West Street began in April 2009, following the circulation of letters to local residents in February and March. The refurbishment of Guanyin Temple Street with clean walkways and gray painted shop frontages was finally completed to coincide with the sixtieth anniversary of the founding of the People's Republic of China on October 1, 2009. Amateur video footage taken on the day revealed an immaculately tidy street without a soul in sight apart from a small dog. Unlikely looking flowerpots with bright orange blooms stood in front of the newly painted shop fronts. As the camera panned up over the walls of the buildings, it came to rest on people sprawled over the rooftops watching the massive military parades taking place in Tian'anmen Square.[29]

If the outside appearance of Guanyin Temple Street seemed to hail a clean and orderly future, inside the courtyards little had changed. Dashalar's dilapidated infrastructure and overcrowded residential conditions presented the local government with particular challenges.[30] Inadequate investment and population growth during the 1950s hampered the overstretched local government's plans for demolition and reconstruction. Some dazayuan housed twenty or so families, with neither sanitation nor hot water, who shared an outside stove burner.[31] There were frequent conflicts between registered residents, tenants, and private owners who wanted to reclaim their property. In a property in Guanyinsi Street, for example, a family with three children, registered as Beijing residents, wanted to return to the neighborhood from Shanghai only to find that another family was living in their former, publicly owned accommodation.[32] Under the system of government allocation of employment (*guojia fenpei*), and the *hukou* household registration system that restricted mobility between cities, it was formally impossible for urban residents to move their place of work and residence of their own accord. Local government attempts to mobilize households to vacate rooms in order to accommodate new residents only added to the overcrowding without providing any new services. In January 1962, a local survey, conducted by the Xuanwu District Workers Union, noted many instances of "six people of three generations in one bed, with only enough room to turn around in, and sleeping on wooden planks in summer."[33] Another undated document about the problems caused by the "communist wind" of the Great Leap Forward, signed by the Dashalar People's Commune, noted that between 1958 and 1960 the commune made two attempts to mobilize one thousand households to leave two thousand rooms in order to provide living space for the growing population. According to this document, this only exacerbated the difficulties. In 6 Shaanxi Alley, just off West Street, the two rooms occupied by a seven-person household were reduced to one, in which four of the five children had to sleep on the floor. Private owners wanted to take their property back, sometimes so that sons could have somewhere to live when they married, and sometimes because of conflicts with the tenants.[34] Despite official declarations of full nationalization of property in 1956, and the imposition of the household registration system in 1958, in part to control population mobility, private ownership of residential property still continued to facilitate movement of individuals and families between cities as far apart as Beijing and Shanghai. As plans to expand Tian'anmen Square and widen Chang'an Avenue got under way, a report from the State Planning Commission in 1954 commenting on "draft regulations on reconstructing and expanding the city of Beijing" noted that "there is an excessively high building and population density in the old city areas, so the numbers of buildings that will have to be demolished and residents who will have to be resettled are very high." The report further stated, "On a rough estimate, the construction of a seven-story building of 1 million square meters requires the demolition of 180,00 to 280,000 square meters of old buildings, meaning the relocation of 20–30,000 people. So we not only have to resolve the housing issues for residents, but the influence on their employment and lives."[35] By the mid-1950s, demolition affected vast numbers as the government launched its project to construct its "Ten Great Buildings," including the two monumental buildings in Tian'anmen Square.[36]

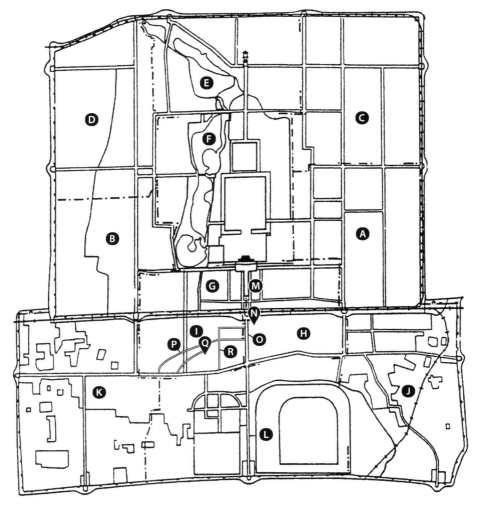

A. Inner One District
B. Inner Two District
C. Inner Three District
D. Inner Four District
E. Inner Five District
F. Inner Six District
G. Inner Seven District

H. Outer One District
I. Outer Two District
J. Outer Three District
K. Outer Four District
L. Outer Five District

M. Tian'anmen area before enlargement as Tian'anmen Square in 1959
N. Qianmen Gate
O. Qianmen dajie
P. Dashalar: Guanyin Temple Street/West Street
Q. Guanyin (Bodhisattva) Temple
R. Meishi Street

Map 1.3 Based on map of the Old City before the enlargement of Tian'anmen Square, in Madeleine Yue Dong, *Republican China: The City and Its Histories* (Berkeley: University of California Press, 2003), 45. Courtesy of the University of California Press..

Large "repair rescue teams" were organized by the housing authorities to assist those in need, particularly during the rainy season.[37] However, repairs failed to keep up with the pace of dilapidation and demand, and pressures mounted as the effects of the Great Leap Forward and famine began to hit home in the rural areas surrounding the capital, pushing large numbers of destitute peasants to seek survival in South City.[38] By 1965, it was reported that the amount of "old and dangerous housing" had doubled since 1949.[39] Now that private housing had been entirely absorbed into public ownership, a snowballing approach, described as "demolishing three and building one," was adopted to deal with the housing problem. But by the mid-1970s the housing situation was no better. The earthquake in 1976 further exacerbated the situation, and subsidies to enable people to undertake repairs were woefully inadequate. In all, under a policy of "not letting the roof fall in, not letting the walls collapse, but repairing serious leaks," the area suffered from extreme neglect. A combination of scarcity, population density, inadequate investment in housing and services, and an overwhelming policy emphasis on productivity repeatedly undermined the designs, intentions, and plans formulated for Beijing's older districts between the 1950s and the late 1970s.[40]

Various plans were drawn up in subsequent years, but nothing much changed in Dashalar until well into the 2000s. An urban plan to transform Beijing from an industrially based city into a "political and cultural center" to attract business and tourism designated Dashalar a cultural protection area in the early 1980s. Following the commodification of urban housing in 1988, Dashalar was marked for regeneration in a city plan to "transform old and dilapidated housing" (weifang gaizao) by 2000, the date when the government initially hoped to stage the Olympics. By 2002, Dashalar appeared in another protection plan as one of the "twenty-five historical areas of Old Beijing city," two-thirds of the housing of which was graded as dilapidated.[41] Demolition of parts of the neighborhood finally got under way in late 2004 with the widening of its main north-south road axis and the relocation of large numbers of local residents, powerfully recorded in Ou Ning's documentary film.[42] While pedestrians had to pick their way through piles of rubble, debris, and litter, posters appeared on courtyard doors and walls explaining the government's concern for local residents. Evacuation orders were put up, and notices appeared urging inhabitants to "say farewell to dangerous housing" (gaobie weifang) in return for monetary incentives offered for voluntary relocation. Enormous billboards displaying computer-generated images of the reconstructed neighborhood celebrated the commercial splendors of Dashalar's history, and in preparation for the Olympics, shop owners were ordered to refurbish their shop fronts with new signage and gray paint, at their own expense. Street vendors and pedicab cyclists were cleared from the lanes as the local government implemented a policy of physical, spatial, and social cleansing of the neighborhood.[43] Full-scale reconstruction of Guanyin Temple Street began only in the winter of 2008–9, with migrant workers laboring alongside bulldozers late into the night to lay new pipes and wiring in the excavated street, leaving a tangle of open wires and piles of rubble in the tiny pedestrian margins left at the sides.

In 2011, global design began to make small inroads into Dashalar, with the arrival of the "Dashilar Project" as part of the Beijing Design Week in some of the small streets just north of West Street. Some of the contributions featured pilot designs for dazayuan of the future, with courtyards containing sci-fi-looking modules constructed out of environmentally friendly materials. Others were pop-up exhibitions by young Western graphic designers and artists. None of the people I knew in Dashalar could be convinced to visit the installations with me. Between 2011 and 2014, most of the hutong had new paving, new plaster on the walls, and new gray paint. However, the dazayuan behind West Street remained virtually untouched.

For my Dashalar friends, having lived in Dashalar for decades, everyday life had been long been shaped by experiences of what, with few exceptions, they saw as disregard and neglect, exacerbated in recent years by the emotional and social stress of living with the relentless noise and detritus of demolition and reconstruction. The overlapping boundaries between the ramshackle dwellings of the crammed dazayuan already made hutong life very complex; dazayuan residents generally all knew each other's names and occupations, where their children attended school, and what kind of people visited them. As Zhao Tielin once graphically put it, "Everyone knows everything, even when a blade of grass moves in the wind." Far from the nostalgic tones of recent narratives about the "loss of the hutong," the spatial arrangement of the dazayuan and the hutong sustained a hotbed of gossip about local relationships and family quarrels, and hutong interpersonal relations (*hutong shenghuo de renji guanxi*) were fraught with potential conflicts that frequently spilled over into street brawls and fights with the local patrol officers.[44] By 2014, most of those who remained in the neighborhood did so because they were too poor, without family or social connections, or too demoralized and psychologically exhausted to find the energy to think of alternatives.

The following chapters show how the terms and temporalities of local people's memories of life in the neighborhood indicated a tacit rebuttal of the state's attempts to cast them as its obedient subjects. Their spatialized routines of everyday life were significantly shaped by the state—through its policies and regulations concerning housing, employment, and education; through its political campaigns; and, visually, through the signs and slogans covering public space, including the recent big white "chai" character and exhortations to contribute to building the "harmonious society" (*hexie shehui*)—omnipresent public reminders of the state's power. The state was also inversely present in its objective neglect of the neighborhood, effectively holding local people hostage to a rhetoric of development that could never ring true. At the same time, while the presence of the state shaped the neighborhood as a site for the "operation of large historical forces" of the state, the bureaucracy, and most recently the market, local residents' experiences of what they saw as the government's neglect produced the paradoxical effect of reaffirming a sense of ownership of their homes and neighborhoods.[45] This was apparent, as we shall see, in their creative everyday strategies of survival, in their intractability, silent defiance, and determination to keep going against the odds.[46] Their lives thus simultaneously revealed the extent and limits of the party-state's power.

2

Old Mrs. Gao

The oldest person I knew in Dashalar was Old Mrs. Gao. She moved into the neighborhood around 1937, when, at the age of seventeen, she married a local man. She had never left Beijing and had never been on a train. The only time she left the neighborhood was in 2011, when after the death of her younger son and together with her daughter-in-law, she moved to Tianqiao, a popular area south of Dashalar, commonly represented as the epitome of popular "old Beijing" traditions and the epicenter of South City. Over her long life, she earned the reputation of being determined, feisty, resilient, and, above all, absolutely committed to keeping her family going; she was the matriarch of the family. She was by all accounts very striking in her younger years—tall, with long black hair tied back in a chignon—and never reticent in voicing her opinions. But by the time I met her in 2006, she was bent and frail. Without much energy—or maybe inclination—to talk, she spent much of her time sitting observing the comings and goings in her home, briefly interjecting comments when she thought necessary. By contrast, she seemed to enjoy talking about the hardship of her early childhood, as if telling tales of endurance was a defiant response to a world that had brought her little material comfort or joy. Old Mrs. Gao exemplified a mixture of dogged resilience and an attachment to culturally embedded and gendered notions of ethical living that centered on family unity and solidarity.

As a young wife, Old Mrs. Gao lived in one of three dazayuan rooms that belonged to her in-laws. Her husband worked as a security guard for the Nationalist (Guomindang GMD) police. Then, in the early 1950s, just a few years after the founding of the PRC in 1949, and largely as a result of Old Mrs. Gao's persistent requests to the authorities, she and her husband, now with three children, were allocated another dazayuan accommodation, with two rooms on the same lane as their first room. She gave birth to her youngest child, a son, in 1960, at the height of the famine years. One of her in-laws' three rooms was reallocated to another family during the early 1960s, when the local authorities appropriated rooms from dazayuan residents to house the growing population of rural people who flooded into the district during the famine years. Then, during the Cultural Revolution, one of the rooms in her larger dazayuan was taken over to allocate to another family. Old Mrs. Gao's elder son lived for many years in her first dazayuan, but moved out around June 4, 1989, to leave it to her younger son and his wife. The elder son went into the army and married only when he was thirty-eight.

Thus, when I first visited Old Mrs. Gao's home in 2006, it consisted of the single dazayuan room where Old Mrs. Gao lived and her original room on the same lane, where her younger son and daughter-in-law slept. The main living space, where Old Mrs. Gao spent her days and where family members used to gather, consisted of a single room divided by a partition wall to make an inner small bedroom and the outer living room. This had a double bed—the *kang*, as Old Mrs. Gao called it, harking back to earlier times when the bed was a raised brick platform—a dresser supporting a television, and a few shelves with a framed picture of the Buddha, a few ornaments, tea caddies, a water flask, cups, and household bills. A picture of the Bodhisattva over a framed print of a couple of golden carp hung on the wall beside Old Mrs. Gao's bed. Another wall featured a faded picture of Chairman Mao in military uniform, against a faded red backdrop of the entrance to the Forbidden City, with white doves flying across the sky. There was also a large fridge and a microwave, a small table at which the family used to eat, one small armchair, and a few stools. A small lean-to built outside to the left of the entrance to the living room served as the kitchen, with a single stove burner and a single cold tap. The smaller bedroom at the back contained a big wardrobe and a double bed under which were numerous boxes storing the family's extra bed linen, clothes, and other household objects not needed for daily use. The place was warm, and full of family bits and pieces—a few photographs, a couple of soft toys, sauce and wine bottles, and so on. But it was badly in need of repair, with dilapidated walls and peeling pale green paint. The bed linen was worn and gray looking. As in all other dazayuan homes I knew in the neighborhood, the floor was bare concrete.

Old Mrs. Gao became bedridden in 2009. Painfully thin, and very frail, she used to spend her days on the big bed, lying back against a pillow, knees raised in front of her, sometimes looking at the television on the dresser in front of her, but often dozing or just looking around.

Her gray hair was always neatly arranged, pulled straight back from her face and caught in a clasp at the back. She kept a small wooden box at her side with her immediate necessities—cigarettes, lighter, and tissues. The family's

Fig. 2.1 Entrance to Old Mrs. Gao's dazayuan, 2008.

little dog often lay snoozing at her side. Her unemployed son, Young Gao, used to spend most of his time with her, sitting at the small table at the side of her bed. His wife, Xiao Xi, did the cooking and used to eat sitting on the bed at her mother-in-law's side. Xiao Xi was often out at work, and so apart from mealtimes, it was up to Young Gao to help his mother use her bedpan, to fluff up her pillow, and generally take care of her. But when Xiao Xi was around, he left these tasks to her, as well as the daily food shopping, the tidying, and the cleaning. Despite clear evidence of his wife's role as the physical mainstay of their home, Young Gao nevertheless complained that she didn't do enough. "How can I tidy the room?" Xiao Xi once responded to a reproachful comment Young Gao made about her domestic performance. "How can I possibly tidy the room? I'm too exhausted. If I spent time tidying it up I'd just keel over, and then you'd be really alarmed."

The first time Old Mrs. Gao talked with me in any detail about her life was one day not long after she had returned home from the hospital in June 2007, when Zhao Tielin, Huang Mingfang, and I went to visit her. A despairing

Fig. 2.2 Inside Old Mrs. Gao's home, 2008.

gloom seemed to shroud the main living room. Old Mrs. Gao had spent the previous two weeks in the hospital with pneumonia, and the doctors had told her relatives to prepare for the worst. It had been a difficult time for her children and their spouses, with most of them taking turns to stay with her in the hospital, taking her the food and toiletries she needed, and tending to her basic nursing needs.[1] Old Mrs. Gao's eyes lit up as we arrived, and although she remained more or less motionless in her chair, she was clearly pleased to see us, particularly Zhao Tielin, whom she knew very well. She needed little prompting from Zhao to tell me her story, but her elder daughter showed little interest in listening. "You never want to listen to me when I tell you that I suffered much more than you," was Old Mrs. Gao's comment, to which her daughter jokingly said, "That's right, I don't want to listen; I'll just watch the TV, but you'll still be talking when it's over."

From Child Marriage to Motherhood

Old Mrs. Gao was born with a "bad fate" (*ming bu hao*), as she put it, because she was born on what her mother told her was an inauspicious date. Her father had been away working for the Nationalist police and returned home through a rainstorm one late April to find that his wife had given birth to a fourth daughter. He developed a fever and died twenty days later, apparently "brokenhearted" at not having another son. Elder relatives on his side of the family suggested giving the newborn baby away. One reportedly said that had it been his wife's baby, he would have left it at the barracks. Another apparently said, "She's a girl, let the dogs drag her off."[2]

Old Mrs. Gao was the youngest of five, with an elder brother and three elder sisters. Her eldest sister was already fifteen when she was born; the second sister died in infancy; her third sister was eight; and her brother, three. Life was extremely tough. "Without a father, who would take you seriously?" (*Mei you fuqin shei na ni dang hui shi*?) In her early years, she lived near Deshengmen, one of the old city gates north of the Forbidden City where merchants and vendors coming into the city used to have to pay taxes. Just a small child, she used to follow those coming in by foot, particularly those carrying scrap metal that they would sell to make into objects such as vases. She and her brother would pick up bits and pieces that dropped to the ground and stuff them in their pockets to take them to a small depot near Deshengmen, from which these scraps were taken to a workshop to be smelted down.[3] Masters and apprentices who worked in the workshop needed coal for their work, so Old Mrs. Gao used to take coal to them. She looked up to her elder brother, the sibling she talked about most, who, although illiterate, eventually—after 1949—found a job as a cook in a party school. Her widowed mother, already thirty-seven years old, had no chance of remarrying—"Who would want to marry a widow with five children?" Old Mrs. Gao remembered with gratitude that her mother received a bit of help from one of her dead husband's uncles. She also recalled how her brother always told his son, her nephew, to be grateful to this uncle for his kindness, but how, in contrast, her own children didn't seem to care too much about acknowledging his past help.

Without independent resources and without a husband, Old Mrs. Gao's mother tried to make ends meet by picking up whatever work she could—cleaning, gathering fuel left on the streets, making shoes for people in the neighborhood, and sometimes working as a maid. She sometimes used to take her small daughter along with her. Beijing for poor people was a grim place at this time, and outbreaks of fighting between armed militia of different warlords made life extremely precarious. "We had to run off when we came across the soldiers. What kind of life was that? That's how we lived." Because Old Mrs. Gao's mother was often not at home and was consequently unable to properly look after her daughter, she felt that the girl would be better off if she stayed with another family.[4] Her idea was that her daughter should return home at agreed times of the year, when she would go out with her mother again to collect coal. So, at around age five, Old Mrs. Gao was sent to a household—"a place where I could eat"—as a "child-bride" (*tongyangxi*), where she collected coal, washed clothes, and did menial, dirty jobs as she was asked to. But this household was also poor. "If you were poor, how could you find a good husband?" Three times each year, including the New Year, her mother went to fetch her home, then after a few days returned her to her in-laws. But the girl repeatedly ran back to her mother's and elder sisters' homes. Tossed to and fro, the child lived in a state of relentless uncertainty: "I didn't know where I would eat next," was how Old Mrs. Gao described it. Insecure and miserable, she finally succeeded in leaving her in-laws at the age of ten, when her repeated attempts to escape made it clear to her mother that there was little point in sending her back anymore. Her mother was then working as a maid in a household outside Beijing, earning three yuan a month, so the girl went to live with her married elder sisters, earning a bit of money doing odd jobs for neighbors. At night, she stayed with her third sister, by now already married and with children, and in the morning, after lighting the fire, helping with the children, and buying coal, she would go off to her eldest sister's house. The husband of her third sister later hanged himself in a Buddhist temple; he had been a transport policeman and was reportedly accused of letting an elderly woman die when he let a rickshaw pass before going over to help the woman who had collapsed at the side of the road with what turned out to be a heart complaint.

Then, at the age of thirteen, the young girl decided to try to find work at a local labor market, but her former mother-in-law kept looking for her, waiting for her to appear. Children the young girl knew would rush to her to tell her to hide because her mother-in-law was around. She eventually found a job in the house of a local vendor, collecting bits of coal off the street and cleaning, but when her eldest sister discovered her and read her the riot act for her impropriety in leaving home, she returned to her mother.[5] At fifteen, her mother found her another household in the countryside outside Beijing, but the man couldn't afford to marry her, so she just stayed there a couple of years until her mother realized that he couldn't formalize the marriage, and so took her daughter back. Then her elder brother disappeared, apparently to escape conscription by the Japanese forces, and the girl and her mother spent days searching for him. They eventually discovered him near the Guanyin Temple in Dashalar, where he was learning to make shoes in a household with three sons, the youngest of whom was not yet married. At seventeen, Old Mrs. Gao was tall and beautiful, with long shiny hair. Her encounter with the third son quickly led to marriage: his father liked her; the eldest brother took on the responsibility for making due arrangements and found someone to act as matchmaker; her mother and elder brother were both content with the arrangement; visits were arranged for the groom's family to visit the bride's; and a bride price was agreed: two quilts passed down from the married sisters-in-law and a couple of metal rings.

The in-laws' family was poor, and couldn't afford a wedding for their third son, so for a while, the young bride lived with her eldest sister while her mother continued to work as a maid outside the city. Eventually a date was fixed, and the new bride was carried in a sedan chair from her eldest sister's home to a hotel on the day of her wedding, which Old Mrs. Gao insisted was March 26—one of the few precise dates that I heard her mention.[6]

The bride's new mother-in-law was a tough taskmaster, and regularly used to shout and swear at her daughters-in-law. She had no daughters of her own, so she demanded that her daughters-in-law work long days in the household. Their daily diet was just two corn buns and a small bowl of rice. "We were really pushed around. Even if something wasn't your responsibility, she made sure it was." Old Mrs. Gao gave birth to two children in the first years of her marriage, both of whom died. She then gave birth to a daughter in 1942, followed by a son and another daughter before and after 1949, and finally by her youngest son in 1960, when the famine had already reached the cities, with particular effects on the poor. Old Mrs. Gao's comment on the hardship she endured during this period was one of resigned acceptance: "You had to have children, didn't you? What would you do without children?" Her second sister-in-law had seven children, one of whom died during the famine—"Who could afford to see a doctor then?"—and another of whom was sent off to live in another household (*songzou*).

Life was thus extremely difficult, and Old Mrs. Gao had to struggle to keep the family going. The year 1960 was particularly prominent in her memory because of the lack of food, but her memories of the early years around 1949 were also pretty dismal. "During the war," as she put it—presumably before 1949—she described how she used to use a small knife to cut the clothes off dead people, including soldiers, who were laid out in a nearby park on blood-covered stones. Then, in 1949, she worked briefly in a makeshift "clothing factory," where along with other women she pulled small bits of shrapnel and metal from clothes that had been removed from corpses, and discarded any buttons that were broken, then washed the blood and filth out of the fabric to remake it into trousers and jackets. Zhao Tielin's comment was that this was something no one talked about. Despite the gruesome detail of such descriptions, Old Mrs. Gao recalled her work with some pride, and associated it with a vaguely articulated memory about Chairman Mao in the early 1950s. "I unpicked and remade so many clothes, several hundred cotton clothes, really well made they were. The cotton was really good then. Excellent. I didn't understand much then, but now when I think back, Chairman Mao was very impressive. In '49 I made clothes, and big leather coats, and sewed on buttons. I sewed the buttons really well."

Her memory as to how long this work continued was unclear; on the one hand, she commented that she was unable to continue with it since she had a small baby, but on the other, that she used to pay her mother twenty cents a month to look after her baby while she went to work at the clothing factory. Thinking back, she also commented that had she been in a position to leave her children to work full-time later on in the 1950s, she would have liked to, in order to obtain a state pension commensurate with her husband's. His pension made him eligible for 85 percent of his medical costs when he was sick. But, she complained, "It was not like that for me. For me, it cost 20,000, with no insurance. The street committee used to say they'd compensate me for 10,000, but they didn't. They then said 2,000 for 20,000 expenses. You'd have to spend 100,000 to get 10,000."

Old Mrs. Gao remembered her husband as a mild-mannered man. At first, she thought him very good-looking, but as time passed, so her story implied, she began to think he was somewhat inept. Before Liberation, he worked for the Nationalists household registration police for six yuan a month, but was sacked from his job for allegedly bribing someone to give him a couple of cakes to celebrate his wife's birthday. He then attempted to fend for himself in random jobs before finding a job selling vegetables for a local vegetable market that was nationalized under the public amalgamation of private enterprises (*gongsi heying*) in 1956, or when, as Old Mrs. Gao put it, "he joined the organization [*ru zule*]. All the vegetable vendors were organized, this group, that group, each with its own boss."[7] But according to Old Mrs. Gao, he rarely brought much money back home, since he always undersold his produce by weighing out too much, rather than too little, on the scale.

Old Mrs. Gao's memories of the famine years, when her youngest child was born, were particularly acute. She recalled feeling really upset that she couldn't find any red dates to eat.[8] She spent many cold mornings and evenings queuing up alongside thousands of others for a bowl of millet gruel served out of big wooden vats. With little to eat, and a family to keep going, she had to scavenge on the lanes, and send her older children out to the suburbs at night to forage for wild plants.

There was no grain in 1960. We were so hungry. Fucking radish peel. My daughters used to go out looking for wild plants, they were so hungry. I don't know how it got to this, but there was no grain anywhere, all over the country. And there were no wild plants left. In the dining hall near our yard we had cabbage hearts boiled in gruel, half a pound per person. And half a small steamed bun. Just enough for two mouthfuls. . . . Even if you had money there was nowhere you could go to buy grain. . . . They said it was natural disasters, but I was really puzzled. You mean to say that there's no grain just because it doesn't rain? It was really difficult for [my husband's] father to find work, but he did, and that gave us some security, so we got some grain coupons, and ate in the dining hall. You couldn't even buy medicines in Tong Ren Tang. When I was pregnant with [Young Gao], a boy, I longed for sour, tart things to eat, but we didn't have anything, just empty pots, so you couldn't even make a sauce. How can you explain that? How come it got so bad?

Even later, after the famine years had passed, corn dumplings continued to be the staple, with noodles at New Year and when relatives came to visit. Meat was always a rarity, even when the bitter years of scarcity had passed. Fast-forward to the years when I used to visit Old Mrs. Gao's home and when local shops sold a wider range of produce than was available during the Mao years: the household's main meal was generally still very basic noodles and preserved vegetables. I usually took either fruit or meat with me when I visited the family and was often invited to eat lunch with them, but only very occasionally did we eat a pork or chicken dish.

Old Mrs. Gao didn't talk much about political activities. Her eldest daughter thought that at one time she had joined in literacy classes, and may have participated in "speak bitterness" sessions.[9] Old Mrs. Gao did not have any specific memory of this, but she repeatedly reminded us how bitter her life had been, and that although "everyone talked about how bitter their own lives had been [*zhe ye su ku, na ye su ku*] [hers] had been far worse than everyone else's [*wo bi shei dou ku*]." The term she used here to refer to her own bitterness was *su ku* (speak bitterness), one of the very few terms derived from Party discourse that I heard her use. The *nannü pingdeng* (male-female equality) discourse of the '50s and '60s seemed to have completely passed her by, and when on one occasion I asked her if she had any recollection of campaigns to publicize "male-female equality," she responded with a somewhat puzzled negative.[10] She did, however, remember the Cultural Revolution, when she joined a local rebel group (*zaofan pai*) that criticized the local neighborhood committee. She joined this group mainly to get back at the head of the neighborhood committee, a woman who used to bully her to get her to wash clothes and cook for her, without pay. Old Mrs. Gao said she withdrew from the rebels when she realized that they were going around beating people up. Her most prominent and forcefully articulated memory of this period was her glee when she refused to make a padded jacket for the neighborhood committee head, even though she used to make padded jackets for others in the neighborhood as a way of bringing in a little extra money.

Between 1958 and the mid-1960s, Old Mrs. Gao worked in a collective that she recalled as the May 7 Company (*wu qi lian*), organized under the neighborhood committee largely for women who were not in the formal social labor force.[11] As members of the collective, local "housewives" (*jiating funü*) made shoes and clothes, stuck matchboxes together, and folded paper into what became the pages of books, including, so Old Mrs. Gao noted, the Little Red Book of Mao's Quotations sold by the New China Bookstore. For this she was paid two cents per one hundred pages. Old Mrs. Gao's work for this collective took place not in the physical space of a work unit but in the informal space of her home.[12] She and her neighborhood "sisters" (*jiemei*) would take their shoes and paper to work together in her back room, where they would chat and smoke cigarettes. Illiterate and without any publicly recognized skills, Old Mrs. Gao commented that "this was all someone like me could do." Tellingly, her eldest daughter once commented that her mother might have done better had she stayed with the man to whom she was "married" as a child bride. In her own view, however, even though she regretted not having been able to participate in the full-time labor force in 1958 and thus receive a full pension that would have covered her health costs, she acknowledged that if it hadn't been for the May 7 directive and her work in the May 7 Company, she wouldn't even have been given the five hundred yuan monthly pension that she subsequently received.

Old Mrs. Gao enjoyed a local reputation for her determination to keep her family united and stable through the hard years of her marriage. She was also celebrated for her strength in being able to pull through illness and hospitalization—"to live on again" (*you huoguolaile*), as her eldest daughter put it. Zhao Tielin used to say she had a "big fate" (*ming da*). She put it in more humble terms: "At least I haven't been a bad person [*bu chi de ren*], and when I die, there'll still be a family—sons, daughters-in-law, daughters, aunts, and they've all looked after me. And none of them have ever done anything bad." By the time I got to know her, her brother and elder sisters had long since died, and despite her evident sense of achievement in having kept her family

Fig. 2.3 Old Mrs. Gao's dresser, 2008.

together—"there'll still be a family"—she often used to hark back to the bitterness of her life. "What good things have I had? Me? Our family's always suffered, never had enough to eat. Never. At that time, all we had was a couple of corn buns. But I still did everything, making rope, odd jobs, making cotton-soled shoes for thirty cents a pair."

Old Mrs. Gao was also known for her generosity to neighbors down on their luck, and had a very affectionate relationship with an immediate neighbor, Meiling, a widowed former prostitute, who lived in a nearby dazayuan. Old Mrs. Gao's infirmity did not diminish her role as the matriarch and emotional mainstay of her household. People used to come and go; they would sit at the table to eat and watch television, or they would chat, drink, and smoke cigarettes, accompanying her as she dozed.

Meiling often used to drop in for a chat, and sometimes cooked for the old lady. Old Mrs. Gao loved her company; Meiling was an endless source of ribald humor, gossip, and repartee that drew on the popular traditions of South City. Another elderly woman who lived in the same dazayuan from time to time used to drop in for advice from Old Mrs. Gao about her family and housing difficulties.[13] However, as time passed, Old Mrs. Gao became less and less talkative, only really perking up when some visitor, or some TV program, prompted her to recount stories from her past. From time to time her daughters would jokingly tell her that she was talking nonsense, or that they did not want to hear any more about her tales of woe. Her eldest daughter occasionally became quite impatient with her, and rejected her claims to have suffered more than her children: "I tell you, the work you did, making rope, making shoes, was light compared to mine in the factory. Those big heavy metal rods." But her children were extremely respectful of and attentive to her, and not only to her physical needs. Her youngest son— effectively the male head of the household, since his elder brother lived in another district and did not often appear—would often turn to her from his table with some comment or a gesture to include her in our conversations. She no longer spoke very clearly, and seemed to find it difficult to follow conversations; or maybe she simply wasn't interested in following others' conversations. Nevertheless, Young Gao and others would consult her when they needed details about past events on their lane. Her memory for the names of former neighbors, or for the dates of local births, marriages, and deaths, remained sharp. Zhao Tielin often tried to cheer her up by celebrating her "big fate," and even though her eldest daughter and Xiao Xi were some-times quite curt in their manner with her, their respect for her was evident in their deference to her when she spoke or asked for something. Young Gao repeatedly commented that "she was second to none in her lane, and every-one respected her capacity to help people sort out their difficulties." She had kept her family going with limited resources, and had also offered her home as a kind of haven to neighborhood acquaintances in need of support and comfort. She was the linchpin of family unity and the pillar supporting her family's survival.[14]

After she became bedridden in 2009, Old Mrs. Gao sometimes said that she had lived too long and just wanted to die. Her neighbor Meiling had fallen out with Young Gao and his wife over a money matter, and so no longer came to visit. This was an irreplaceable loss for Old Mrs. Gao, and she used to com-ment on how much she missed Meiling. Lonely, frail, and bedridden, she spent her days on her bed, moving her skeletal frame only when she reached to the little table at her side for a new cigarette.

Fig. 2.4 Old Mrs. Gao's bed, 2008.

Young Gao

The first time I visited Old Mrs. Gao's home in early 2006, the only person there was her youngest son, Young Gao. His mother was in the hospital, and he had been at home resting since his left arm was in a cast after he'd broken it in what he said was a collision with a pedicab cyclist. He was initially taken to the Friendship Hospital, where he was asked for a deposit of twenty thousand yuan. "We were stunned," was his sister's comment. "How could we possibly come up with that kind of money? A hospital like that's inhuman, it's just out to make money. Totally unscrupulous. There are some things that just make ordinary people boil over with anger." Young Gao then went to the Jishui Hospital, where he was charged one thousand yuan for a cast. "Nowadays you can't even think of getting sick," he remarked, sardonically. "I've got two cracked ribs as well. If I could arrange insurance I'd still get 80 percent of my wages. But I can't. You're only eligible after you've worked a full twenty-five years, and I'm still two years short. . . . And in any case, I only broke two ribs. They said you'd have to break three ribs to be eligible for early retirement on the grounds of sickness."[15]

At forty-seven, Young Gao was still far from retiring, but he was no longer employed. He used to work in the vegetable company where his father had worked and where he used to earn six hundred yuan a month, but he left this job in 2001 well before completing twenty-five years. In fact, he had been sacked for punching his boss, a man who used to regularly slough off but who repeatedly pulled rank in telling Young Gao to get on with his work. On this occasion, when the boss gave him the same order, it was too much for Young Gao. He just flipped, and let rip at the boss, without thinking about the consequences. After this he spent a year or two working in construction but soon had to give that up due to sickness. He received welfare payments (*dibao*) of three hundred yuan for a couple of years, but apparently when his wife, Xiao Xi, then forty-five years old, retired, he was no longer eligible for this, and so had to rely on her pension and on temporary work.

Xiao Xi was an able and hardworking woman.[16] When I first met her she had just returned from visiting her mother-in-law in the hospital. She then used to work six night shifts every week in a local leather factory. Previously, she had worked in the sales department of the vegetable company where Young Gao had worked, which counted as light labor, but managed to change her dossier to machine worker, which counted as heavy labor and therefore boosted her pension. By 2007, even though formally retired from her work, Xiao Xi continued to bring in a small income in other ways, mainly as a pedicab cyclist until pedicabs and street vendors were officially ordered off the streets as part of the neighborhood's "beautification" in the run-up to the 2008 Olympics.[17] Between her pension and her work, she brought in around fifteen hundred yuan a month, around eight hundred yuan beneath the basic average required in Beijing at that time.[18] "It would be better if I had divorced her, that way I'd get welfare," was Young Gao's rather mean comment. Their only child, a daughter, then worked for an insurance company for around twelve hundred yuan a month, and so didn't need extra support from her parents.

Childhood, Courtship, and a Daughter's Marriage

Young Gao was six years old when the Cultural Revolution began. I asked him and Xiao Xi about their schooling and how they met. Young Gao started reluctantly by saying that he found it embarrassing to talk about his education, since it was all a "real mess." Xiao Xi then commented that he was "out on the streets all day long, and didn't go to school much," and this gave Young Gao his cue: "I was famous for fighting. Everyone knew me. I beat everyone up so they were scared of me. I even hit the teacher once. He hit me first, kicked me and punched me in the face when I complained of a stomachache when we were out in the countryside. I was just furious. He was later criticized, because he had committed this mistake. Not taking me to see a doctor but kicking me and saying I was making it up."

He was happy not to have had to go to school during what he called the years of the Gang of Four, but came to regret his lack of schooling later. "No one wants you if you're not educated." And although he felt that society under reform was generally more stable than during the Cultural Revolution, he said he still "missed the Mao era." For her part, Xiao Xi said that she really only started regretting not having been properly educated in 1987, when their daughter was born. "Now when I think of it, it was a brutal environment. We had to learn about Zhang Tiesheng." Zhang Tiesheng became a household name in 1973 as a figure of protest against academic exams that discriminated against those from working-class backgrounds. Instead of answering questions in a national exam in physics and chemistry, he handed in a blank exam paper, on the back of which he denounced the outdated character of the academic exam system and its failure to reward "workers, peasants, and soldiers" with political credentials.[19] This then led to a real difference of opinion between husband and wife, with Young Gao insisting that despite what he called Mao's small peasant mentality, "I still believe in Mao Zedong. There was no stealing in those days, no mugging, very little." By contrast, Xiao Xi stuck to her view that "we regret Mao Zedong and the whole . . ." Before she finished her comment, she decided to lighten the tone a bit by turning to the early days of their courtship.

Once this slight friction had dissipated, the couple settled into a shy but enjoyable banter about their courtship. Young Gao described it as a relationship that was low-key and drawn out, due to the conservative and constrained circumstances of the time.

> We got to know each other as a laugh, and went skating and swimming with friends. At that time students weren't allowed to have a boyfriend or girlfriend, so you had to do it secretly. And if you were seen by someone, that was it. I said to her go and talk to your parents, see if they agree or not, and if they do, we'll just go ahead and get married. Five years. Lots of people were chasing me then, from our work unit. They still are, but I'm not up to it anymore. We married after knowing each other for five years, in 1984. Things were very strict then, and men had to wait until twenty-five and women until twenty-three. But we were really conservative, too, and didn't know anything. We didn't even hold hands.

Xiao Xi concurred, with the comment that someone once told her that you could get pregnant just by touching hands.[20] "And we never got really passionate, like going out to eat, holding hands, having a kiss."

The wedding was a frugal affair, as was standard practice at the time. The wedding banquet consisted of food the couple cooked themselves, sweet tea, peanuts, and candy. Young Gao borrowed tables from neighbors to set out in the family home in Dashalar. He also managed to find three cars to bring his bride's relatives over to the celebration from Tianqiao, where they lived.[21] He himself drove over to Tianqiao to fetch his new bride.

Young Gao's daughter's experience of courtship was a very different matter, although when she visited the family home in Dashalar with her boyfriend, she behaved as her father wanted. Young Gao didn't like what he considered to be young people's immodest public behavior. "When my daughter used to come over here I'd say you have to be well-behaved. What you do in your own place is up to you, but here, you have to be well-behaved." In fact, Young Gao was very happy with his daughter's partner, and indirectly indicated that his approval had played a part in his daughter's choice: "If I hadn't been satisfied, she wouldn't have married him." Not long before they married, Young Gao's daughter and her fiancé decided to study to become taxi drivers, since this would give them a stable income. But marrying also depended on having somewhere to live. Indeed, in Young Gao's view, it was impossible for men of his son-in-law's generation to find a wife if they didn't already own an apartment.[22] Fortunately for Young Gao's daughter, her fiancé's parents were in a position to buy their son an apartment—"really cheap, for around 700,000 yuan"—beyond the second ring road. By August 2009, they had obtained Young Gao's approval to marry, but Young Gao was reluctant to wait until 2010, the date they initially wanted, because it was his daughter's zodiac year, and therefore not an auspicious date. The date was brought forward to December 2009, and Young Gao was determined to make it a proper affair, with a professional cosmetician, a formal MC for the wedding banquet, and hired cars for the bridal couple and important guests. The wedding ring the fiancé bought for his bride was a mandarin duck of white gold, but Xiao Xi didn't like it very much and so gave her daughter another one. Young Gao contributed some 30,000 yuan for the dowry—"of course we had to give her a dowry—quilts, a cell phone, and money." When I commented that he must have been saving for some time, he responded with "I prefer a daughter, because you don't have to spend so much money on them when they marry. You wouldn't be able to afford it if you had a son." The wedding banquet alone, financed by the groom's family, came to around 50,000 yuan, not including the car hire. The wedding was a grand affair, with officials from the Sanitation Bureau sitting with Young Gao at the head table, and a party secretary who gave a speech. "It's really important that the party secretary speaks," was Young Gao's response when I asked him about her presence at the banquet. A video of the celebration showed the party secretary speaking and then leaving before the banquet started. But Young Gao was in no way fazed by the rapid exit of the honored guest. On the contrary, he was very happy for his daughter.

> He's got a stable job; he's reliable. College graduate, and my daughter [went to] high school. So we can relax. We don't have a lot to do with their family . . . just visits at Spring Festival, but the most important thing is our daughter. The party secretary grew up around here, so knew our family well. She also knew the groom's aunt and uncle . . . both in the same work unit, the Sanitation Bureau, so understood them well, too. To tell you the truth, I was really worried about [my daughter], but now with a stable job and a good house, she's stable for life. And I stopped drinking a bit, tried to look after myself. And when she has a kid, I'll be able to look after it. She's no good at that [pointing to his wife].

His wife concurred, "It was him who looked after her when she was little."

Gossip and Politics

Much of the conversation sitting at the table with Young Gao and his wife revolved around the goings-on of their immediate neighbors, and the intricate web of ties that bound their near neighbors together. One abiding topic of fascination concerned the movements of a near neighbor, nicknamed Young Fox, who was a well-known local figure but whose recent history was cloaked in mystery. He had disappeared from Dashalar to evade punishment after he had been reported to the police for mugging someone who was apparently quite well-connected. The mugging took place in Tian'anmen Square and involved some violence. Young Fox and Young Gao had grown up together, and Young Gao continued to receive secret phone calls from him and so would urge him to meet for a drink, but a meeting never seemed to happen, and no one had any precise knowledge of his whereabouts. Meiling's name invariably cropped up in gossip about Young Fox. She had known Young Fox for a long time, and years earlier, when he had operated as a pimp, he used to introduce her to clients, including Brave Li, her long-term lover. Brave Li apparently used to give presents to Young Fox's children, but once he was seduced by Meiling, as Young Gao put it, he stopped. Young Gao added that before he disappeared, Young Fox used to get angry about Meiling's comings and goings, and insisted that she owed him something since it was he who had introduced her to her clients. Young Fox's wife, who had been a close friend of Meiling's, also stopped seeing her.

Behind this gossip, however, lay considerable resentment at what the Gao family considered to be Meiling's manipulation of her social and kin relationships for material gain. Young Gao was particularly disparaging about Meiling, calling her a "small/mean person" (*xiaoren*) for refusing to repay his mother the two hundred yuan she had borrowed on one occasion. He also disdained her for her habit of repeatedly swearing at her mother-in-law. When on one occasion Xiao Xi claimed that Meiling was the "lowest of the low" (*zui diceng*), Zhao Tielin retorted, "No, she isn't, Young Fox is." Hearing this, it didn't take much for Young Gao to turn his scorn on Young Fox, forgetting his customary reticence: "He was a small person, too, and if you made any money he would try to ruin you. One time, the boss, my wife, had just come back home on her bike, and he got up in the middle of the night to go to the toilet, and got angry and threatened her with his belt. That's what he was like. And he was always scared you might make a bit of money, and come out stronger than him. He was bad. He hated people who laughed at him for having nothing." To justify his usual protectiveness about his former friend,

Young Gao claimed that he had not initially known much about Young Fox's "crime" but over time came to the realization that he "had no defense" against the accusations made against him.

After years of hearing similar kinds of stories, and never being able to precisely work out the nature of the ties that held these erstwhile friends and neighbors together, or what made them fall out with each other, I decided to accept as it was this impenetrable network of dazayuan relationships for how it came across to me, the outsider: as an incomprehensibly dense series of relationships, passions, tensions, intrigues, and conflicts. It seemed to be a perfect example of what Zhao Tielin meant when he told me that dazayuan relationships were very complex. Old Mrs. Gao was deeply hurt by what she considered to be Meiling's disloyalty. Meiling had been a dear favorite of Old Mrs. Gao's over many years, and so was treated not as an "outsider" but rather as one of the Gaos' inner family circle. Old Mrs. Gao was therefore understandably distressed by an unfortunate incident about a loan for two hundred yuan she had made to Meiling. Once it became apparent that Meiling was not going to return it, Young Gao and Xiao Xi were openly vexed. Though apparently quite trivial, Old Mrs. Gao saw this issue as Meiling's betrayal of her trust as one of the "inner" family network. It thus resulted in a complete halt to their neighborly contact. For his part, Young Gao's relationship with Meiling was entangled with complex childhood relationships, animosities, and attractions, including her former activities with clients introduced by Young Fox. Even though Young Gao was critical of her behavior, he did not hide his enjoyment of drinking and flirting with her, and on one occasion when we all went to lunch at a restaurant where Meiling was working, he asked me to take a photograph of them both hugging each other in the snow.

Over years of visiting the family, and hanging out in the Gao household, I had come to expect conversations that focused on the goings-on of the neighborhood and its residents rather than bigger social and political issues. So I was surprised one day when Xiao Xi became very animated talking about her experience of the protests in Tian'anmen Square in May and June 1989. We were chatting about Young Gao and his wife's early years of marriage and where they lived. Neither could remember the exact date when they moved into the single room in Dashalar that had formerly been occupied by Young Gao's elder brother. But they eventually agreed that it was around the time of the "turmoil" (dongluan), the term that both of them used to refer to the 1989 protests.[23] Almost as soon as this term appeared in the conversation, Xiao Xi launched into an impassioned description of her experience of the protests in Tian'anmen Square between May and June 1989:

We all went, every day. Listening to those students talk, they were so good. People pedaling their pedicabs just stopped in their tracks to listen. There were tons of people standing around listening. He [Young Gao] sent his nephew to go and have a look, but he didn't dare hang around for too long. There were plainclothes police everywhere. The second day at five in the morning, the two of them were still sleeping, so I ran out. I wanted to go there again in the night, when I woke up and looked out of the back window. I told him to wake up, they're shooting bullets, I said. He didn't want me to go out. He said if I went, I'd just die there. . . . But I hadn't seen a tank before, so wanted to go and have a look for myself. Three of them appeared just as I reached Zhengyi Road, so I ran off, to Tian'anmen. But police lined the sides of the road, so we had to run along the middle. We were terrified. Police were everywhere. It was really brutal that students died. They were from outside Beijing. "Leave the square, leave the square," blared out from the loudspeakers, but they refused to leave. . . . There were lots of army units too. There was someone who had just stood up to talk in the square about how they should fight, and all of a sudden he was covered in blood. . . . I heard Wuerkaixi once, I didn't know who he was before, but he spoke really well, without notes, just spoke. Mostly about corruption, and how he wanted a dialogue with Li Peng.

Recalling these events, Xiao Xi spoke as if she couldn't get her words out fast enough. Not only was I surprised by the topic, but I was also surprised by her passion.[24] She generally did not say much, and I had never heard her talk at such length about anything before. Sadly, I was not able to follow up with her on these recollections, since when I visited the household there were always people around and things to attend to. It was not until some time later, after her mother-in-law's death, that I began to be able to apprehend her determined assertion of what she felt to be morally right and link this back to her admiration for the protesters of June 1989.

Depression and Deaths

The general atmosphere in the Gao household in 2006–7 was pretty gloomy. Old Mrs. Gao was barely eating anything, and was extremely weak. While she was still in the hospital, the consultant advised the family that she was unlikely to make a full recovery. Young Gao was indignant at such a suggestion—"the hospital always tries to frighten you"—but his wife, Xiao Xi, concurred that her mother-in-law was in a perilous condition. Old Mrs. Gao's daughters and daughter-in-law took it in turns to look after her in the hospital; she had neither the resources nor the desire to employ a nurse. Young Gao was not in a position to help since his arm was in a cast, but financial pressures were clearly on his mind, as well as his mother's condition. However, there was more than this. By June 2007, he had just been sacked from another job as a night watchman after being discovered drinking while at work. Too ill and unfit for regular employment, he largely depended on his wife's income.

Young Gao's health was not good; he was diagnosed with a chronic lung condition in 2006, and also suffered from back problems that used to surface when he tried to lift his mother from her bed to take her outside to the public toilet. He wanted to keep this from his mother, and asked his sisters to say that his pain was from a cold draft. He drank a lot, and would pour out rice liquor from a large plastic container whenever Zhao Tielin and I turned up, whatever the time of day. His mother sometimes found this annoying, and on one occasion when Young Gao and Zhao were pouring the liquor into cups, she told them she didn't like them drinking like this. However, her son, so it seemed, took whatever opportunity he could to drink, sometimes drinking, so he said, until the early hours if a willing relative or neighbor turned up.

One morning in the hot summer of June 2009, when the lane outside the Gao home was covered in rubble from an adjacent small temple—the Zhenwu Temple—that was being rebuilt, Young Gao seemed unusually depressed, and had lost a lot of weight. He, his wife, and his mother, the latter now bedridden, were the only ones at home. Old Mrs. Gao had had another spell in the hospital, and it was left to Xiao Xi and a nurse they hired for seventeen yuan a day to look after her. Xiao Xi was exhausted; a comment she made to the effect that she welcomed it when Young Gao pulled his weight a bit could not mask the reality that he basically did very little. His elder sisters and brother did not visit much, since they lived some distance away and physically were not in great shape. In all, the Gao household seemed devoid of sociable energy. The atmosphere was not helped by the news we had to bring, that Zhao Tielin had died the previous month. The Gao family was the first he had gotten to know well in the neighborhood, when he started his photographic project there in 1997, and he had been a frequent visitor to their home ever since, sharing a drink with Young Gao and memories of past events with Old Mrs. Gao. Huang Mingfang had been unable to get through to Young Gao on the phone, nor had she been able to contact near neighbors to pass on the news. Neither Young Gao nor his mother said much: "It's too sad for words, and I wasn't able to get to his funeral," was Young Gao's comment. Old Mrs. Gao simply said, "How come I don't die? So many people have died."

Young Gao complained about not being able to sleep, and how drinking a bit in the evening helped him feel better. He talked about how sometimes he got so angry that he couldn't sleep at all. His mood was not helped by the sweltering heat and the constant noise of bulldozers excavating the nearby lane. Though it was only ten in the morning, he had already started drinking strong spirits. His mother's condition had clearly deteriorated, but it was his father's death in 2004 that was on his mind. He told me how before his father died, he, the son, had been quarrelling with one of his elder sisters, and had been unable to sleep properly for some time. Exhausted and run down, he had developed pneumonia. His father was already in the hospital, and so Young Gao tried to ignore his own condition to be able look after him. Eventually, however, Young Gao was told that he would have to be hospitalized if he was going to recover from his pneumonia, and his father died before he was discharged. "So I couldn't make it in time before my father passed away. What regret. I cried, I really cried. Aiya! It was so hard. I just wailed when I saw his body." Old Mrs. Gao used to make repeated complimentary references to the care her younger son gave her. Yet for Young Gao, there seemed to be a painful contrast between his daily sedentary presence and attendance at his mother's side and what I came to understand was his sense of inadequacy at not being able to work and sustain his familial and filial duties.[25] His distress about his father's death and his mother's condition seemed to convey a deep sense of abject failure.

During a visit in the winter of 2007, Xiao Xi asked me "whether women or men enjoyed a 'higher' position in Britain." When I responded by saying that generally men did, and that women had to take care of their families as well as work, she agreed, but then added, "but sometimes women make more money than men, and if they didn't work . . ." She broke off when she realized that this might go down the wrong way with her husband, and quickly added, "I'm not talking about you, I'm just making a general comment. This is not about you," to which Young Gao said, "I might as well go and drown myself." His wife tried to ameliorate the situation by saying that in the past, women like her mother-in-law didn't go out to work, since they had to stay at home to look after the children, while in contrast, "now women go out to work, we are liberated, and in any case the housework is simple, quick, cooking, tidying the room." Young Gao's taunts about her domestic performance that I mentioned at the beginning of this chapter did not seem to unsettle her. On the contrary, their effect, for me, was to reassert his sense of his own inadequacy. His claim that it was the "Communist Party that doesn't let me work" could not hide his awareness of his own shortcomings as a husband unable to support his wife.

His embarrassment (*miantian*) was, moreover, compounded by a parallel sense of failure as a son. On one occasion, his mother even rebuked him for a remark he had made to the effect that it would have been better had she not given birth to him.

Young Gao died unexpectedly in the hospital in the autumn of 2010, at the age of just fifty-one. His lung condition had finally gotten the better of him. Photographs of his funeral at the crematorium revealed a solemn ritual, with four pallbearers dressed in full military uniform leading a procession of his relatives, neighbors, and friends, and a small brass band. The solemn ritual was a clear indication that his family wanted to grant Young Gao the recognition he had not received during his lifetime by giving him the send-off he would have welcomed and could not give his own father. Old Mrs. Gao was too frail to attend the funeral, but photographs taken of her after the event revealed a face etched with deep lines of misery and exhaustion.

Housing Uncertainties

The question of housing and relocation to another neighborhood became a prominent and explicit issue of concern for the Gao household in June 2009, when work to widen the lane outside the family home began. However, various comments in previous years, coupled with Old Mrs. Gao's recollections of the changes in the space of her dazayuan home in the years after she married into the neighborhood in 1937, made it clear that the allocation of housing between the family members had long been a source of tension. It took me several visits and attempts to piece together small snippets of conversation before I began to understand what the tension was about.

When Young Gao and his wife married in the early 1980s, they didn't have a place of their own. It was not until 1989, when the elder brother moved out of the old dazayuan room inherited from their parents' early years of marriage, that the couple finally had their own single room. "My elder brother already had a place allocated to him by his work unit, but he still didn't want to leave [our place], so I got angry with him. I said you've got a place to live, but you don't leave this to me. Do you want to make a mockery of me by asking me to move into my wife's home? Finally, he moved out. If he'd left a bit earlier, he would have been eligible for two places with two bedrooms, so there would have been enough for my daughter when she marries." Ever since my first visit to Dashalar, rumors abounded about imminent demolition, and circulars to the effect were occasionally distributed to local households by the street committee. Local people were long accustomed to a political system that churned out plans for neighborhood regeneration that were rarely implemented, and they found different ways to live with the uncertainties this produced. Some, like Xiao Xi, were quite pragmatic in their response to the prospect of moving. Xiao Xi had grown up with three brothers and two sisters in cramped conditions in the popular district of Tianqiao, south of Dashalar. After years of living in equally cramped conditions in Dashalar, she was ready for a change: "If we have to move out, then that's what we'll have to do, but we won't be able to come back." In retrospect, she said she would have moved when demolition began, when many younger residents decided to take the compensation offered to leave, but, she said, "I didn't know anything about it then. Like if your house was worth 250,000, they would find you something with two bedrooms out in Tong County, for example, for 35,000. The apartment blocks were good and clean but not very convenient. But [it would have been] better than living in the hutong. And you don't know anyone there, so you can avoid the hassles of living in a dazayuan. [But] a single-story place would be the best, particularly for the elderly."

Young Gao was more reserved about the prospect of life in an apartment block: "No one knows anyone, no one talks to you." He chose not to confront the idea, and resigned himself to a future he could not face: "We can't think about the future," he said, "since all we can do is get through today. All we can do is wait." By mid-2009, however, a move seemed to be imminent, following official news that their lane was to be widened. It was only at this point that Young Gao made direct reference to me about what might happen, when he said that if their house was demolished, they would have to leave, and if they accepted compensation for having to move out to the suburbs, they would not be eligible to return. His view, however, was that if their house wasn't demolished they would be able to remain.

The end of the Gao family's life in Dashalar came, finally, in the summer of 2011, when, after Young Gao's death, Xiao Xi made the decision to move back to Tianqiao with her mother-in-law while they waited for the local government to complete building the apartment block allocated to them in the southern suburbs. Sometime earlier that year, the local government had given Dashalar residents three choices: to move to accommodations in the far southern suburbs allocated by the local government, to move to accommodations they found independently, or to stay in Dashalar, in which case they would be moved to a small area of the neighborhood along with the other households that did not want to leave. In Xiao Xi's opinion, it was only a matter of time before the entire neighborhood would be demolished and rebuilt, so the last option was not realistic. With only two people in the household—she and her mother-in-law—they would not receive enough compensation to rent decent accommodations on the private market, and so they were left with the first option. They were then informed that the apartment block allocated to them would not be built for another three years. So Xiao Xi decided to move back to Tianqiao, where her siblings could help her find rented accommodations. Not even a year after Young Gao's death, Old Mrs. Gao and Xiao Xi moved from Dashalar to a two-bedroom apartment with a small shower and hot water, on the first floor of a small block in Tianqiao. The few belongings they decided to take with them—a bed, a dresser, and a few kitchen utensils and clothes—Xiao Xi piled onto the back of a three-wheeler pedal cart. One of her sisters-in-law took their mother there in a taxi. Xiao Xi was extremely matter-of-fact about the move, and openly welcomed the prospect of more space and better services. Old Mrs. Gao was silent on the matter, both before leaving Dashalar and on the only occasion I saw her in her new apartment in the autumn of 2011.

The occasion was her birthday, and all her children, their spouses, Xiao Xi, and a couple of grandchildren were there. The men sat at a table playing cards, while the women moved about laying out dishes and carrying food in from the kitchen. Old Mrs. Gao had a bedroom to herself, separated from the living room by a windowless wall; she was lying back on the bed, watching the television, in much the same way as she had done in Dashalar, but physically removed from the comings and goings in the living room, she was no longer a part of her family's activities and conversations. She said little as I went into her room to greet her; to my mind, her eyes had an almost bewildered look, and she did not respond when I asked her, as I always used to, how she was. Who was I? What was I doing there? Separated from the places, objects, and even people who gave form and substance to her everyday life, she no longer seemed to be the central figure of her family's history. She was now more than ninety years old and, spatially cut off from access to the sociality of her family's everyday lives, had little to live for. She died in the spring of 2013.

It was only after Old Mrs. Gao's death in 2013 that I came to understand the nature of the reasons explaining Xiao Xi's insistence on moving, despite the discomfort it brought to her mother-in-law. She told me that she hoped that the contract for the new apartment would pass to her after her mother-in-law's death. In the event, Old Mrs. Gao's remaining offspring attempted to buy her out, but resentful at being treated as what she called an "outsider," Xiao Xi stuck to her guns and insisted that having spent so many years looking after her mother-in-law and husband, she had a moral right to the apartment.

Interlude 1

The narratives of Old Mrs. Gao and her son were undoubtedly inflected by my interests in their family and neighborhood. Had I approached them with different interests, or had I gotten to know them earlier, they might have talked about their lives in different terms. Like many elderly people, Old Mrs. Gao liked to dwell on her childhood and youth: "I'm happiest when talking about the past, however bitter." Her recollections of her mother's destitution and her own childhood suffering were particularly acute, sometimes bringing tears to her eyes. Reaffirming the bitterness of her childhood highlighted her achievements in having kept her uterine family going through long years of extreme hardship, while at the same time these same achievements explained her lowly status as a "dependent housewife" outside the formal state system of employment. It was through producing children, and nurturing bonds with them, that a poor, uneducated woman such as Old Mrs. Gao could manifest her agency as a subject deserving acknowledgment for having maintained her husband's ancestral line.[1] The ethical status this gave her in the face of huge hardship and personal loss underwrote her locally acknowledged authority in family and neighborhood matters. The bitterness of her past life, therefore, became the pivot of an agency expressed as self-legitimation and a claim for recognition articulated through her role as mother, wife, and dependable neighbor. Her son's narrative, in contrast, fluctuated between resentment against a state that, in his view, subjected him to its power without bringing any benefits, and his sense of inadequacy as a husband and son.

In the context of their physical positioning in their home and neighborhood, surrounded by family members and neighbors whose preoccupations centered on the everyday routines of getting by, Old Mrs. Gao's and her son's choices of events and concerns to articulate were telling, however selective or partial they were. For Old Mrs. Gao, recalling the bitterness of her past could sustain a claim to virtue as the core of her sense of being an ethical person who, against huge odds, had managed to pull through and keep her family going without harming anyone. As his health deteriorated, her son, in contrast, looked to associations with more performative, even ritualized, practices to consolidate a sense of self-respect. His insistence on the importance of the party secretary's presence and speech at his daughter's wedding was neither a sign of political commitment to the party-state nor of pandering to the authorities in return for some material or political gain but of performing a ritual in a manner that he deemed appropriate to the occasion and within the parameters of what was available to him. In this sense, his desire to do things right at his daughter's wedding may be seen as the effect of a search for recognition in a world that heralded status in specific and publicly observable ways but that condemned him to the margins.

At first glance, the stories of both Old Mrs. Gao and her son could suggest a relatively abject self-positioning, the former as a victim of poverty, hardship, and illiteracy, and the latter as hapless subject of the neglectful yet controlling party-state; recall Young Gao's explanation for his unemployed status: "The Communist Party doesn't let us work." In contrast, Old Mrs. Gao exercised a palpable sense of agency in turning her "victimized" status around to make it work for her in a different way, as a source of virtue. Moreover, as I argue below, it was this agential capacity that enabled her to metaphorically hold her head up and make sense of her life in everyday social and political conditions that over long years held her hostage to the predictabilities of scarcity and precarity.

It goes without saying that the life experiences of mother and son covered much more than they shared with me. This was particularly the case with Old Mrs. Gao, whose long life spanned huge changes between the early Republican period and the new millennium. The urban environment of Old Mrs. Gao's childhood and adolescent years in Beijing was dominated by poverty, vagrancy, sickness, infant mortality, and endemic violence. The city was overrun by warlord infighting and banditry, and the streets teemed with beggars, mendicant monks, and prostitutes, alongside street vendors and rickshaw pullers. By the time Old Mrs. Gao married and moved to Dashalar in 1937, Beijing was occupied by Japan. Between 1945, when renewed civil war between the Nationalists and the Chinese Communist Party (CCP) erupted, and 1949, Beijing was under Nationalist control.

Throughout this entire period, everyday life for those at the bottom of the social ladder, such as Old Mrs. Gao, was a grim struggle for basic survival, as Lao She's famous novel *Rickshaw Boy*, first published in China in 1937, graphically reveals.[2]

The events of Old Mrs. Gao's childhood and youth that she shared with me made no direct reference to these broader conditions, even if basic survival was a recurring and prominent theme in her narrative. She repeatedly noted, for example, how she and her mother used to scavenge on the streets for bits of coal. However, as I got to know her better, and became accustomed to her local accent and manner of talking, I realized that her memories of her early years tended to rehearse the same themes, in the same language, with the same gestures, and in the same sequence of events, almost as if she had performed them on many occasions.[3] Looking back through my notes, it was clear that the story had hardly changed at all since the first time I met her in 2006, together with Zhao Tielin, when she needed little prompting from Zhao before launching into descriptions of her early childhood. As Zhao Tielin and Huang Mingfang already understood, it was this story that was the template she drew on when she talked about her past. It established the frame through which she retrieved her past when the occasion invited her to narrate it. It was thus inseparable from how she saw herself in her waning years. It was as if narrating and renarrating her past in a particular way, performing it in the way I observed and heard, had become an integral part of herself.

Narrative enables us to place ourselves within a "historically constituted world," and is essential to enable us to make the world and ourselves intelligible.[4] Old Mrs. Gao's narrative certainly did this, as a performative exercise of self-validation and agency in claiming recognition for a long life of hardship, poverty, and resilience. In the terms of the CCP's discourse, it bore many features of the practice of "speak bitterness" that was deployed by the Communist Party before and after 1949, as a means of enabling the oppressed to take cognizance of the class-based and collective nature of their oppression. Seen as an expression of agency, Old Mrs. Gao's narrative articulated events and experiences in terms that were inextricably mediated by the discursive contours of her life. In voicing her memories of particular experiences, she drew on social scripts established in the social and cultural world she inhabited. Yet, in contrast to the key moment of rupture—1949—in the "speak bitterness" motif, there was little in her narrative that could be construed as a break from her past suffering and a celebration of the bright present of socialist society. Rather, her story continues after 1949 and into the Mao years as one of relentless hardship and scarcity: bringing up young children in crowded conditions, with no running water or basic sanitation, with few employable skills, in social and political conditions of unpredictable turbulence. Hardship and precarity were the constant features of her life; her claims for recognition crucially revolved around her resolve to keep going in the face of adversity. That she was able to do this and was acknowledged by all as the mainstay keeping her family together makes her a telling example of Stafford's "matriarch."[5]

Old Mrs. Gao implicitly acknowledged that her life had improved materially in recent years, yet her words registered no more than an equivocal comment that contrasted the poverty of her youth with how "good" the city's construction (*jianshe*) was in the present. "Now is better. . . . [We] don't have to unpick quilts, or spend long hours mending clothes. It was poor in those days, but now, in this city, it's really good [*zhen bucuo*], with construction [*jianshede*]. But thinking about it then, Mao really did a lot." If Old Mrs. Gao's admission of improvements since Mao was tempered by her implicit praise for Mao, it was also tempered by the everyday pressures on her household that mounted as chaiqian gathered speed in the neighborhood in the mid-2000s.[6]

Across the years that I knew Young Gao, his narrative exuded an increasing sense of hopelessness, fatalism, and inadequacy, conveyed on the one hand by his tendency to denigrate himself, whether as a school student or a son, and, on the other, by holding the party responsible for denying him opportunities for self-improvement. He did not dwell at length on his personal regret at not having attended more to his studies during his youth, and in any case, such regret was counterbalanced by an evident pride in his childhood reputation as a good fighter.

The key moments of rupture in the progressive view of history— 1949 and 1978—thus barely surfaced in either the mother's or the son's narratives. Without these, their accounts of their lives were framed by a temporal and agential quality that was rooted in the mundane and exhausting grind of everyday survival. Neither mother nor son offered glimpses of hope for a different future for themselves. If for Old Mrs. Gao this could plausibly be explained, partially at least, by her advanced age and the limited time left to her, for her son it was because he felt he had been beaten down by a system that had never given him cause for hope. In contrast, he was determined to celebrate his daughter's well-being and transition to her new future by proving to the world his paternal authority as a responsible father in cutting back on his drinking and making proper arrangements to observe the necessary rituals of the occasion. At this bleak stage of his life, his resolve in rising to the occasion of her wedding and investing such signs of hope in his daughter conveyed a claim to a symbolic and gendered recognition that he had not achieved in his roles as son and husband.

In different ways, then, that were commensurate with the specificities of their individual life experiences, both Old Mrs. Gao and her son transformed their stories of injustice, powerlessness, and victimhood into testimonies of resilience, determination, and, in Old Mrs. Gao's case, virtue. The same stories became witness to the exercise of agency, not in order to resist the external conditions that perpetuated their powerlessness but to assert an ethical claim to recognition as human subjects. Agency in this sense is distinct from normative ideas of resistance or subversion of established authority. Rather, following Saba Mahmood, it refers to the multiple interests and motivations involved in people's assertion of self, whether as individuals or as members of collectivities, including families and households.[7] Furthermore, understood in its historically contingent forms, the exercise of agency may not correspond with the notions of individual rationality and rights that invariably inform its association with progressive change. As such, agency may be oriented to conservative ends, including the maintenance of profoundly gendered relationships of authority and dependency.

As mother and respected elder, Old Mrs. Gao's life's achievements lay not in political or income-generating activities but in sustaining her family against forces of fragmentation and disunity. Her main source of self-legitimation echoes Stafford's argument about the crucial role of women in safeguarding the kin group from separation and disintegration.[8] Coming not long after the death of her youngest son, and soon after her departure from her long-term home in Dashalar, the timing of her death thus had a particular poignancy. Compelled by material circumstance, her daughter-in-law's decision to return to the neighborhood of her natal family while awaiting completion of the apartment promised by the local government confirmed the dissolution of Old Mrs. Gao's family once she was no longer around to hold it together.

Young Gao, in contrast, saw himself as the male head of the household, despite his evident incapacity to realize the role. He repeatedly, if indirectly, invoked his imagined authority, on the one hand, by deprecating himself as son and, on the other, by affirming his role as father. Recall, for example, his distress at his failure to attend the funeral of his father and his self-reproach for not having been a good son to his mother, alongside his assertion that his daughter would not have married a man without her father's approval. It was only in his death that his lament about his father could finally be put to rest, when he, the son, was given the ritual send-off that he would have wanted to give his father.

Old Mrs. Gao's claims to virtue as long-suffering mother, and her son's insistence on doing things right at key moments, alongside his abject sense of failure when unable to do so, constituted a historically mediated gendered agency, asserting an entitlement to a dignified ethical status in a world that had refused to treat them as full persons.

For both Old Mrs. Gao and her son, the spatialized present of their home in Dashalar created a physical, emotional, social, and temporal container for narratives that conveyed a palpable, if muted, sense of agency. In their different ways, they revealed a desire for recognition in a local world that after years of neglect was finally thrust aside by the political and market imperatives of the party-state. As social subjects of Beijing's various transformations, mother and son survived in the margins of the shifting policies and strategies of the urban planners, whatever the moment and political emphasis. Both were effectively silent about the terms of these strategies and policies despite their inescapable influence in their daily lives. Their silence, however, signified neither passive acceptance nor subversion of these terms. Old Mrs. Gao's narrative distance from the state could only be construed as subversion by stretching the term to include her stubborn deafness to the appeals of the party-state. Rather, her self-positioning vis-à-vis a state that reinforced her social marginalization buttressed her resilience in keeping her family going. This became the evidence for and source of her exercise of agency in claiming ethical recognition for her humanity and subjectivity.

In contrast, a combination of unwillingness and incapacity made it impossible for Young Gao to shake off the abject conditions of his existence. Instead he preferred to drown his sorrows in alcohol and wait to get by until the next day. In effect, this was a rejection of the party-state's claims to uphold the interests of the disadvantaged, even though he occasionally and ironically stalled this rejection by a conscious desire to use the party-state's trappings of authority to assert his own. His determination to demonstrate this at his daughter's wedding expressed a yearning for recognition that he was unable to claim in other forms.

The everyday focus of the preoccupations of Old Mrs. Gao and her son was a product of the material precarity of their existence. Their stories (whether about childhood, family, or neighbors) were dominated by concerns with the present (material, bodily, emotional, and social) always framed by the place of their home and neighborhood. This denied them a share in the sense of a future represented by the temporal rhythms of the urban planners, whether of the Mao era or since then under market reform. Indeed, the stories Old Mrs. Gao shared with me never made any reference to hopes or aspirations that might be associated with either the heady collective passions of the Mao era or with the material opportunities of post-Mao consumerism. In retrospect, her resilience took the form of a dogged refusal to give in, not in the name of any hope but just to be able to keep going.

Toward the end of her life, as Old Mrs. Gao became aware of the destruction of her neighborhood, it was not surprising that she, like many elderly people, was drawn to memories of her younger days. Nor was it surprising, given her advanced years, that she could not or did not want to talk about her future, because—at least by the time I got to know her—that future threatened the literal destruction of the physical space of her home. For Old Mrs. Gao, the place of her home was crucial to her sense of being. Stephan Feuchtwang has argued in his work on the making and remaking of place as a centering process that a temple may give territorial place a sense of interiority not through establishing boundaries but by affirming a center. In similar ways, the interiority of Old Mrs. Gao's home was affirmed by the status she gave it as the temporal and physical center of her sense of self-worth. To take this away, or to remove her from it, was tantamount to denying her the material and emotional foundations of her self-legitimation. As Feuchtwang forcefully put it, "Dislocation and displacement are vertiginous and can be deadly."[9]

73

3

Zhao Yong

Zhao Yong is a man of many talents and interests. He reads, brews his own wine, cooks, practices martial arts, cultivates vegetables and flowers, and is a practicing Buddhist and an attentive follower of international news. He has an apparently limitless capacity to talk about almost anything at great length, from the environment and philosophy, child education, and ethics to religion, human rights, and politics, and the impassioned and magisterial tone his voice often takes on fully compensates for his height. Just under five feet tall, Zhao Yong blames his height on his poor diet when he was growing up. Born during the famine years in 1961, to parents who were classified as small landlords by the communist government in the early 1950s and then counterrevolutionaries in the 1960s, he learned bitter childhood lessons in how to survive the joint pressures of political discrimination and poverty.

Zhao had a variety of short-term manual jobs before finding stable employment in a state-owned factory in the late 1980s. By the mid-1990s, China's engagement with the global capitalist economy heralded the rapid privatization of social property and employment and the full-scale marketization of society. Many state factories closed down in the mid-1990s, with particular effects on the unskilled, middle-aged workforce. Zhao Yong was laid off, pushing him into the ranks of the permanently unemployed. Already disadvantaged by class background and poor education, Zhao found himself hostage to the discriminatory effects of the widening differentials between wealth and poverty.[1] To make ends meet, he turned to the informal economy of odd jobs and street trading.[2] To make things worse, he had to endure the social stigma of belonging to a family locally known as crazy. But neither his background nor the everyday responsibilities of caring for an elderly mother with severe mental health problems seemed to dent his capacity for resilience, hope, and good cheer.

Zhao Yong lives with his immediate family in a two-story dazayuan off Dashalar's West Street. His household consists of his wife, stepdaughter, and mother. He spends much of his time looking after his elderly mother, who, now more than eighty years old, suffers from an extreme form of paranoid personality disorder that makes it unsafe to leave her on her own. When she is not out at work, Zhao Yong's wife, Qian, also cares for her mother-in-law. Zhao's stepdaughter, who was only five years old when Qian and Zhao married, sometimes used to appear after school but generally left in the evenings together with her mother to sleep in a small room nearby that Qian kept on after her first husband died in the early 2000s.

Qian was no stranger to hardship, and she seemed to have a boundless capacity for resilience and good cheer. Always smiling, her eyes sparkled with merriment and curiosity, and she rarely seemed to sit still for more than a few moments at a time. While Zhao sat on a small stool expounding his philosophies of life, she busied herself washing dishes, cutting up vegetables, keeping her mother-in-law occupied by asking her to fetch water or wash the fruit, and only occasionally interjecting a wry remark into her husband's flow of words.

Old Mrs. Zhao, Zhao Yong's mother, was a force to be reckoned with. She made up for her diminutive and wiry build with a commanding presence, often overwhelming me with expressions of physical affection—hugging me, pulling at my arms, or stroking my hair—and loud tirades of questions: "Why don't you dye your hair black? Why don't you wear a watch? Why don't we both run away together to find ourselves new husbands?" Between one minute and the next she veered between demonstrating her skill in martial arts moves, sullen silences—particularly when reprimanded by her son—and loud, terror-stricken assertions that the government had issued orders to hunt her down. She repeatedly interrupted conversations, sometimes with terrified panic (her neighbors wanted to burn her out of her home, the police wanted to arrest her) sometimes responding to news items on the television with demonstrations of her knowledge about current affairs ("You see, I'm not ignorant, I know the names of African countries"). Her son and daughter-in-law were both adept in devising strategies to occupy her attention, asking her to help wash the dishes, fetch water, or tidy up the plates. From time to time, Zhao's exasperation with his mother's incessant demands reduced him to shouting at her: "Just put it over there! Just do it! Not there! You're so stupid. What kind of a person are you? You don't understand anything." But neither his occasional impatience nor his mother's angry responses swayed him much from his train of thought.

When I first met him in 2007, Zhao Yong lived in a small room divided into two at the back of the dazayuan where he still lives. This used to be a low-grade brothel (xiachu) during the late Qing and early Republican eras, and as in other such buildings in the neighborhood, the rooms ran along an interior

Fig. 3.1 Former two-story brothel in Dashalar, converted into a dazayuan, 2008.

corridor on the ground floor and a balcony on the first floor, each with its own doorway.

Zhao's two rooms—or rather one room divided into two—totaled no more than about nine to ten square meters. The main part was the living space, with high walls painted a faded pale pink and a coal burner. On the back wall opposite the doorway hung an unframed picture of the Buddha, beneath which was a black-framed Buddhist saying—"Tea and meditation are the same taste" (*cha chan yi wei*). The only furniture was a cabinet with a small statue of the Buddha and incense, a small low table, and a couple of low stools. The adjacent part of the room on the other side of the partition wall was entirely taken up with a double bed, at the end of which was a television. There was no kitchen, and Zhao cooked outside in the corridor on a small stove burner he shared with his neighbors.

Zhao Yong lived in these two rooms for more than forty years after his parents were moved there during the Cultural Revolution. When he was born in 1961, they lived in a slightly more spacious accommodation in Zhushikou, just south of

Dashalar, in a single-story house next to an oil company and near the steam basket factory where his father worked. The family's move to Dashalar, so the family story went, happened because his mother used to enjoy smoking a long-stemmed pipe, and one day, just as a policeman from the local police station was passing by, a spark from her pipe caused a fire in the building. She and her family were then rehoused on the grounds that her smoking in a building next to an oil station was too dangerous. According to Zhao's wife, however, it was because of the family's political difficulties, and, she added, her mother-in-law's mental health problems. The room allocated to the Zhao family in Dashalar was smaller than their Zhushikou accommodations, but they had no option but to move there, since, as Zhao Yong put it, "You had to live where the unit told you to live." There were eight or nine different households in the courtyard at that time, each with five to seven people. By 1973, when Zhao's younger brother was born, the household had six people—he also had two sisters—one older, one younger, "but we managed to live together. When we were small, we all slept on wooden boards that fitted into one another, like those wide beds for lots of people in the countryside. Not like one person per bed. We didn't have that. Like when I was small, we didn't have a table, so I used to write on the floor. Later we had a square table, then a long narrow table. That was when things were a bit better. Then, we had a wide bed, and a wall cupboard, and one of those heavy, old style dressers." It was not until the third time I visited Zhao that I realized that he shared his time between his Dashalar home and his wife's single-bedroom flat in another nearby neighborhood. The only person who regularly slept in their Dashalar home was his mother, although Zhao Yong used to stay overnight if he felt concerned about his mother's condition or had urgent business in Dashalar early the next day. Nevertheless, he and his wife spent their daytime hours working in or near Dashalar, always on hand to tend to Old Mrs. Zhao's needs. She rarely went out, unless it was with her son; or, as she put it, she was not allowed to go out on her own because her son didn't let her, since in his view, she would get lost or run into trouble. Without the resources to finance either hospitalization or a care home, Zhao and his wife had little choice but to look after her themselves.

In early 2010, Mr. Zhao and his household moved into a larger room left vacant by a former occupant, just inside the main entrance of the same dazayuan. A small inner room dividing this from their former rooms served as a general storage room as well as his mother's bedroom. More than double the size of their former space at the back of the building, the main room was full of color: in contrast with their room at the back of the building, it felt spacious, with big, high windows that opened onto the lane outside to let in the

Fig. 3.2 Buddhist shrine in Zhao Yong's home, 2013.

daylight, bright plastic flowers, a Buddhist shrine in the corner festooned with offerings of fruit and small gourds, and a square prayer cushion featuring a lotus design on the floor in front of it.

A single bed in one corner served as a sofa, and a new gray metal bookcase laden with books, wine cups, and bottles neatly packed in boxes stood against the back wall. Big wooden Buddhist beads hung from a hook by the left-hand window, outside of which were flowerpots in which Zhao grew green beans and sugar snap peas in summer. A small electric stove on the floor was surrounded by pots and cooking utensils, and on the wall above was a large flatscreen TV, bought, so Zhao told me, to keep his mother occupied. He had also bought a small talking parrot, kept in a birdcage hanging from the ceiling, as an amusing distraction for his mother, but nothing, he commented with an air of resignation, helped improve her state of mind.

Early Years

Both sides of Zhao Yong's family were businessmen during the Republican era. His paternal grandfather was originally from a rural area near Tianjin, where together with his elder brother, he set up and ran a successful artisan workshop making steam baskets. During the Japanese occupation, another brother served in Shanxi as an official for a local warlord, for whom he apparently ran a private militia.[3] His grandfather moved the basket workshop to Beijing sometime before 1949, where he also set up a number of shops in South City, selling handmade wooden pots and small barrels. Zhao's father and uncle took over their father's business, but it was nationalized after Liberation and renamed the July 1 Agricultural Tools Factory. Zhao's father's real passion, however, was for art. He had been educated in a small private school in Beijing, and as a young man, so Zhao related, was accepted into the Central Fine Arts Academy. He excelled in landscape painting, and Zhao recalled with pleasure moments during his childhood spent watching his father paint landscapes and flowers. He was also "good with his hands," and Zhao remembered how when he was a small child, since there was no money to buy a toy go-cart, his father made him one out of strips of wood he retrieved from his work unit.

Zhao's maternal grandfather was also from Tong County, where he ran a successful optician's business—the Big Bright Opticians. He was a notable martial arts practitioner, and at one time was head of a Bagua Research Association.[4] In his spare time he ran an amateur martial arts training school for young men, which was closed down during the 1950s.[5] His family lived quite near to Zhao's paternal grandfather, and the two families knew each other through their entrepreneurial activities. It was through these early connections that Zhao's parents' marriage was arranged.

By the time they married, however, in the late 1950s—Zhao was unsure about the exact date—their families' fortunes had changed drastically. Both families were classified as small landlords in 1949, and their family property was nationalized in 1956 during the amalgamation of state and private business, when with the collectivization of agriculture and the nationalization of industry, classes were officially declared to have been abolished. To avoid further stigmatization, the families were quick to register their company with the state, and agreed to pay the taxes demanded of them, but this failed to secure them any benefits, and all their property was confiscated.

Zhao's mother had no formal education. She claimed that she had learned to read, but her reading skills were very limited. She had learned basic martial arts moves from her father, but not, she somewhat resentfully noted, to the same standard as her brothers, since, as a girl, she was not allowed to attend her father's training school. One of six children, she spent much of her childhood and teenage years working on the land, where she insisted that she had done everything, despite her son's doubts.

Who? Me? Me? I have dug ditches, dug reservoirs, but you didn't see any of that? You weren't born then! I still hadn't married. My mother had to live. Just go and visit my old home and ask. My mother could do everything, the same as me. I can't do this and can't do that, but let me tell you, if I was working in the fields, let me tell you. . . . Don't okay, okay, okay me. . . . I've built fences and used a pickaxe, I've dug ditches and land, weeded the courtyards. . . . I could do anything when I was young. But I didn't go to dig the Miyun reservoir.[6] My mother said I couldn't go. She said, "They send the riffraff there . . . you're not going. Weren't there those two girls who were raped?" But if you didn't go, they didn't give you anything to eat. They gave food to my brothers, but not to me, so my mother used to steal corn buns for me. Have you ever eaten from the collective pot [*daguo fan*] like that? I've suffered a lot, you know, but what's the point of talking with you?

Zhao Yong dated his mother's psychological condition back to the Cultural Revolution, when the Red Guards ransacked (*chaojia*) their home; poverty did not protect his parents from their class background.

They smashed everything, the dresser, the doors and beds, everything was all over the place. That was the worst time. They smashed the paper in the windows so we covered them with clothes. Whatever they found to confiscate they confiscated, and we handed over whatever they asked for. My mother was left with nothing. We slept on the floor, in the old room, on rush matting. You know, the big mats used to cover vegetables? Think of it. I went barefoot in winter . . . and then I had loafers, eighty cents a pair, but they went up to one kuai, and then I had white sneakers, but that was in winter, so my feet were still cold.

Zhao's maternal grandfather decided to support the Communist Party after the nationalization of private property, and so was spared being targeted by the Red Guards. Without the protection afforded by such political credentials, his father and paternal grandfather were both beaten up and persecuted. Zhao recalled seeing his father being forced to kneel outside his dazayuan doorway as the Red Guards hurled abuse at him. He was then sent back to the countryside in Tong County to be "transformed" (*gaizao*), as his son put it, and was allowed to return to Beijing only when he was rehabilitated in the early 1980s, when open-door reform was taking off. He was given no more than a few hundred yuan in compensation for the confiscation of his property, and his family continued to live in poverty, despite a slight increase in his wages in 1987. He and his wife, Old Mrs. Zhao, had endless quarrels provoked, according to Zhao Yong, by her mental difficulties, and his father "never really enjoyed anything." His experience during the Cultural Revolution scarred him "in every way, mentally, socially, and at home." He died of cancer in the hospital in 1999. Zhao's younger brother died a few months later—one story was that he died as a result of an infection that developed from a ricocheting bullet wound in Tian'anmen Square in 1989, and another was that it was cancer—and his mother's condition continued to deteriorate. "Why did our family degenerate into the state it's in today?" was Zhao's rhetorical question. "It's all to do with the Cultural Revolution. If you want to talk about human rights . . . I don't oppose the Communist Party, but it's gone too far in some things. And if you talk about democracy, you can't go into it in much depth, because, truthfully, it's enough just for people to be able to survive before we can start talking about democracy."

Zhao's mother accompanied her husband back to the countryside in the 1960s, taking her two youngest children with her. Although both still very young, Zhao Yong and his elder sister were left in Dashalar to care for themselves until their maternal grandmother stepped in to look after them. The street committee gave them some grain, and their father's work unit gave them a bit of corn flour, which they cooked on a small open fire they used to make from scraps of coal and wood they picked up off the street. Local primary schools had all closed down, and it was only when they reopened in the early 1970s, when Zhao Yong was already nine years old, that he started attending school. He didn't mind being three years older than his classmates; on the contrary, he quite liked it, he said, because "no one could beat me up." He described himself as having been a somewhat undisciplined child, climbing up onto rooftops, up electric poles and trees, and spending time with his schoolmates throwing clay balls into potholes in the local roads and alleys. He found it difficult to keep up with his studies. "Our home was awful. There was no table or stool to study. I used to use a stone slab outside. Then the lights, there were always electricity cuts. I studied every evening until eight or nine, then supper, bed at twelve, and then had to get up at six to go to school. Without breakfast, because we didn't have any money."

After having to repeat a year, he only just managed to complete the sixth grade when he was nearly sixteen years old. Nevertheless, what he lacked in academic skills he tried to make up for in other ways.

They taught us painting at school, so I'd paint something and take it home to use for the fire. Matchboxes used to have pictures on them, and I used to cut them up, twenty at a time, and put them in my satchel to sell to the kids at school. A teacher once asked me why I had so many in my bag and I said I've got to make the grade [so need the money]. I also used to cut up foreign reproductions in newspapers I came across to sell them to fellow students for twenty cents a go.

One of Zhao's teachers was a kind man who used to help the young boy by giving him food when he arrived at school. According to Zhao, this teacher had had a tough life, and sacrificed his own interests to care for his elderly mother, and it was only when he was forty and she died that he married. Zhao was extremely grateful to this teacher for his support, and when the teacher married, he, Zhao Yong, and a fellow student went to his house to give him a wedding present—a porcelain bowl decorated with the "happiness" character and little birds. The occasion remained in Zhao's memory as a minor epiphany: "It was then that I thought I really wanted to change my circumstances, to make some money to change our lives—not too much, not for conspicuous spending, but to change our life circumstances."

On finishing primary school in 1979, Zhao decided to start work while studying part-time at night school. Adult education was not expensive then, sixty to eighty yuan each term, and Zhao brought in enough of a wage to continue his studies for another three and a half years. He tried his hand at different jobs, making enough to give his parents and leave a small amount for himself. He first worked as a rubbish collector and street sweeper, and then for three years as a manual laborer digging ditches, for which he earned one yuan fifty cents per square meter, totaling between seventy to eighty yuan a month. He used his first three months' wages to follow through with his commitment to improving his family's life by buying a wardrobe. After another three months, he had saved enough to buy a desk, later followed by a nine-inch black-and-white TV for 120 yuan. He lived on a frugal budget in order to save enough money for these purchases, and retained a precise memory of his expenditures: "Thirty-five to eighty cents for food . . . stuffed savory buns [shaobing] were really cheap then, a big one was twenty-five to thirty-five cents, but later they went up to fifty cents. Then tofu [doufu] soup for eight cents, that later went up to twenty cents. . . . But you'd wake up one morning and things would be more expensive again. So sometimes I didn't eat breakfast. Buns and noodles were all too expensive."

He decided to try to earn a bit more by loading sacks of sand and other heavy materials onto trains for three and a half yuan per shift, but working two shifts a day was too demanding. "I couldn't take it after three months. Up and down, you had to count everything . . . and to do this work you had to eat four buns in the morning to keep you going," in other words, more than he could afford. Through the street committee he found another job in the Beijing Sewing Machine Factory, followed by another mixing sand and cement on a construction site, and then as a scaffolder. "At that time, I ate two big shaobing every morning, and three big pieces of bread, and a plate of pickles for two cents. My father made fifty-five kuai a month, later went up to fifty-seven. My wages went up from thirty-one to seventy a month. Why did I work in scaffolding? Three and a half kuai every day, up from two and a half to three and a half every day, so I started subsidizing our family."

He had to leave this job when he developed an allergy, and around 1989 finally found more stable employment working in a state-owned motor vehicle factory, earning around five hundred yuan a month. By 1996, however, as state companies started laying off huge numbers of workers, Zhao was made a contract worker, and was finally laid off in 1998 when the factory became a joint venture under US management, producing four-by-fours. As an unskilled, unemployed worker approaching middle age, he had few employment options, so decided to go it alone selling fruit. "I got to work at seven in the morning and returned home at two to sell fruit. I had to wake up at four in the morning to go to buy the fruit on my rickshaw. I bought seven, eight, or nine pounds of fruit. I used to finish at ten at night. So my life was completely irregular [meiyou guilü]. I never had time to eat and didn't rest enough."

Despite his efforts and exhausting work, Zhao's income was barely enough to put food on the table, let alone cover any additional expenses. He had not had any contact with his elder sister for many years. His younger sister, whom I never met, apparently had mental health problems and was unable to work. His younger brother was hospitalized for two months in late 1999, at the same time as his father, and between them their medical expenses came to 110,000 yuan. His father had 80 percent of his medical insurance costs paid by his former work unit, and between what he earned and could borrow, Zhao managed to pay the remaining 20,000 yuan. However, this left Zhao without any resources, not even enough to buy his brother's funeral garments. "If you don't have any money, they just watch you die."

Strategies and Struggles for Everyday Survival

Qian, Zhao Yong's wife, was as accustomed as her husband to making do with limited means. She was born in 1964, the youngest of four children, and grew up with her family in a single small rented room in another popular neighborhood of South City. "We were so poor when I was little. We had paper windows then, and when we didn't have anything else to play with we'd poke holes in it. We didn't have windows like we have now, then, no way." She recalled that her entire family slept on a *kang*—a raised platform structure—since there was no room for beds. Marriage did not bring her much comfort either, and when her first husband died in the mid-1990s, he left her with little to support their daughter, then only two years old. "He couldn't give me anything, could he? He was dead!" was her wry response to my question about whether he left her anything. Three years after the death of her first husband she was introduced to Zhao Yong, then divorced from an unhappy first marriage. Zhao was initially reluctant to consider another marriage, since his first wife had brought him little but misery. She was disrespectful and unfilial toward his mother, and repeatedly pressured Zhao for money. But Qian was persistent, getting neighbors to visit Zhao and making numerous phone calls to him. She eventually asked him out for a meal, and they took a couple of day trips out of Beijing.

Qian was clearly a very different kind of person from Zhao's first wife. She helped look after Zhao's father before he died, and was extremely attentive to his mother. "She cut her hair and her nails, and washed her clothes. Much better than my first wife. She's very filial. So I was happy to get on with her daughter. We got on well." For Zhao Yong, Qian's respect for his mother more than compensated for the additional responsibilities of taking on a stepdaughter; Qian, for her part, was more interested in creating a stable environment for her daughter than in making money. "Money, your arse . . . money is what people fight over. . . . His mother wanted to give me a gift [of money] when we met, but I said I didn't need it, and told her to keep it for herself, since she didn't have much." One of Zhao's cousins repeatedly warned Qian against marrying him, on the grounds that his mother's and younger sister's mental health problems would put too many demands on her. Qian, however, reminded this cousin, "I'm marrying him, not his mother or his sister. I'm marrying this man, and whatever his family is like has nothing to do with me." The couple agreed not to have another child, even though as a childless man entering his second marriage, Zhao was entitled to have another.[7] As he put it, "You have to give them a good environment [to grow up in]." But Zhao was a good father to his stepdaughter, and treated her as his own child, advising her about her schooling and doing his best to instill in her a moral code of respect for her elders. He was determined that she should benefit from education to explore better opportunities in life than he had had. This opportunity presented itself in 2012. As resourceful as ever, Zhao took advantage of what he described as "a new policy introduced by Premier Wen Jiabao, to give disadvantaged students access to schools without necessarily meeting the exact entry requirements." With a bit of online research, he discovered a horticulture course in a boarding school in Beijing that found employment for its graduates. His stepdaughter was not an academically minded student, so when this school crossed Zhao's horizons, for the cost of seven hundred yuan a term, he leapt at the opportunity it offered.

Qian's and her husband's everyday life revolved around work and domestic chores—fetching gas cylinders, buying coal and food—and looking after Zhao's mother. Zhao Yong's main source of income when I first met him derived from driving a pedicab and selling Buddhist trinkets on a small mobile vending cart he used to park on Dashalar's West Street. He did not have a license for his pedicab, so generally worked on the stall during the daytime, handing it over to his wife in the evening when he felt it was safer to work the pedicab. Nevertheless, he was fined on numerous occasions, particularly around 2008, when stringent regulations were implemented to clear the neighborhood of street vendors and illegal trade, as I noted in chapter 1.

Qian also worked the pedicab and helped with the Buddhist stall, alongside a number of other jobs. When I first met her, she had a job washing dishes in a nearby Kentucky Fried Chicken outlet. By 2009 she had given this over for a more flexible job cleaning for a single elderly man in the neighborhood. This work, however, was both time-consuming and frustrating; her client often slept late in the morning, so Qian would turn up expecting to be able to start work, only to have to return home since he did not like people cleaning while he slept. He did not have a telephone, so Qian had no means of contacting him to confirm the times of her work. And although his veteran's pension brought him in four to five thousand yuan a month, he paid her minimal wages. Her next job as a garbage collector brought her one thousand yuan a month, but she had to work eight hours a day, every day of the week. By 2013, she had found yet another job, cooking lunch for some twenty employees of a bank in Chaoyang District. With a monthly wage of 1,300 yuan and one day off a week, this was clearly preferable to the thankless task of trying to keep the streets clean of rubbish.

Both Zhao and his wife were hard and resourceful workers. Nevertheless, the pressures of having to pay a monthly rent of eight hundred yuan plus the school fees for their daughter were relentless. There was scarcely enough to pay the water, electricity, and coal bills, and rising food prices were a constant source of indignation. All around them, they could see evidence of the achievements of China's global economic success. The stark contrast with their own situation further fueled their resentment. On one occasion, loudly indignant at having been arrested for refusing to pay a minor traffic infringement fine, Zhao told me that I had to find a way to help him to move to London. "There are no human rights here," he shouted. "You've got to get me to London." By 2013, he had begun to think about Canada, a country he felt was "more stable" than China, where—"I've checked online"—in return for bringing in fifty thousand dollars, he said, he could obtain a visa and work permit.

Zhao's concerns for his mother were never far from his mind, and despite his frequent impatience with her, and the exhaustion of attending to her needs, he was resigned to his responsibility to care for her.

> Why does she have to remind me about things, like how I haven't done this or that, or what things need to be arranged? I remember everything, and if something hasn't been done, I do it right away. I'm emotionally tired, and physically tired, sometimes it's really too much. Like you, you have to work and take care of the children. You and I have to put all our mental energies into attending to others, and don't do an awful lot for ourselves. Like me, as long as I have something to eat, that's enough. But my old mother is a different story. I have to think about clothing her properly, keeping her warm, making sure she doesn't get too cold. Then the kid, how is she today, is she studying okay? So, emotional exhaustion is even more than physical exhaustion. I wasn't like this before. Before, I made money and kept the family going, and we got by fine, but now it's a different story, you have to think of everything. The old lady can't [do much], so you have to think about how to deal with everything.

Awareness of the injustices of their social and economic environment only added to the constraints Zhao and his wife had to face in their everyday lives. Local patrol officers (*chengguan*) who routinely used to fine local pedicab cyclists caught without a license sustained what Zhao called a completely arbitrary system of individual control (*ge ren guanli*), "where anything can happen. They just want to get money off you. If you give them money they let you go and give your bike back. If they say you are okay, you are okay, and if you have connections, or conditions, they might give you some concession, but if you don't, no one gives you anything."

The changing social environment of his neighborhood was another source of local tension, in Zhao's view.

> In the past, if there was any problem at home, the neighbors on the lane would all help you. If you asked anyone for help, they would all be totally willing to help you, unselfishly. Now it's not the same. When you knock

on someone's door, they don't answer. People keep their distance from each other. Older people still get on with each other [*jiang dian qinqing*], but young people don't. Like people of our age, we are okay, but people younger than thirty, those who were born after the reform, I really don't understand what they are on about.

The Cultural Revolution, Zhao Yong argued, made social relations so tense and cold that neighbors scarcely dared talk to each other. His own distance from his neighbors—through the many visits I paid him in his house, I rarely heard a neighbor calling out to him or knocking on the door, let alone coming in—was compounded by the social stigma his family had to endure as a result of their reputation for madness. It had been a long time since he had had any social contact with his local boyhood friends, and one of these—Jia Yong, one of the few local people I knew who made good from market competition—was openly disdainful of Zhao's family situation, as I note in chapter 7. It was, Jia claimed, the consequence of a history of family madness and child neglect.

However, the most significant changes in Zhao's social environment occurred, in his view, after the onset of market reform, with the massive arrival of labor migrants—"outsiders" (*waidiren*)—from other parts of China, and the gradual erosion of what he called the "taste of old Beijing." Many of his former acquaintances in the neighborhood moved out, but even more outsiders moved in. Eight other households lived in his courtyard when I first visited him there, none of whom were from Beijing.

Before 1990, there was still the kind of feeling [*ganjue*] of the old Beijing courtyard, like a big family. Some people were quite selfish, but others quite considerate. . . . [T]here were a few tensions between people, but there was still the taste of old Beijing. But after 1985, after 1990, these things gradually disappeared. It no longer had the same feel as before, eating old Beijing street food [*xiaochi*], ambling along the old Beijing lanes, looking for that old Beijing feeling or a kind of taste. That lifestyle no longer exists. When people started moving in from all over the country, and other things from outside started pouring in, the old feel of Beijing was destroyed. . . . In fact it's the poor quality of outsiders plus the things from outside. . . . Real old Beijingers are . . . how to put it? Like, I'm really friendly to you, really polite, and happy for you to live here, but now these people from outside, they are secretive and damage things, they are bad, rapists, tricksters, and greedy. And the greedy ones don't go out to work. So lots of the old Beijing things have been lost, and have been badly mixed up with other things, and there are lots of bad things from outside. . . . In the past people considered justice and righteousness [*yi*], and feeling [*qing*]. Now the feeling has gone, leaving people empty. Because there are too many false things, so it's just empty.

While Qian was grateful for Zhao's supportive attentiveness to her daughter, this by no means meant passive acceptance of all that he did. Indeed, she not infrequently demonstrated a slight suspicion of what he did when he was out and about, and hinted on a number of occasions, sometimes in the presence of her husband, that he was involved in all sorts of activities that he kept in the dark. He was often out "on business" (*ban shi*), as his wife put it, when I called on the family unannounced, and on his return rarely gave any explanation for his absence. I too was occasionally surprised by him, though for different reasons. One day he suggested taking me to watch him practice martial arts in a park toward the west end of the city, and he wanted to drive me in his car, a convenience, as he put it, for getting over to his wife's apartment when his mother went to bed at night. It had not occurred to me that he had a car, nor that he was a regular practitioner of martial arts.

Zhao's delight in talking about "big things" and his dreams about life elsewhere took him into worlds of existence that were doubtless far removed from Dashalar. Nevertheless, Dashalar was the place to which he was attached, and apart from those occasions when frustration and anger got the better of him, I never heard him make any reference to a desire to leave the neighborhood. His wife, in contrast, longed to travel and see the world. She went with a tourist group on a short holiday to Hong Kong in 2010, and told me that had she had the resources, she would have relished the opportunity to live in another part of Beijing. In contrast, Zhao's anecdotes and memories of Dashalar's lanes and alleys, its temples, brothels, and small opera houses, anchored his philosophical and spatial meanderings in place. He repeatedly listed the names and locations of its old artisan shops, restaurants, and temples, even though most were demolished or destroyed some time ago. And although the opportunity never seemed to present itself, he often suggested giving me a guided tour of the places he remembered from his childhood. Dashalar gave him a grounded place-based personal history shoring up the constraints of his present.

"Big Things" and Personal Philosophy

Zhao Yong was in his element when talking about "big things" (*da shi*)—politics, comparisons between Europe and China, the histories of the famous artisan trades of Dashalar, food, morality and filial piety, child upbringing, and Buddhism. On more than one occasion when his mother attempted to join in our conversation, he interrupted his flow of thought to tell her to be quiet and let him speak: "You be quiet, let me speak. We are talking about big things." He moved seamlessly from one topic to another, interjecting rhetorical questions into his philosophical musings, his voice becoming louder and louder, even overbearing, as he spoke. An apparently simple question about how his work was going could launch him into an impassioned exposition on morality, Confucianism, and traditional Chinese culture. References to the colors of China's imperial tradition could lead to a discourse on such apparently unrelated topics as the meaning of good fortune and the shortcomings of modern parenting. He could quote entire poems of Mao Zedong, and without pausing for breath could move through war and China's political system to critiques of Chiang Kaishek, corruption, and power. The meaning of his meanderings was frequently opaque:

> I like Mao Zedong's poems, but I don't like his political thought and ideas. I can't say that I oppose him, because he changed things for China. What did he change? He changed the dynasty, he changed history, but he didn't change people's lives. He was just like Cixi; he wanted to control people.[8] All he wanted was to be high up, on top, and everyone else was just dumb and stupid. But people, geography, the environment, individual elements, plus the state, plus the Second World War. The war was chaos. There's always war in the human world, and then there are dictators and tyrants. Why do you not dare to speak out in China? Because it's still a single-party system, it's not a multiparty system. It's not like Europe. China has a slave system. What do I mean? I'll put it another way. Why do parents nowadays not focus on bringing up their children to work hard? Today's parents focus on their children being good. As long they don't get into any big trouble then everything's okay. I don't share this view, because you have to be strong, and go out and fight. But there's a problem with this, because you have to learn how to be a good person and how to do good things. You can't just do as you want. That was what Mao Zedong was like. Why did Wen Jiabao say that children should be educated? I really approve [zancheng] of this. But all that people think about now is just making money. You can do anything, you can cheat and harm people, and it's all okay if it's to make money. Not even Chiang Kaishek did this. The local patrol officers and the people in the local police stations make it their specialty to control the small traders. They don't dare touch the big people. Chiang Kaishek wasn't like that, because he specialized in the big entrepreneurs, he didn't bully ordinary people. You want to say something? They don't let you speak,

no way, they just want you to die. "I'm the one who calls the shots [*shuole suan*]." You've got even less of a chance if you're uneducated. So, I would tell children, "Arm yourselves; knowledge is the way to create wealth."

Buddhism occupies a central place in Zhao's personal moral code. He converted to Buddhism in 1993 when he was hospitalized with a kidney infection, and his doctor introduced him to a Buddhist monk who talked with him about "life release" (*fangsheng*). When he left the hospital, he decided to find out what *fangsheng* meant, so he went to a temple the monk had mentioned, where he found a group of people "releasing life" and "releasing souls from misery" (*chaodu*).[9] After this experience, he felt completely recovered from his infection. So began his belief in Buddhism, which he described as a kind of "destiny" (*yuanfen*). Ever since his conversion, Zhao Yong has kept a small Buddhist shrine in his home, and he lights incense at it every day. The Buddha's protection, so he and his wife think, has enabled him to survive many difficulties, including a foot wound resulting from stepping on a nail, when he nearly died of septicemia; his younger brother's death; and his family's mental health problems. His conversion also inspired his decision to start selling incense and Buddhist ephemera.

Alongside Buddhist beliefs, Zhao's personal philosophy is an eclectic mix of ideas that combines many other elements, including random thoughts about cultural difference and political power.

> I like hearing about these things. Buddhism, Daoism, Christianity, God. Buddhism's very purifying. What does it purify? The soul [*linghun*]! In Buddhism we say "linghun." In the West you talk about purifying your soul, and purifying your heart and mind, and then you go from your heart to wisdom and knowledge. Why do I say that people at the top all understand this? Including Chiang Kaishek, he moved from Buddhism to Christianity, because the Song family was from the West, Western culture, and he was from Eastern culture. . . . It's the same with Mao Zedong and today's leaders. They are all the same, really. They all moved from Eastern culture to Western culture and back to Eastern culture.

As these short excerpts from his narrative suggest, Zhao's logic was quite difficult to follow, but his attempts to formulate some understanding of the relationship between class, culture, and power demonstrated an interest in matters and ideas outside and beyond his immediate environment that I did not encounter much among others I knew in Dashalar. While confused and confusing, and sometimes blatantly prejudiced, his musings released him from the imprisoning constraints of his material and social existence.

Like his beliefs and interest in "big things," Zhao's personal philosophy revealed an intricately but unevenly woven tapestry of diverse and apparently inconsistent ideas drawn from traditional concepts of filiality, fate, self-cultivation, the meaning of individual responsibility, the ethical boundaries of individual behavior, and much more. While acknowledging that he was but poorly educated, Zhao felt he possessed a sense of responsibility and morality that many others, particularly younger urban people, who were much better off materially than he was, notably lacked. "If you're responsible to your family, parents, and children, then you can feel that you haven't wasted any time as a person." He also took a certain pride in what he considered to be his achievements in having created opportunities for himself, including being able to study China's moral tradition.

> I have my own value, and haven't let my family down; I know what I'm capable of. Some sons and daughters have their road paved well for them by their parents. Who paved mine? It was me alone who created it. Some say people of value are those who turn their life around. This is like what I think. . . . Culture lets you absorb things and develop . . . and to be able to take the measure of yourself and all living creatures. If you don't take the measure of yourself, how can you take on everything else? Studying traditions . . . teaches you how to be a person, how to do things.

Between his comments about family and personal value, and his exhaustive efforts to care for his mother, Zhao Yong was thus not above attempting to demonstrate a certain superiority by taking the moral high ground. This was particularly apparent on one occasion when he lapsed into comparing his own situation with that of his childhood acquaintance, the local restaurateur, whose story I tell in chapter 7. "That restaurateur has got it good. . . . [H]e's in a much better situation than I am. No matter what it was like to begin with, he's now got the ground firmly under his feet; his mother set things up well for him. But me, I have to think and do much more than him. His son, people say he's like a little lord, but who does he save for? For his son, and who does the son then pass it on to? To the father, so it all starts again."

Frustrations and Face

Zhao Yong was at his most animated when talking about "big things" he cared about. However, he could also direct his animation at his mother, as we have seen, sometimes loudly shouting at her to stop being stupid or to stop interrupting him. My presence did not stop him from giving vent to this kind of frustration. On one occasion, however, I realized that his frustration could take other forms when I wasn't there.

It was late on a Saturday evening in early summer 2009. I was walking north back from West Street to the subway at Qianmen when I heard someone shouting at me from the other side of the street. Turning, I realized that the person shouting was Old Mrs. Zhao, who seemed desperately anxious. I crossed the road to find her frantic with fright, telling me that the police were behind her and wanted to break her knees, that she had been locked out of her home by her neighbors, who wanted to set fire to the place. She was terrified, and kept pointing behind her to where she said she could see the policemen. I managed to calm her down a bit, and walked back arm in arm with her the short distance to her home, where the door was open, with no evidence of a fire. I saw Old Mrs. Zhao to her room at the back, and phoned Zhao, who asked if she was okay, and said that this behavior was not uncommon. He instructed me to shut the padlock on the door of her room, and that he would be there in the morning to check that she was okay. I returned the following morning to hear loud angry voices coming from inside, in what seemed to be an extremely heated argument. I left and returned an hour or so later, by which time things had quietened down. As I entered the yard, I asked Zhao how his mother was, and told him that I had been alarmed to see her in such a terrified state the night before. Zhao told me that she not infrequently used to wander off and get frightened, so the only way to deal with the situation was to lock her in her room when he left to stay the night with his wife. He assured me that if anything really dangerous were to happen, he would of course stay with his mother. What this revealed to me, apart from the evidence it gave me about how much worse Old Mrs. Gao was than I had previously witnessed, was that Zhao Yong was quite circumspect about how much of his domestic situation he shared with me, or let me see.

However, he knew that I was sympathetic toward him, and I had realized sometime before this incident that he welcomed my visits both as a kind of escape from the relentless and exhausting mundanities of his everyday life, and as recognition that he was a person with needs and interests as much as anyone else. Over time, I came to realize that he wanted to use his connection with me to boost his social capital—in local language, to give him face (*mianzi*). One occasion was one I have already mentioned, when he invited me to go with him to watch him practice martial arts in a park on the outskirts of the city. It was a bitterly cold Sunday morning. We arrived at the park in Zhao's car to find a small group of people, all middle-aged men, standing around a small clearing. They had hung their jackets and scarves up on the branches of nearby trees. All were dressed in trainers, training trousers, and traditional Chinese martial arts jackets. After a few minutes standing around chatting, we were approached by an imposing-looking man dressed in full martial arts gear. Zhao Yong introduced him to me, saying he was his teacher, and cousin, and that he, Zhao Yong, was extremely fortunate to have a cousin who was an expert in martial arts. He also told his cousin that I was a friend from England, and that I was conducting research on the history of Dashalar and wanted to watch Zhao practice his exercises. Did his cousin mind? The cousin was polite enough but seemed completely indifferent both to what Zhao had to say and to my presence.

The class started, initially with group exercises. After a while, the teacher, Zhao's cousin, asked individual members to perform. The first two, both men, rehearsed their routines at a measured pace and finished without the cousin saying anything. It then came to Zhao Yong. He started off the same routine as the others, but at a rather faster pace, whereupon his cousin told him to slow down. Zhao continued, only to be interrupted again by his cousin, who stopped him and demanded that he watch him, the teacher, go through the same routine so that Zhao could see how it should be performed. Finally, Zhao managed to get through the routine, with his cousin standing at the side, chin in hand and shaking his head. On finishing, his cousin put his hand on Zhao's shoulder and declared to no one in particular that if you tried hard enough, you could get through the routine. The class came to an end after the final two students performed their routine, again without any comment from the teacher. As Zhao and I got into his car to go home, I asked him how he thought the class had gone, to which he responded by saying that his cousin was an "excellent teacher" and a "real expert." All I could do in response was to remain silent, as, in my awkwardness, I tried to absorb the import of Zhao's inter-nalization of and reinterpretation of his cousin's attempts to show his own authority by belittling Zhao in front of me.

The only other occasion when I became conscious that Zhao might be concerned about losing face was when he insisted on inviting me to lunch in a restaurant in Chaoyang District, a short distance from Dashalar. The occasion was to celebrate the birthday of one of my daughters, whom he had met several years beforehand. However, as soon as we looked at the menu, I realized that it was much more expensive than I was prepared for him to pay. I felt foolish for having accepted his invitation. So, at the risk of offending him, I decided to tell him that I was very happy for him to decide on the dishes (*dian cai*), but that *I* wanted to invite *him* because that was what my daughter would have wanted. Rather than argue, as has happened on numerous other occasions when Beijing friends and I have gone out to eat in Beijing, Zhao just accepted my suggestion. It seemed that no offense had been caused.

Pleasures and Disappointments

After an absence of several months, I returned to Beijing in the mid-autumn of 2013. I called Zhao to arrange a time to visit him at home. It was a sunny day, and I arrived to find Qian busy rolling dumplings and cutting up vegetables for a big lunch. As was her wont, Old Mrs. Zhao greeted me warmly and immediately plied me with questions about why I had not been to see them for so long. Zhao greeted me like an old friend, asked me to sit down, and affectionately asked after me and my daughters. His home seemed a bit different; most noticeable was that the bird and the birdcage had gone. He said that his mother had lost interest in the bird, and the bird had stopped talking, so he had given it away. Over lunch we talked about how he had had to give up his Buddhist trinket stall, since he did not have a license, and how he now depended on doing bits of business to make ends meet. As we ate, Qian talked about her job and, very briefly, about her daughter, who she hoped would go to the horticultural college I mentioned earlier.

After a prolonged lunch, Zhao invited me outside onto the lane to admire his crop of sugar snap peas, growing up from a vast pot leaning against the outer wall of his home. There were not many left, but he decided to harvest them so that I could taste them. To access the peas, he had to climb on top of a flimsy lean-to shed, and looked alarmingly unstable as he reached up to pick them. Qian came outside with a plastic bowl, looking slightly worried. But Zhao was totally confident that the roof of the lean-to shed would hold him. His delight was palpable as he threw each pod down into the bowl that his wife, standing on the ground, held up for him.

Back inside, he announced that he had changed. He no longer yearned for exciting activities, and didn't want to struggle any more, but was content to feel that as he approached his later years, he had fulfilled his family obligations. He enjoyed doing simple things at home. Smiling at her husband, Qian said that she was not yet at that stage. She was not yet ready to give up ideas of traveling abroad.

Unperturbed, Zhao embarked on a description of his ideal of an elderly couple, comfortable with each other, walking out and about together, exchanging the odd comment, peeling an apple for each other, companionable, relaxed, and content in their later years. He also claimed that on his retirement he would receive a monthly income of around two thousand yuan, partly from the pension fund he had been paying into over the past ten years, and partly from the unit where he used to work. He ended this conversation by announcing again that he intended to go to Canada, where the younger brother of his brother-in-law lived, where he would buy a house and maybe teach martial arts.

The last time I visited the Zhao family was in May 2017, after an absence of three years. I turned up unannounced, together with a friend who over the years had accompanied me on many visits to local people in the neighborhood. I shouted out to Zhao Yong from the alley. The plant pots in which he had grown his peas and beans were not in evidence, and since none of the doors on the alley were numbered, it took some time for me to identify his home. Zhao clearly heard me outside on the lane because he rushed out to greet me and invite me inside. I had not anticipated what I found. He and his family had moved out of the more spacious room just inside the entrance, back into their former cramped subdivided room at the back. But they now had much more furniture and bits and pieces than when they had occupied this small room before. Inside the main living space was a single bed that served as a sofa, a cabinet, and a dresser. It was also quite dirty. There was just enough room to fit a small table for the bowls of fruit and nuts that Qian laid out for us. Zhao, my friend, and I sat on the bed while Qian, her daughter, and mother-in-law busied themselves outside in the corridor, rolling dumplings. Neither Zhao's mother nor his wife seemed to have changed much. Qian initially seemed as cheerful as always. Old Mrs. Zhao couldn't get her words out quickly enough as she asked me about what I'd been doing all this time, and why hadn't I been to see her. Qian's daughter then appeared, rather shyly. I simply did not recognize her. She was no longer a child but a young woman. She was also much plumper than she had been, a result Zhao said of eating too much fast food. It was only when she opened the gift I had brought her from London, a pencil case and a purse with a shoulder strap, that she relaxed enough to say hello and ask me how I was, but then made a hasty retreat back to help her mother prepare the meal.

Zhao seemed more subdued than I remembered him. He started by telling me that the owner/landlord of the front room had raised the monthly rent, and since he, Zhao, was unable to afford it, he had no choice but to move back into his former, smaller room. This was unsatisfactory, but what could he do? Qian had stopped working and his mother's situation hadn't changed, and he was extremely tired. When I asked him whether his daughter had graduated from the horticultural college, he launched into a complicated story about a confusion about her final exams. From what he told me, I understood that he had registered her to sit the final exams for her course under his Dashalar address, but since the examinees apparently had to be registered in the same district as the college, she had not been eligible to sit the exam. She had therefore finished the course but had not obtained the qualifications she had anticipated. Moreover, the initial plan, advertised by the college, to help their students find employment through a work placement scheme, had come to nothing. Given that it was this that had initially attracted Zhao's attention, he felt extremely frustrated with the college authorities, who in his eyes had gone back on their word.

Zhao and I sat there chatting while Qian, her daughter, and Old Mrs. Zhao kept appearing at the doorway to ask Zhao's advice about eating arrangements, specifically the dish they should use to serve the dumplings in. The first they wanted to use was broken. "So why don't you use that other one that I picked up the other day?" When his daughter responded by saying "You mean the one I had to scrub clean?" Zhao became very impatient and ordered her out of the doorway back to help her mother. He also muttered something about how his mother made a habit of picking things up off the street that were too old or broken to use. A brief loud exchange between Zhao sitting inside and Qian cooking outside in the corridor finally resolved the matter, and after a few minutes Qian came in with a large plate of steaming dumplings.

As we ate, Zhao brought me up to date on his martial arts practice. He continued to practice every weekend, often in the same park to which he had taken me earlier. His older cousin, whom he addressed as "Brother Teacher" (Shixiong), had started up his own martial arts training school, at which Zhao's class had been invited to give a performance. Zhao himself had not participated in the performance. His cousin's son, who was also a student in this class, suggested that Zhao join them for a celebratory lunch and photograph. His cousin responded by saying this would not be appropriate, since Zhao had not participated in the performance. To cover his disappointment, Zhao then showed us a photograph of him practicing martial arts together with his cousin's son, who addressed him as "Uncle," thus affectionately acknowledging him as close kin. The implicit contrast Zhao was drawing here between his "Brother Teacher" and the latter's son did not, of course, escape my attention.

Interlude 2

Zhao Yong and his family were the most disadvantaged of the long-term local residents of Dashalar I knew. Zhao Yong inherited a burdensome legacy of social and political discrimination associated with his family's classification as small landlords in the early 1950s, a family history of mental health difficulties, and local neighborhood disdain. During his early childhood, his family's impoverished situation was not enough to prevent attack during the Cultural Revolution. The wrath the Red Guards hurled at his father and the ransacking of his home had devastating consequences, resulting in his father's depression and his mother's paranoid delusions. Despite the government's official pronouncements in the 1980s, his father received no compensation for the earlier destruction of his home and property. Between the 1990s and the new millennium, as sweeping market reforms took effect in the fuller spatial and social reconstruction around Dashalar, Zhao's situation became even more precarious. Now unemployed, he had to rely on a combination of his wife's fluctuating income and his own ad hoc earnings in the informal economy to make ends meet.

At first glance, Zhao's account of his family's experience during the Cultural Revolution seems familiar: it echoes the narrative of violence and suffering of those with "bad" family backgrounds that abounds in autobiographical accounts. However, while the incidence of Zhao's experience, per se, is not what makes it unusual, the memory and narration of its occurrence in a disadvantaged urban household is distinctive. The abundance of literary, filmic, artistic, biographical, and media depictions of the Cultural Revolution now available to global audiences address a diverse range of subjects, urban and rural, Han and ethnic minority, young and old, female and male. Academic writings on the social, cultural, and political processes and experiences of the Cultural Revolution focus this range on a largely urban demographic consisting of intellectuals, professionals, writers, artists, musicians, and students—in other words, those whose skills, training, connections, and backgrounds facilitated the writing of diaries and letters, fictional stories and memoirs. The social and political status of these groups has earned them the attention of biographers, chroniclers, and documentary filmmakers; it is these whose stories feature as testimonies of the numerous ranks of urban residents who were sent to cadre schools, or sent down to the countryside to learn from the peasants; it is these we are told who were killed, imprisoned in labor camps, or committed suicide. It is arguably through the lens of "victim literature"—the body of literature that focuses on the experiences of these sectors—and its concerns with the suffering perpetrated on the nation's educated elite, that the Cultural Revolution is best known to Western and, arguably, young Chinese audiences.[1]

By contrast, research on the Cultural Revolution has given little attention to the urban poor—the kinds of people I write about in this book—who, like Zhao Yong, make no claims to a privileged victimhood in their accounts of the late Mao era, who have no social or political stake in debates about the legacy of the Mao era, and who do not have the social or cultural capital or skills to record their own or their families' experiences. Zhao Yong construed the Cultural Revolution not as a state of exception, or a blip on what would otherwise have been a smooth transition between the Republican era and market reform, as mainstream accounts commonly imply, but as one moment, albeit distinctive in its particularities, in a bigger history of hardship, neglect, discrimination, and precarity predating and following the Cultural Revolution years.[2] Without privileged access to compensation enjoyed by the wealthier and better socially connected sectors of the population, the absence of any financial or material backup for the Zhao family either during or after the Cultural Revolution confirmed a decades-long condition best described as a state of unremitting material and social subjugation. If this began as an effect of political discrimination against private entrepreneurs in the early years of the PRC, it was confirmed by the family's poverty, isolation, and lack of beneficial social and political connections.

The formal end to the mass political "campaign" (*yundong*) as an appropriate political practice, announced in 1981, was in part to thwart a recurrence of the arbitrary use of violence by both the state and individuals associated with the "politics in command" policies of previous decades.[3] The extent and character of the violence visited upon the urban professional, intellectual, and political elites during the Cultural Revolution did not recur on an equivalent scale in subsequent decades, despite the target of the protests of the 1980s.[4] Many members of those elites, moreover, went on during the reform era to become well-known academics, professionals, and entrepreneurs. For the urban poor of Dashalar, in contrast, the vicious and destructive effect of the Cultural Revolution came to an end in its particular localized form with the disbanding of the Red Guards, but in contrast with the new opportunities available to the professional and intellectual class after the Cultural Revolution, neither the demise of the political campaign nor the advent of new educational and economic opportunities under open-door reform offered the urban poor relief from the uncertainties of everyday existence. Their all-round disadvantage meant that local residents of Dashalar were unable to benefit from the educational, professional, and economic opportunities and recognition that post-Mao reform offered the emerging urban middle class.

Into the 1980s and 1990s, wide-ranging market reforms reshaped the labor, social, and spatial conditions of the urban poor, further entrenching the uncertainties of their existence. Many of my acquaintances, including Zhao Yong, found themselves without access to stable employment at the same time as the demolition of inner-city neighborhoods near their homes began to gather steam, and as the privatization of social property and employment heralded the arrival in the neighborhood of large numbers of migrant workers, willing and able to earn a basic livelihood picking up odd jobs in the informal economy. Zhao Yong, without much education or skills, found himself even more disadvantaged. Laid off from work as many enterprises went under in the late 1990s, Zhao found himself without a reliable source of income. As a local and historically specific manifestation of the larger configuration of increasing social and economic differentials that accompanied the spread of the neoliberal global economy, the effects of marketization seemed to threaten even the possibility of engaging in the informal economy. Precarity became a way of life, pushing Zhao Yong to make ends meet by scavenging. Meanwhile, his powerlessness to effect any change in his circumstances found expression in his abusive resentment of "outsiders."

Zhao's survival at the margins of the global market reminds us about how claims to modernity and progress are substantiated by their counterevidence. In conditions dominated by a rabid form of neoliberal capitalism, the spatial situation of Dashalar and Zhao Yong's home, just a stone's throw from Tian'anmen, the monumental seat of the government's power, gives forceful visual, material, and architectural evidence of this contrast. Zhao's survival also highlights how the market successes of the new rich under the commercialization of China's economy acquire apparently spectacular dimensions and are celebrated across the globe but at the same time reproduce the poverty, marginalization, and eventual exclusion of those unable to benefit from them.[5]

Neither Zhao Yong nor any others I knew in Dashalar sought any kind of formal recognition of their past suffering. Their class and educational disadvantage denied them access to the critical expositions of the Cultural Revolution and the Mao era in general in the form we have come to associate with the "wounded literature" or the Fifth Generation films of the 1980s and 1990s.[6] None, as far as I know, ever took up explicit or overt forms of protest to articulate their anger against a system that had systematically failed them. Rather, by the time I met the Zhao family and others, the cumulative effect of decades of scarcity, neglect, and inadequate education took shape in rather different forms that emerged in family tensions, personal stress and depression, and quarrels and aggression—all widely chronicled in the comparative literature on deprived populations living in conditions of extreme pressure and hardship.[7] The everyday wretchedness of living with long-term precarity found an outlet not in overt protest, such as has been described elsewhere, but in individualized anger and extreme family tension, which Zhao did his best to hide from me. After all, I was a guest from afar, and both he and his wife were nothing except hospitable toward me. Hospitality in the form of cooking and sharing food was fundamental to their understanding of proper behavior toward a guest. But their hospitality could not mask the extreme stress of their domestic situation, as Zhao Yong's occasional outbursts of anger toward his mother and wife indicated.

Based on what I observed and what Zhao and his wife told me, the Zhao household's situation had been one of relentless adversity throughout Zhao Yong's life. With no social connections or educational opportunities to offer an escape route to a different kind of existence, and having to care for an elderly sick mother without any institutional or professional backup, Zhao developed a strategy of survival—of getting by—which in some ways was reminiscent of one of the major characters of China's early twentieth-century fiction: Ah Q. The *True Story of Ah Q* was written by Lu Xun and initially published as a serial between late 1921 and early 1922, before appearing as a novella in 1923.[8] In this story set in 1911, Ah Q was a poor, illiterate man from the countryside who was immortalized as a metaphor for what Lu Xun called "spiritual victories"—in other words, self-deception. Alternately bullying toward those he saw as inferior to him and fearful of those above him, Ah Q was known for deluding himself into believing he was the victor every time he lost a fight. He always managed to find a way to explain away defeat or humiliation, even in the face of public mockery, right up until the moment when he faced public execution.

I do not want to stretch the analogy with Zhao Yong too far. During the aftermath of the May Fourth Movement in the early 1920s, Ah Q came to symbolize all that was backward, despicable, and tragic in Chinese society. As Gloria Davies has argued, the image of Ah Q offered progressive Chinese intellectuals a kind of negative standard "against which they could measure China's and their own advance into modernity."[9] Zhao's story describes a situation more than a century after Lu Xun's call to arms, featuring material, social, and emotional entanglements of poverty, hardship, and wretchedness that neither the transformative projects of the Mao decades nor of the post-Mao market era have been able to shift in their attempts to build their own versions of modernity.

If on a certain level Zhao Yong's behavior reminds us of Ah Q's capacity to delude himself into imagining that right was on his side, I think of Zhao's repeated ability to bounce back, remake himself, and explain himself—as when his cousin insisted on belittling him in front of me—in ways that were commensurate with his sense of personal dignity, as the exercise of a kind of strategic agency oriented toward buttressing his own survival. Thinking "big things" was his way of indicating a refusal to succumb to the depressing grind of his everyday existence. My occasional presence in his house gave him arguably the only opportunity he had to talk about matters that interested him, however muddled they were, knowing that in me he had a willing audience. Linked to his desire for recognition, his delight in talking with me during my visits indicated an exercise of agency as an act of being listened to, as an act of recognition. We nearly always met in the crowded conditions of his home, where there was a poignant contrast between the constraints of his physical and spatial reality and the flights of imagination that his monologues launched into, expressing a desire to transcend his worldly existence and to experience something removed from it, whatever it might be. While many things that Zhao said were objectionable, as occasionally was his behavior toward his wife, his self-indulgence in talking big indicated his resilience and refusal to succumb to the status of victim. In this his narrative can be read as the assertion of agency in claiming recognition of his subjecthood. In contrast with Old Mrs. Gao's enactment of agency in her self-legitimation as a long-suffering mother, Zhao Yong expressed his agency in his insistence on loudly expounding his personal philosophy. Both can be apprehended as different modes of a subaltern agency associated not with subversion or protest but with qualities and capacities constituting their subjectivity within a discursive environment dominated by deeply embedded social and gendered norms.

The gendered quality of Zhao Yong's persona is prominent in his story. His delight in talking about "big things" corresponded with one of the stereotypes of Beijing men, who are known for their loud and authoritative displays of knowledge, whatever it might be. Zhao Yong was an example of what in Beijing and elsewhere in northern China is termed *yemen*—a kind of heavily male masculinity—displaying the qualities of strength, loyalty, knowledge, dominance, and face, all associated with being a real man. Local Dashalar culture—the environment in which Zhao had grown up and lived his entire life—was steeped in the gendered evidence of this, whether in groups of men sitting on stools in the lanes in summer, arguing with each other over the rules of the card game they were playing, or in motley gatherings of men loudly issuing instructions on movements to chess players sitting around makeshift tables in front of local shops, or even more in the loud exchanges between men as they sat around tables in local restaurants, smoking and playing drinking games. Zhao Yong's assertion of knowledge and his impatient putdowns of his wife and mother when they interrupted him were mild forms of what I call the "thick masculinity" of local expressions of Beijing men's sense of their own authority.

Young Gao's sense that being a filial son and responsible father were core elements of being a good person was mainly articulated through his distress at his failure to be a good son and breadwinner. For Zhao, in contrast, his commitment to a practice of filial behavior gave him a resolve that enabled him to preserve a sense of his own integrity and dignity, despite and in the face of his neighbors' and relatives' disdain. A passionately expressed attachment to the idea that personal integrity lay in his fulfillment of his gendered obligations, as son, as husband, and as father, offered a rock to cling to in a world that had repeatedly threatened to overwhelm him.

Finally, Zhao's sense of integrity also extended to his concern to maintain face. Face, as the anthropologist Yan Yunxiang argued, is fundamental to the "moral domain of *renqing* ethics," in other words to the combined moral, social, and affective qualities of "human feeling." Respect of the other's face, therefore, conveys an ontological recognition of claims to being a full person.[10] On one notable occasion in my experiences, namely when Zhao invited me to go to watch him practice martial arts, his interest in face was mainly social, to demonstrate to his elder cousin, his teacher, that he, Zhao, had access to a social capital that his cousin did not have. Zhao's desire for recognition in this instance conveyed an exercise of agency as an act of being seen to possess a certain face. No words to the effect needed to be spoken to make this clear. And it doesn't take much to interpret his cousin's explicit attempt to denigrate Zhao in front of me as an attempt to demonstrate that he, the cousin, could still call the shots. Apart from this occasion, however, Zhao's concern with face referred instead to a basic and highly gendered sense of integrity and morality, along with a desire for recognition that defined his presentation of self. As a moral concern, his concern with face was simultaneously an internal *and* external quality: internal, in that asserting his cultural and moral principles granted a sense of dignity that kept him going through the relentless and complex demands on his time and energies; and external, in that performing his cultural and moral convictions in my presence granted him social and intellectual capital to affirm his sense of dignity in a neighborhood and domestic environment that withheld it from him. At root, then, what came across as a desire for face—combining both its social and moral meanings—was a desire for recognition, and Zhao Yong's warm hospitality to me was his response to the recognition I gave him.

4

Hua Meiling

Hua Meiling, now in her late fifties, lives with her twenty-nine-year-old daughter, Xiao Hua, in a small room in a dazayuan two doors down from where the Gao family used to live. Meiling's mother-in-law, Mrs. Zhang, now well into her seventies, lives in the same dazayuan, with her daughter and grandson.

Meiling has been living in the same room since she married Mrs. Zhang's son in 1990. The room is immaculately tidy. Meiling puts considerable energy into keeping it in order, and every time I have visited her there, there has been something new or different—a photograph hung in a different place, a new tablecloth or bedcover, small soft toys and ornaments, rearranged furniture, and, on one occasion, a new coat of paint on the walls. For a while she had a small dog, but by October 2013, she had sold him, since she no longer wanted to pay the five hundred yuan annual license fee to keep a domestic pet. She had also dispensed with a sofa that used to be pushed back against one of the walls, and had acquired a low dresser on which she kept a simple stove burner. On the opposite wall hung a large photograph of herself in semiprofile taken in a studio when she was forty or so—smiling, intelligent eyes, long black hair falling in gentle waves over her shoulders, and wearing a red blouse. The room had a double bed that Meiling shared with her daughter, a computer that her daughter used, a television, a small table, and a large wardrobe for her daughter's and her own clothes. The bed was always beautifully made, covered with a neat coverlet, which Meiling said she always changed after visitors sat on it. The room exudes a decidedly feminine feel, with pink cushions, flowered pillow covers, pictures of cute puppies on the wall, and a lace mat on the small table. Meiling always keeps the door shut, and so the only light that comes in is from a small window above the dresser, decorated with a hanging plant and a few trinkets.

Meiling's presence and personality are striking in their contrast to the soft calm of this small space. Until the last time I saw her in May 2017, she invariably dressed in black or red, in silky, lacey blouses and tight-fitting trousers.

She was always well made up with foundation and powder on her face and eyes framed with dark gray eye shadow and black eyeliner. Her fingernails were a matter of great care: long, finely manicured, and flawlessly painted in pale beige or pink nail polish. Plump, loud to the point of being raucous, fast-talking, quick-witted, funny, and chain-smoking, Meiling used to swear like a trooper and never missed a chance to crack a joke at the expense of those around her. She talked in a broad local accent, and between her loud jokes and quick repartee, she was an intimidating presence. No one, as Huang Mingfang often remarked, could outtalk her, even if they tried. I saw young colleagues whom she was keen to introduce to me—in a restaurant where she used to work, or in a cosmetics store where she worked as a cleaner for a few months in 2011—reduced to embarrassed silence by her loud comments about their appearance or their behavior.

Meiling's life has not been easy. The youngest daughter of demanding parents, she grew up in a family atmosphere that lacked warmth and affection, and spent a lot of her adolescence hanging with "bad boys." In the early 1980s, she was arrested for prostitution and held in detention for three years. She married soon after her release and gave birth to a girl. Her husband was then imprisoned for several years on charges of violent robbery. He died several years before I got to know her, since which time she has had to depend largely on her own resources. When I visited her in the autumn of 2013, her monthly household income consisted of nearly 600 yuan of basic welfare (*dibao*), 1,500 yuan she earned from working as a domestic helper and companion to an elderly woman living on her own in Dashalar, and 2,000 yuan that her daughter earned from her job. She also received 300 yuan a month from Brave Li, her lover of fourteen years, whom she had not seen for two months, since, as Meiling put it, his wife had begun to kick up a fuss. Over the years I regularly visited her, she had a succession of short-term jobs, preferring these to depending on meager welfare payments from the local government. Between 2008 and 2009, she worked in the kitchen of her elder sister's restaurant until she decided to quit because she felt that her sister was treating her badly. She then worked in another restaurant, washing up and cleaning the floors, and in 2011, found a job as a cleaner in a cosmetics shop near Wangfujing. In all these places, she had to work long hours, arriving on her bike early in the morning and returning home in time to make dinner for her daughter and herself. Some of her jobs meant a bike ride of an hour each way.

What her daughter might get up to at home without her mother around was a constant source of concern for Meiling. But by 2014, her daughter had left her job, so now as the only breadwinner going out to work, Meiling had little option but to leave her daughter on her own. From her early teens, Xiao Hua had been more interested in running off with boys than studying. Her lack of education was compounded by minimal social skills and a lack of self-confidence, exacerbated by a facial disfigurement due to a childhood illness. With no more than basic literacy and numeracy skills, it was difficult for her to find a job, and when she did, she found it all too easy to throw it over when she decided she'd had enough, preferring to rely on a combination of her mother's and a boyfriend's resources.

Meiling's difficulties were further complicated by her estrangement from her natal family—she had virtually no contact with her parents between her marriage in 1990 and 2015. Without resources from either family or husband, she was proud of her independence, energy, and self-reliance, and felt that her daughter respected her for her hard work and her care. Her determination to maintain a livelihood by relying on her own resources did not get in the way of looking to her lover for monthly support, or turning to neighbors and others, including me, for small loans.

Growing Up

Born in 1962 to parents who worked as low-level cadres in a state ministry, Meiling was the youngest of four daughters, followed by two younger brothers. She grew up in what she described as an austere and violent family environment. Her parents were bullies and, in her eyes, were more interested in their public status than in caring for their children. Her father used to "beat the hell" out of the girls for tiny misdoings, such as buying the wrong bottle of vinegar or being seen walking with a boy. He even beat one of his daughters on her marriage day, since he did not approve of her husband. Such physical abuse was compounded by callous disregard. Meiling recalled how her second sister, married and with one child in Ningxia, telephoned her parents to ask for their help when her husband decided to divorce her, but they just refused.

The family home where Meiling grew up was in Hepingmen, a popular area north of Dashalar. Meiling was intelligent and completed her high school education but had no inclination to continue her studies. In her own terms, she had begun to "go bad" during the third year of high school, when she began hanging around with neighborhood boys. All she wanted to do was to have fun. Through her father's work connections, her parents found her a job in construction, but Meiling found it physically tough and uninteresting, and so did not pull her weight. Her parents' response was to beat her, repeatedly, to the point that she decided to run away from home. She then got in with a "bad

crowd" around the popular neighborhood of Tianqiao, renowned as a catch-
ment area for pickpockets and thieves. Since she was young and naïve, her new
friends made full use of her as a foil for their activities, offloading stolen goods
onto her, hiding their money with her, and generally demanding that she behave as they wanted. Having left home, and with nowhere else to go, Meiling
felt powerless to leave them, even though she eventually realized that they were
manipulating her for their own ends. But she was attractive and vivacious, and
was often invited to go out and eat with the crowd. It was not long before she
"learned bad ways." But her life with the bad boys was preferable to staying at
home. On several occasions when her mother came across her on the street,
she pulled her away to take her home, where her father would beat her again.
Eventually, she told her father that she would not put up with it any longer, and
would rather die than continue to be the target of his abuse. But even this was
not enough to convince her father to modify his behavior. When she downed a
bottle of poison that was kept under the dresser in her home, her father, aided
by her sisters, bashed her on the back to make her throw it up, only to follow up
by threatening her with an axe. She ran away again, and ended up with a young
man from a workers' family, who lived in Caishikou, an area between Tianqiao
and Dashalar. In her parents' eyes, however, he was too shabby and poor, and
they did not approve of him as a prospective husband until they found out that
Meiling was already pregnant, when they insisted that she marry him. Meiling
had no such intention, since many other young men beckoned; she wanted to
go on having fun. At the age of twenty, she had her first abortion.

Detention

Not long after the abortion, in 1984, a group of policemen turned up at Meiling's home early one morning to arrest her for prostitution. Her arrest, Meiling noted, was part of the campaign to "severely attack" (*yan da*) social and
moral misbehavior in major cities.[1] Meiling was sent into detention without
trial to a center in Hebei on the outskirts of Beijing, where she spent three long
hard years making sweaters for foreign export. Meiling laughed with bitter
irony as she commented that the only time she ever left Beijing was when she
was sent to detention. She also emphatically pointed out that as a detainee
under the system of administrative "detention for education" (*shourong jiaoyu*),
she did *not* have a criminal record.[2]

Life was tough in the center; it "really messed you up." Physical and verbal fights were common. Fifteen women slept in one crowded room, each
with a small wooden bed, covered with a single sheet of newspaper in place

of a mattress. They lived and worked separately from the men, although they sometimes caught sight of the men when they were taken to the well to fetch water. Some women became "activists" (*jiji fenzi*), acting as informers to the detention center authorities in the hope of reducing their sentences. Meiling was given responsibility for leading three work groups, each of fourteen or fifteen people, and as such was in a position to obtain favors from the authorities. She preferred, however, to get on well with her fellow inmates, never reporting any misdemeanors or doing anything she "might be ashamed of." She used to cover up for other women if they were caught smoking or fighting. She also used to join them in picking up the cigarette butts the male inmates used to leave near the well, taking out the remaining tobacco and rolling it into what they called "big cigarettes."

Meiling generally managed to find a way to get by in detention. Not all did, however, and one woman's escape attempt was prominent in Meiling's memory. Lights went out every evening at nine o'clock, when a roll call of names was taken. One evening, a woman in one of Meiling's groups did not respond to the roll call, and not long after, the alarm sounded. The woman had tried to escape but had hit the electric fence surrounding the detention center, and was dragged back and punished with a further six months added to her term.

Meiling often claimed that it was in the detention center that she learned to be tough. "I learned everything there. Pimps, prostitutes, there were lots of them. I didn't understand anything before I went inside." She described her life there in detached, even calm, tones, as if she were talking about another person, distanced from her present self. In contrast, her references to her parents when she was inside the detention center evoked memories of pain and anger that she did not try to hide. One day her tongue was so swollen that she could not eat, so she was sent to see a doctor at the police hospital. Two policewomen accompanied her there and back to the detention center, but she was so ill that they sent her father a letter asking him to come and take her back home to recuperate. He was unwilling to do this, such was the shame he felt his daughter had brought on his family, but he asked Meiling's sisters to go to the detention center to pick her up. Meiling was particularly touched by her third sister's care, and her later decision to work in this sister's restaurant was motivated in part by a desire to repay her. Her account of her parents' response, in contrast, revealed the intensity of the pain they had inflicted on her and that she continued to feel now, decades afterward.

They were really scared when they saw me and said how much I had changed, and how tough and horrible I seemed. They were really scared.

Once a criminal, always a criminal. You are not the same as other people. But you can't just blame me alone. Who asked you to throw me out? Not to care for me? If you had been a bit kinder, just given me a bit of care, would I be in the situation I'm in now? At root, I was a good child, but what kind of people were you? You were just nasty people, so I just hate you, I don't have even the tiniest bit of love for you. Today I really hate my parents because they pushed me out, they pushed me out onto the streets. They didn't see me once during those three years; they disowned me.

Several years later when Meiling took her daughter Xiao Hua to see her parents, Meiling described how her mother gave her daughter one hundred yuan, and said, "This is for you, not for your mum." "Xiao Hua just stood in front of them and said, 'I'm giving this to my mum, because bringing me up has been really tough.' I just cried. And she just turned around and walked out. That was the last time I saw my parents."

Husband

On her release from detention, Meiling's father found her a job in a pastry factory, where she was introduced to the elder brother of a friend and fellow worker. She had been working there for two or three years, giving her monthly wages to her parents, but when she decided to marry, all her mother gave her was a watch. "Can you guess what she said to me? She said, 'I don't have any money to give you because you still haven't repaid me for feeding you when you were little.' How do you want me to marry? What do I have to do for you not to look down on me? I said I never asked you to give birth to me, and I didn't ask for you to bring me up. I never thought she could say something like that. It just left me cold." Meiling's marriage did not last long, because her husband was jailed for violent robbery for eight years, in 1994. "He robbed someone who was a National People's Congress delegate. It was in the evening news . . . 'Savage activities under the national flag.'" Meiling had nothing good to say about him—on the contrary. "He's a cunt. I don't even want to mention him. He's worth nothing around here." He was unemployed, and so largely depended on Meiling's income.

> Almost everything we had came from what I made. To begin with Xiao Hua's dad used to give me three hundred kuai a month, but what could I do with that? What option did I have but to go out and work? He didn't take care of anything, not even the kid. I brought her up myself. Seven days after she was born I started working again. . . . I washed his clothes,

cooked for him, and attended [*cihou*] to his needs and whims. I also bought all my daughter's clothes. . . . But I was married to him, and like a fool cared for his whole family all those years, and went to see him in prison. Was he worthy of me? He rented a room in Caishikou, where he had another woman. I went over and she saw me and said she really didn't know he already had a child and a wife. I even went to her work unit. Everyone knew how difficult things were for me. . . . He never treated me like his wife. But I never stopped running around to look after him. I didn't do anything to him that I'm sorry about. . . . Fuck it, this life has been bitter, one step wrong and everything goes wrong.

It was a violent and unhappy marriage. Her husband frequently beat her, but despite sometimes imagining divorcing him, Meiling stuck things out during the years he spent in jail. But she was constantly anxious about how she was going to make ends meet for herself and her daughter, and was always on guard against the local police. "I really thought about finding someone else to marry, to get away from home. I was always worried, and the police always used to turn up to check me out. Everyone in the courtyard knew; they saw everything." This too translated into bitter anger against her parents.

My parents were really vain and conceited, which had a terrible effect on me. When Xiao Hua's dad went inside, I told my mother that I wanted to divorce him, but she said, so when he's around, you don't divorce him, but when he's not around you decide you want to divorce him. Okay, so just leave and take your child with you, we don't want you. So my mother didn't let me return home. I told Xiao Hua to say that when anyone asked after her grandmother to tell them that she was dead. . . . Later, I used to say that I wouldn't have shed a tear even if my parents died. They never gave me any help at all. The biggest tragedy in life is when your close family throws you out. I was on my own when I gave birth to Xiao Hua. I think I deserve a bit more happiness; my life so far has sapped everything out of me.

Meiling's husband died two years after he was released from jail, but this did not alter her opinion of him. In her eyes, he was a callous man without any capacity for human warmth.

Life in the courtyard was fraught with tensions, mutual suspicion, and gossip. With their small rooms divided from each other by flimsy partition walls, and within earshot of all but the softest whisper, neighbors had little privacy. Stories about neighbors' comings and goings, missing husbands' whereabouts, telephone calls secretly made and received, fights and separations, family quarrels, and lax parenting could easily turn into malicious accusations. Small arguments could rapidly escalate into angry standoffs, and close friendships could descend into vindictive recriminations. Affairs, sexual intrigues, and suspicions of prostitution were particularly present in my conversations with Meiling, in large part due to the particular family and marital histories of her dazayuan neighbors. Soon after she married, Meiling's already difficult relationship with her husband was complicated by new tensions with his sister, Xingyuan, after she, Meiling, introduced her to an acquaintance of hers, a man reputed to be quite well off, "because she liked a bit of money." According to Meiling, Xingyuan used to steal this man's money, and eventually fell out with him, leading to the end of her friendship with Meiling. Even though the two women lived in the same courtyard, they had not spoken for years. Meiling was often scathing about Xingyuan's casual affairs and made many oblique references to her willingness to exchange sex for money. Her own past practice of selling sex, in contrast to Xingyuan's apparent wantonness, she claimed, had been motivated by poverty and the need to keep her and her daughter going at a time when she had no access to other employment. Now that she could rely on more stable sources of income, she had no further need to prostitute herself. Xingyuan, on the other hand, had a really poor example in her mother, a woman whose dubious morals had, in Meiling's view, rubbed off on her daughter. She had had four children with three different men, so her children had never been accustomed to stable family relationships. Mrs. Zhang, Xingyuan's mother and Meiling's mother-in-law, was also an inveterate gambler, and used to spend her evenings drinking and playing mahjong with her friends, turning up in the early hours of the morning to sleep in Meiling's room since her own bed was often occupied by her daughter and grandson. In Meiling's eyes, mother and daughter were two of a kind. Her moralistic disdain of her mother-in-law for having failed to instill in her daughter the kind of ethical values Meiling claimed she, herself, embodied was matched by her contempt for her sister-in-law. "Who except her would share a bedroom with her teenage son?"

Meiling's friendship with another dazayuan neighbor, Qingmei, ended when Meiling—according to local hearsay—became involved with her husband, Young Fox. Young Fox had been rumored to make money out of facilitating introductions between local women and clients. He was known for his hot temper and had fled the neighborhood to evade arrest after being involved in some violent incident just before I started my research there. Zhao Tielin had known him well, and always used to ask about his news and whereabouts.

Old Mrs. Gao's younger son, who, as I mentioned in chapter 2, had grown up with him, occasionally referred to telephone conversations he had had with him since his departure, but always claimed that he didn't know where he was. Young Fox's absence did not diminish his neighbors' references to him as a colorful figure, despite his abandonment of his wife and child. In fact, people talked about him as a minor legend in the neighborhood. For Meiling, however, his name evoked memories of past injustices; her neighbors' gossip about her former affair with him continued to mar her attempts to present herself as a woman with integrity and a mother trying her best to make ends meet. "Other people have said a lot of good things about me, and they also said bad things, and what people say can feel like a terrible pressure. But wherever I have been, I've never owed anyone anything, there's always been a give and take, I've always repaid things, and people have helped me when things have been difficult."

Lover

The person on whom Meiling most relied to help her out during the years I knew her was her long-term lover, Brave Li. Meiling first got to know him soon after her husband's death, when she was introduced to him by Qingmei's husband. Brave Li ran a small clothes factory where he gave Meiling a job as a cook, and she liked him. He used to "do things for people, and arrange things for people," and even though by the time I got to know Meiling he was unemployed, he always seemed to find ways to make enough money to give Meiling three hundred yuan a month and, occasionally, to take Meiling to a local hotel. He was also good to her daughter, who called him "Uncle," even though she rarely saw him, since she was usually out, at school or then work, when he visited Meiling. "He's not like other people, and I'm really grateful to him. . . . He's a man, and men stand up to pee, not like women who have to squat. But he's not easy, he's always fighting, and outside, he's pretty aggressive [*zhangyi*]. I like people like this. I don't like people who squat."

Meiling was openly proud of her strong man, but being a strong man had its disadvantages, and Brave Li's pugnacious character often landed him in trouble. The worst of his fights occurred in Meiling's dazayuan some years before I got to know her. He was drunk and fell into an argument with one of Meiling's neighbors. The argument soon became heated, and Brave Li slashed the neighbor's face with a knife, leaving blood all over the place and the neighbor in agony. Other neighbors called the police, so Brave Li together with Meiling and her daughter fled Dashalar and returned only two years later, when local memories of the incident had faded and the neighbor had left. In Meiling's eyes, Brave Li cared for her, and offered her protection against the advances of other men. "He's got a strong sense of justice, he plays things straight, so after I got to know him, I felt I would be able to lead a happier life. Things were really hard and I couldn't see a way out, and he pulled me up out of it."

Even so, Meiling did not entirely trust him to have her best interests at heart. When she became pregnant early on in their relationship, his immediate response was to ask, "How on earth can I take care of a child?," which Meiling found unsympathetic and unhelpful, particularly when it meant she had to go through with a painful abortion on her own. "I'm sure he doesn't do anything bad," Meiling commented, "but I told him straight, I can be your lover, but not your wife, because you aren't responsible enough. You might be with me today and another tomorrow. Really, men are totally unreliable." On one occasion when Meiling had helped him out by giving him her monthly wage, he went out to a bar and spent it all on a woman he picked up there. Meiling became increasingly suspicious of his activities, and for a time refused to see him, in part, as she explained, because she was worried that he was going to pass on some disease to her. "Every time I saw some mark on his body, I got scared that he had some dirty disease. I told him not to harm me, but he said, 'It's nothing, it's just something wrong with my skin.' I told him he'd better not harm me, and told him I could hate someone just as much as I could love him. Do men understand women? I just hate men. The more you like them, the less they treasure you."

One of the strategies Meiling used to protect herself from local scrutiny was to shut herself off from her neighbors. When she was not at work, she rarely went out, and always kept her door closed, even in the stifling heat of summer. She went out every second morning to buy food, but did this as quickly as she could and was home in about half an hour. She often commented that she did not have any time to spend with small-minded people whose only interest was dazayuan gossip. She was particularly cautious about publicizing her relationship with her lover. She said she was afraid of the police seeing her with Brave Li and questioning her, and poking their noses into her business and getting into quarrels (shifei) with her. So she spent all day in her small room, cleaning and rearranging things, making up and watching the TV. Occasional references she made to men implied that from time to time she continued to exchange sex for money, but Brave Li was her man. He was unemployed when Meiling first told me about him in 2007, and he seemed to spend quite a lot of time with Meiling in her home. Both of them liked to drink, and Meiling used to cook for him on the single stove burner in her small room. They also used to watch pornographic films together, as I discovered one day when a couple of DVDs fell out from underneath the mattress of Meiling's bed. She used to keep the DVDs there to hide them from her daughter, she said. Occasionally they would go out to a restaurant, or to visit Brave Li's mother, who Meiling claimed did not like his wife. Over the fourteen years they had known each other, they had developed a close and companionable relationship. Despite occasional arguments and fights, Meiling felt that her arrangement with him constituted a sound exchange: in response for the companionship of a protective male partner and the sense of dignity and confidence this gave her despite her reputation as a woman with a past, she was happy to provide the food, warmth, sex, and intimacy that both of them seemed to enjoy.

Daughter

The only person who was exempt from Meiling's derisory barbs was her daughter. She was in Fujian the first time I met Meiling; then at the age of seventeen, she had met a man online who said he wanted to marry her, and decided to take her to Fujian to meet his family. Once there, however, his parents refused to agree to their marriage, and so Xiao Hua returned to her mother in Beijing. Xiao Hua left school at fifteen, and had neither the education nor the skills to find a decent job. She was also shy, to the point that it was impossible to sustain a conversation with her. Without either professional or social skills, she did not have the confidence or the motivation to find work. She liked clothes and makeup, however, and dreamed of doing a cosmetics course. She spent a lot of time online, looking at fashions and films, and although her mother objected, also spent time on dating websites. Meiling was protective of her daughter to the point of total indulgence, and even though she insisted that she was frustrated by her daughter's laziness, as she put it, she regularly gave her pocket money. She explained her daughter's reserve by the fact that she been sexually abused by a cousin when she was six years old. She also suffered from a hyperthyroid condition that affected her facial nerves, leaving her mouth permanently lopsided. "Who wants someone like that?" Meiling asked. "An operation would be several thousand kuai, but I don't have enough money for food, let alone something like that." Xiao Hua eventually found a job as a typist and administrative assistant in a small local office of the Bureau of Trade and Commerce, but since her typing skills were very basic and she was paid according to the number of words she could type in an hour, her wages were minimal. After a year or so she gave the job up, after which, without an income of her own, she took to running up debts of several thousands of yuan on her mother's two credit card accounts. Meiling's response was to give her a mild reprimand. She was anxious about her daughter's future but remained convinced that it lay not in finding a means to economic independence but a man with prospects on whom she could depend.

> If she were really strong, I wouldn't be so worried. I understand my daughter. When you stay at home all day it's not like being out in the world. Your capacity to think through things is not the same. If you spend your days on the internet, you don't understand anything. . . . But a mother always hopes that her daughter will marry a good person. . . . All I want is that she finds a man with a good job, and as long as she treats him well, and he finds a clean house when he comes home, and hot food on the table, he'll be happy.

Xiao Hua continued to spend her energies looking for a suitable boyfriend. By 2013 she had had a succession of short-term relationships, often with rather older men, who Meiling felt were only interested in having a good time. "She doesn't understand that you have to be responsible when you're in love. Today, she'll get together with this guy she likes, and tomorrow another. I always tell her off about this." One of her relationships lasted for nearly a year, and Meiling was hopeful that it would lead to marriage. The young man not only had a job but also access to an apartment in a block to the south of the city. Xiao Hua used to visit him where he lived with his parents, and all seemed to be going well until the parents announced that they did not approve of their son's choice. Mutual recriminations ensued between Xiao Hua and her boyfriend, and, according to Meiling, ended up in a physical fight, leaving Xiao Hua distressed and hurt. Meiling's comment was, "I think she really loved him but was angry with him for not standing up for her." Another boyfriend, a man of about thirty years of age and already divorced, used to visit Xiao Hua at home when Meiling had already gone to work, but on one occasion he turned up before Meiling had left. "He looked terrified as soon as he saw me. I warned him that if you come around harassing Xiao Hua again I'll strip an arm and a leg off you and will bury them in a box under the ground and no one will know. Do you believe me? He just said, 'Aunty, I wouldn't dare do anything.' He didn't show up again. Just never let a man frighten you, because men just make use of women's weaknesses."

On one occasion, when I had taken Meiling out to lunch, we returned home to find the door locked. After a couple of minutes it was opened by Xiao Hua, behind whom stood a young man Meiling had never met. The couple looked somewhat tousled and embarrassed. Xiao Hua said she hadn't expected her mother to return so soon, and that the young man had just dropped by to leave Meiling a bag of dates as a gift from his mother. He left, and Xiao Hua went out to have a shower in the local public shower rooms.

Self and Others

Meiling was a "woman of the people," as she put it, who did not hesitate to speak her mind, or to do what she wanted. She relied on her physical appeal and her loud manner to attract the attention of men, whom she alternately flirted with or hurled abuse at. Once, in a local restaurant where we were having lunch, a small group of businessmen sat down at an adjacent table, and she started exclaiming in a high voice that she had recently seen a book about life in Dashalar and could it be the one that I had written. This elicited a response from the businessmen, with whom Meiling had already been exchanging knowing smiles. One of them was particularly curious about me and about why I was having lunch with her, whereupon she announced that I was her good friend and if he wanted to find out more he would eventually be able to read my book. Banter between them continued and ended only when Meiling agreed to give the man her cell phone number. Other men received less generous treatment, and Meiling did not shy away from lashing out at those she did not favor. Sometimes she got into fights with men who harassed her, and sometimes she had to pay them money to stop them calling the police after she had hit them. "That's what I'm like," she said, "no one had better try to trick me."

Meiling had a local reputation as someone who often borrowed money from neighbors. While this was generally seen just as something that Meiling did in order to get by, it became a source of tension, conflict, and hurt on at least one occasion that I knew about that I related in chapter 2. On this occasion, she had pressured Old Mrs. Gao into lending her two hundred yuan, which for Old Mrs. Gao was a not inconsiderable amount. Meiling could be very persuasive, and Old Mrs. Gao had a soft spot for her, and so agreed to her request. After several weeks, Meiling had not reappeared in her home. Her disappearance was interpreted by Old Mrs. Gao and her son as a sign of not wanting to lose face, since she could not repay the loan. Young Gao's response was sullen anger, and a decision to cut off his relationship with Meiling. The effect on his elderly mother was heartache at losing a person she had considered as an insider, in effect, a member of the family. She often used to say how much she missed Meiling. Although I did not know the details of this particular incident, I knew enough to understand that for Young Gao and his mother, Meiling had transgressed the acceptable boundaries of reciprocity.

I not infrequently gave small amounts of money to Meiling, never in response to a direct request for a loan but rather when she mentioned how expensive things had become, and how difficult it was to pay for the things her daughter needed. She chose her moment to make this kind of comment, invariably as we parted company after a visit. I also regularly used to take her out to lunch, where she would down copious amounts of spirits and smoke her way through numerous cigarettes without really eating much at all. She would then take the leftovers home in disposable cartons, to share with her daughter for dinner. I became accustomed to this kind of exchange with Meiling, but on one occasion, it made me feel intensely awkward.

The occasion was in the autumn of 2013 when Meiling invited Huang Mingfang and me to her home for lunch. She was going to cook, she said. We turned up at the appointed time, but given there was no sign of lunch, we went out to a restaurant to eat. On our return, Meiling took out a letter she had carefully folded away in her bag. As she showed it to me, she was clearly in distress. The letter was a summons from a credit card company addressed to her, saying that this was the third time they had written to her and if she did not pay the bill by the end of the week, they would be forced to take out proceedings against her. The bill was for thousands of yuan, and had been run up by her daughter over a period of a few months. At a loss for words I mumbled something along the lines of what had she said to her daughter and what was she going to do? She said that she had reprimanded her daughter, but neither she nor her daughter was in a position to pay off this amount of money. I decided that I needed a bit of time to think through whether I was willing to help her out, and indicated to Mingfang that I thought it best for us to go. I told Meiling that I was really sorry that she found herself in this predicament, and I would be in touch with her again very soon.

Once outside, Mingfang and I went to have a coffee nearby to talk about how I should respond. Meiling's intention was clear, but I felt extremely awkward about being implicitly asked to give her a loan of such a large amount of money, which would probably not be repaid. It went without saying that I wanted to help Meiling out, but I did not want my willingness to help to be seen as a precedent to other similar loans. Mingfang suggested returning to Meiling in a couple of days when I would tell her how much I sympathized with her, and because of this, I was willing to help her out. At the time, I did not fully understand the wisdom of Mingfang's advice, even though I followed it. What it signified was the possibility of me being able to help Meiling out on my terms in a way that did not mean loss of face for her.

We returned two days later to find Meiling busy making steamed dumplings. When we finished eating, I told her that I really sympathized with her situation, and as a single mother myself, knew how hard it was to maintain a balance between acceding to children's needs and indulging them, and so I would be willing to help her repay the debt. I also said that she needed to do her best to make sure that her daughter did not use her credit cards anymore. Meiling was extremely grateful, and busied herself finding a piece of paper on which she insisted on making a formal record of this transaction. She noted the numbers of the respective credit cards, the amount of money I had lent her, and the date of the transaction. She also committed herself to returning the entire amount within seven months, and repaying a fixed amount each month. She recorded her ID details, Huang Mingfang's ID details, and signed it.

Despite her tough ways, Meiling insisted time and again that she was a "good person" who had never let anyone down, nor harmed anyone. "Everyone says I'm a good person, even if I don't have a good temperament, loud mouth that I am, always quick with words, always swearing. Ha, ha! The kids here all say I'm a really good person." She constantly reiterated how much her daughter respected her and how her daughter had stood up for her ever since she was very young. Meiling never talked with her about her own past on the grounds that she would not be able to understand, and she did not want her daughter to repeat her own experiences. She was, however, "just a bit suspicious of why I hate my parents," and agreed that her daughter possibly knew more about her life than she, Meiling, cared to acknowledge. Nevertheless, Meiling wanted me to write her story because she wanted her daughter to know the full extent of what she had done to bring her up. She was explicit in wanting acknowledgment from her parents, particularly her mother, for her own role as a responsible mother who had managed to bring up her daughter against all odds. "I want my mother to know how I have brought up my daughter. We are both women, and I'm a mother too. I think, okay, as my parents you have ruined me. That's okay, but I still want to show you how I live, and that I'm better than you. I still want to fight because of this feeling."

Home

Meiling was comfortable enough in her dazayuan home, but the constraints of her life there made her long to live in a different social and spatial environment. Local street committee personnel visited her to measure the floor area of her home in 2011, when it seemed that there was a real possibility of relocation elsewhere. The lane adjacent to her courtyard was soon to be widened, and other families in the immediate vicinity were moving out. Only a few, so it seemed, wanted to remain, mainly because they were dissatisfied with the conditions of their relocation. Given that the laws against coercive relocation had been tightened up in response to the local, national, and international condemnation of the practice in recent years, they were to be allowed to remain, but would have to move to another Dashalar accommodation if their homes fell within the chaiqian area.

Meiling's desire to leave was blighted by the complex rental and leasehold arrangements of the occupants of her courtyard. Mrs. Zhang's elder brother lived with his wife in a tiny hutment built against the wall of the small alley outside Meiling's dazayuan. Like many such structures in the neighborhood, the hutment was no more than about one and a half to two square meters, just large enough to house a bed and a tiny table with a small burner to cook on; the couple's few clothes and domestic necessities were piled up against its two sides and on its roof. The brother had spent many years in jail, during which time his only son's household registration was transferred to his sister's address in Dashalar. There were many occupants registered under the two rooms at this address: Mrs. Zhang and two nephews, including her elder brother's son, her daughter and grandson, and Meiling and her daughter. Two former occupants had died: Mrs. Zhang's elder sister and Meiling's husband. Their property in the dazayuan was reportedly valued at around two million yuan in 2011, but the legal requirement was that each occupant registered under the address had to agree to sign a contract agreeing to the amount the local government offered them as a condition of eligibility for government support. One occupant, the son of Mrs. Zhang's elder brother, refused to sign. He rejected his family's offer of fifty thousand yuan in return for his agreement to relocate on the grounds that this constituted but a small amount of his rightful share. His mother was holding out for recognition of her husband's right to be rehoused in the dazayuan on the grounds that it was property inherited from his father and grandfather. Her husband was mentally challenged and unable to talk, and she had written a petition on his behalf, which she displayed in front of her hutment when I saw her in the autumn of 2013. The petition claimed that before Liberation, her husband's grandfather and father had bought a thirteen-room courtyard on a lane off Meishi Street, which had been confiscated during the early Cultural Revolution in 1966. Despite laws stipulating the return of private property to their former owners in 1983, her husband had not been able to assert his rights of ownership. "Why," she asked in the petition, "is my husband unable to benefit from the government's laws? This is also a humanitarian [matter]."

Fig. 4.1 Hutment outside Meiling's home, 2009.

Meiling was thus caught up in a family quarrel that she was unable to re-solve. She had not seen her lover for two months, following a quarrel he had had with his wife. But she was a determined operator who well understood how to negotiate relationships of exchange, "give and take," as she put it, in order to keep going. Though I was familiar with this side of Meiling's charac-ter, I was not prepared for how it manifested itself the last time I visited her in May 2017.

After more than three years of no contact with her, I found her still liv-ing in the same room. I had not told her in advance that I would be visiting her, and I wasn't at all sure that I would find her in her former dazayuan. It was unusually hot, and Meiling was resting when I called out to her from the lane. She looked much older. Her nails were no longer beautifully painted, and the top she was wearing had food stains down the front. In all, she presented herself in a very different way than before. We sat down, and she proceeded to tell me that her life had changed radically since the last time we met. She had finally broken with Brave Li after his wife insisted that he stop the relationship. After years of estrangement from her parents, she had taken up the role of filial daughter, traveling the long distance to the southern suburbs to look after her mother for several months before she eventually died at the end of 2016, then looking after her elderly and frail father for three days each week. Her daughter, Xiao Hua, had found a new job, where she met a man and got pregnant. They married, but this lasted no more than two months, and so Xiao Hua followed Meiling's advice to let her husband take the child, and she returned to live with her mother in Dashalar.

Meiling continued to worry about what her daughter did during the days she spent away each week looking after her father but knew that she had to leave her to her own devices. Meiling insisted that she wanted to let bygones be bygones and was no longer angry with her father. Neither of us mentioned the loan, but on a number of occasions during the afternoon I spent with her, she referred to the property she would inherit from her father when he eventually passes away.

Interlude 3

Meiling was the only woman I knew in Dashalar with whom I could talk at length on her own. The menfolk—husbands, fathers, or sons—unemployed or without regular jobs, generally tended to be around in the other households I visited. After Zhao Tielin passed away, Meiling started sharing with me a range of intimate details, particularly about her relationship with Brave Li, that made our conversations qualitatively different from those we had when Zhao was present and from those I had with others in the neighborhood. With her quick repartee and raucous manner, she had a powerful presence. Initially I found her quite intimidating, but in time, I came to accept a role that, in my view, swung between being a sympathetic respondent on the one hand and a passive audience on the other, struggling to keep up with stories delivered in a thick local accent and loaded with jokes and innuendo.

If Meiling's income-generating activities indicated an itinerant participation in the economy, they also introduced her to experiences, social networks, and longings outside Dashalar; her job as a cleaner in the classy cosmetics store on Wangfujing gave her the opportunity to literally indulge in fantasies of acquiring a fashionable femininity—trying out new powders, perfumes, and shades of nail polish. One of the recurring themes in our conversations over the years was her frustration at being unable to move from Dashalar. Yet though her desire to move away was explicit, her concerns, activities, and significant relationships repeatedly regrounded her efforts as mother, lover, neighbor, and wage earner in the physical place of Dashalar. The entangled web that bound her to the neighborhood formed a dense obstruction thwarting her from realizing longings for a different kind of existence.

Meiling's desire to leave Dashalar hinted at a yearning for relationships and a lifestyle that she could articulate only in negative terms, by deriding those neighbors and family members who, in her view, were responsible for pinning her to Dashalar. She repeatedly mentioned how "small-minded" (*xiaoxinyangr*) she found her near kinfolk and neighbors, and how she had no desire to have much social contact with them. Yet she was tied to the dazayuan she had inherited from her husband, and embedded in an impenetrable tangle of kin and neighborhood relationships and conflicts way beyond my capacity to unravel.

Successive cohorts of local residents started leaving Dashalar when the local government first began issuing incentives to them to relocate in the early 2000s. Then, many younger residents with stable jobs and incomes, who could afford rents elsewhere, decided to leave the neighborhood in favor of more modernized accommodations, either on their own initiative, or by finding ways to marry out, like Young Gao's daughter. Some locals who found the local government's offer attractive enough agreed to move. Others were effectively pushed out when the bulldozers started widening the lanes and roads, as demonstrated in Ou Ning's film on the dislocation involved in the widening of Dashalar's Meishi Street, *Meishi jie* (2006).[1] By the time I started my research in the neighborhood, many migrant workers had moved into rented accommodations. The locals who remained were largely the elderly and the poorest—those who had neither the desire nor the capacity to rent accommodations elsewhere.

Other factors, however, were also at work in explaining why people stayed. One was an interest in hanging on in the neighborhood in the hope that the compensation paid by the local government for relocation would increase as land values went up.[2] Another, which I realized only when I came to understand the reasons for Meiling's inability to move, was family conflict. The issue was complex, and I could grasp only its basic outline. Meiling's mother-in-law's elder brother had spent several years in jail, and on his release had found himself without anywhere to live. When I met him and his elderly wife, the two of them were living in a tiny dilapidated hutment outside Meiling's dazayuan. The mother-in-law, meanwhile, had been offered a reasonable price if she agreed to relocate. However, relocation in return for compensation could occur only if all those registered under the address in question agreed. Mrs. Zhang's nephew, her elder brother's son, who was living elsewhere, refused to agree to relocate on the grounds that the amount of money his aunt offered him in return for his agreement was not enough. The result was a total impasse, leaving the nephew's parents with no option but to continue to live in the hutment outside the dazayuan. Mrs. Zhang's elderly sister-in-law's petition to the local government to resolve their housing predicament came to nothing, so without the resources to move, they had to stay put.

Meiling always had to have the last word, whether in conversations with her daughter, with Young Gao, or with random men. Even in the public contexts of her waged work, she replicated the dominance she exerted in the interior space of her home. She was loud, insistent in demanding her colleagues' attention, whether men or women, and disdainful of anyone, particularly men, who in her eyes were rude to her or who could not stand up for themselves. In sum, there was no occasion—at least that I witnessed—in which she did not have the last word over men.

Meiling was, without any doubt, the kind of strong and impressive woman Charles Stafford described in his treatment of "actually existing Chinese matriarchy."[3] In the first instance, her emotional and physical energies were directed to sustaining her capacity to provide for her daughter, caring and cooking for her, and maintaining order in their home as an enclosed center of tranquility in an otherwise turbulent and aggressive world. In this sense, her efforts were oriented principally toward domestic concerns—the realm of the "private" that Stafford discusses. However, one of the most significant features of the change in gender relations that the Liberation of 1949 brought to women was the formal recognition of their legitimacy as social subjects and productive laborers no longer bound by requirements of sexual segregation and now legally empowered to move about in public outside the domestic domain. Meiling thus grew up in a social world that acknowledged the public legitimacy of women's role as members of the social labor force. Hence, even if in the local world she inhabited her labor did not count as proper productive labor, her activities, movements, and commitments indicated a constant to'ing and fro'ing between her roles as domestic carer, mother, lover, and waged worker, all oriented toward maintaining a basic livelihood. While her main preoccupations were domestic, they necessarily involved her social labor, and she bicycled great distances to work long hours in restaurants and shops. Her movements between domestic and income-generating activities thus remind us of how women's labor is foundational to the social role of the household/family/kin group as a unit of social and economic management and order. They also offer a specific instance of how the boundaries between the domestic/private (*nei*) and public (*wai*) can be blurred, as an effect of the nonrecognition of women's work outside the domestic space as labor, rather than as an extension of their reproductive role as mothers and carers, as Wang Zheng and others have argued.[4] Meiling's struggle was not to obtain recognition for the *condition* of her labor; rather it was to obtain recognition for her status as a virtuous woman who had endured suffering and self-sacrifice in order to be a responsible, hardworking mother for her daughter. While Meiling's age and education granted her opportunities and capacities that Old Mrs. Gao had not been able to explore, her claims to virtue defined a mode of agency that rested on a shared understanding of women's role as ethical exemplar.

Another dimension of Meiling's determination as a mother lay in her desire to direct—as much as she could—her daughter's activities, particularly over matters concerning love and marriage, including, finally, her daughter's decision to relinquish custody of her baby to her estranged husband. By her own account, her indulgence of her daughter was to compensate for her own experience of having been emotionally abandoned by her parents. She also hoped that one day, between the publication of Zhao's book and mine, her daughter might come to appreciate the sacrifices that she, Meiling, had made on her behalf. Cooking for her adult daughter, even when the latter had spent the entire day at home surfing the internet, thus implied a kind of double-bind imposed on her daughter—supporting her while simultaneously exacting an emotional cost for her support.

For her part, Xiao Hua was not simply the docile subject of her mother's authority. She decided to run off to Fujian with a man when she was just seventeen. Later on, her behavior in embarking on several affairs, and in running up credit card debts without her mother's knowledge or approval, could be interpreted as further indication of her assertion of her own desires, despite the cost to her mother. Even though finally, having given birth to a baby, she succumbed to her mother's authority in deciding to give the baby up, her exercise of agency as a young woman was indicative of one of the most significant aspects of gender transformation in China in recent decades—namely the increased leverage that young women feel they have to assert their own desires and aspirations even when they clash with their families'. In this, given that it is contextualized by very different socioeconomic and cultural conditions, Xiao Hua's behavior offers a kind of inverse example of Yan Yunxiang's famous argument that younger women are the main beneficiaries of the increasing focus on individual desires and aspirations that independent economic activity and increased incomes, facilitated by the relaxation of state and collective controls of the market, have generated. Let me explain by reiterating the main outlines of Yan's thesis.

Yan is arguably the most prominent anthropologist to argue, on the basis of long-term fieldwork in a village in the northeastern province of Heilongjiang, that through the changes in marriage, family, and employment structures since the 1950s, gender relations in rural families have recently given new leverage to young women to use their greater education and income-generating capacity to exercise unprecedented influence in family and household matters: "A redefinition of family relations and gender roles is perhaps the most significant change in the sphere of private life since 1949."[5] While such changes have certainly occurred, they are far from producing relations of gender equality either in the domestic or the social/public arena of employment and political power. Nor do they necessarily empower the young women concerned, as Xiao Hua's story reveals. Her experience suggests a *desire* to draw on her environment that incites individual desires but without the capacity or the conditions to be able to benefit from it. Moreover, in the context of the contemporary market-driven economy in urban China, there is considerable evidence that the changing gender division of labor and the consumerist dimension of increasing emphasis on the expression of women's individual desires in marital and family life are producing a reassertion of hierarchical gender relations according to which the male breadwinner and homeowner is not only desired by middle-class women as a source of their own material comfort but also enjoys a legal authority to retain marital property registered in his name in the event of divorce.[6]

Alongside her determination to rely on her own resources, her pride in being able to sustain her independence, and her commitment to caring for her daughter, Meiling's account of her life repeatedly returned to a number of other key themes: her alienation from and abandonment by her family, her disenchantment with men yet, at the same time—paradoxically—her desire for male protection.

Her story reveals an attenuated attachment to reconfigured patriarchal practices and values through her gendered and generational commitments. Meiling does not exemplify a classic accommodation of patriarchal authority any more than she exemplifies a consciousness of the gender implications of her determination to find waged employment. Her status as a single mother living with her daughter removed her from the need to accommodate the constant presence of a senior male, but pragmatic considerations about her residential security tied her to her husband's family. Similarly, pragmatic considerations explained her tolerance of her husband, including the long years he spent in prison and his violent behavior toward her. She was proud of her performance as a hardworking parent, able to keep going and stand up to a social world that disdained her. At the same time, and despite her history of violent abuse by her father and her husband, she continued to rely on men's capacity to offer protection and material security, as evident in her advice to her daughter about the benefits of subservience to the "man's family."

The investment in patriarchal configurations that Meiling made—for her daughter as much as for herself—was premised on the one hand on a realistic and conscious assessment of Xiao Hua's limited chances of finding a decent job and being able to afford independent housing, and on the other on a basic, even naturalized, assumption about the kinds of protection a man, ideally, could offer a woman. Men "did not squat to pee" was Meiling's description; men stood up, and she didn't like people who squatted. Meiling held on to this assumption for her daughter, and to a certain extent for herself, despite her repeated disappointments in men, and despite the evidence of her daughter's difficulties in finding a stable partner. Between the different options available to her, she did not explicitly challenge male authority but rather accommodated it, both when she saw benefit and advantage in such accommodations *and* when such accommodations served to shore up her own sense of ethical self-worth.

The contradictions in Meiling's enactment of agency echo both Deniz Kandiyoti's general suggestions about women's bargains with patriarchy as well as others' arguments about the pragmatic and ideological reasons sustaining women's adjustments to patriarchy in China.[7] But beyond such considerations, Meiling repeatedly referred to her sense of virtue as a wife who had stood by her recalcitrant husband, as a committed mother, and as a constant, if complaining, daughter-in-law. She was a "good person," she constantly reiterated, who had never let anyone down, and had never harmed anyone. Her claims to virtue were rooted in her observance of her familial duties as a woman. With a history that earned her social disrepute, this virtue could become a source of self-validation that she could hurl in the faces of those who disdained her.

Finally, Meiling's story sheds interesting light on the place of exchange and face in local neighborhood life. Her relationship with her lover, Brave Li, was premised on an exchange that endured for many years. Meiling's take on the world—incorporating her attitude toward her parents, her neighbors, and random people, including me—was framed by a notion of exchange rooted in the idea that others, beginning with her parents, had always been responsible for her difficulties and that they therefore owed her something. This never took an explicit form, but her repeated practice of manipulating situations and relationships in which she could obtain money—knowing full well that she would not be in a position to repay it—seemed to bear this out. Not only did Old Mrs. Gao miss Meiling's visits, Meiling also missed them. But rather than lose face by visiting Old Mrs. Gao again, knowing that Young Gao would call her out for having misbehaved, she preferred to keep her distance. As far as I know, she reappeared only once at a later date to attend Young Gao's funeral and to visit Old Mrs. Gao, who was too frail to attend.

Meiling's interest in her relationship with me combined a kind of affectionate trust with a desire for instrumental, financial support and social capital, as her loud displays of her familiarity with me in restaurants demonstrated. On one occasion when we went out to lunch she insisted that I take her to a restaurant from which she had been sacked. Once there, she proceeded to goad her former colleagues into coming over to our table to chat to her English friend. On another occasion, as I have described, she loudly proclaimed me to be her friend who was writing a book about her. If my description of these exchanges seems to foreground her instrumental interests, this is for analytical purposes and should not be interpreted to discount the bonds of affection that made these interests possible.

The coda to Meiling's story, based on my visit to her in 2017, seems to illustrate an inversion of the story I was familiar with between 2007 and 2014. It also, ironically, offered her the possibility of a partial way out from the dense webs of local entanglement that kept her in Dashalar. By 2017, her earlier emphasis on her virtue as constant wife, mother, and daughter-in-law had been replaced by another script emphasizing herself as the filial daughter of elderly parents. In this, again in Stafford's terms, she exemplified the pivotal subject within the main cycles of familial and communal reciprocity—in which relatedness (including of the patrilineal kind) is explicitly seen to be *produced* by human, particularly women's, action.[8]

Even if in Meiling's case, few of her neighbors cared to acknowledge her achievements, her constant reiteration of her determination and integrity also contained an implicit call for recognition and for redress against the injustices of the world in which she found herself but also rejected the status of victim. Her self-identification fluctuated between an assertion of her status as victim owed support by others and her determination to keep things going by depending on her own resources. Poverty, material constraints, knowledge of her disadvantage, and a determination to be self-reliant all folded into a deep sense of ethical responsibilities and sensibilities, of being a good person. Her sense of self as such, despite manipulations of relationships for personal material benefit, was, moreover, maintained through supporting fundamentally patriarchal values. Meiling's strength and resilience were in significant measure sustained by her attachment to patriarchal values.

Meiling's story thus represents a complex paradox of resilience and determination, shored up by instrumental interests, and an investment in patriarchal authority. Instrumental concerns and patriarchal structures held her to place-based entangled webs of family and local relationships from which she longed to escape. It was her often-fractured sense of virtue boosted by occasional pleasures and associated with contradictory gender practices and convictions, played out in having sustained her family in the face of material constraints and diverse exchanges, that served to sustain her through conditions of extreme hardship. Her agency thus took form through the complex articulation of a conflicted relationship with her family and neighborhood. Without access to experiences and forms of knowledge beyond those of her local world, she was repeatedly pulled, paradoxically, to identify with the dominant ideological and gendered themes of the discursive environment of her existence.

5

Li Fuying

Li Fuying and his family were the only migrant family I got to know well in Dashalar. They were a family of four, originally from Shaanxi: Li Fuying and his wife, Zhang Yuanchen, both in their early fifties, a son, and a daughter. After arriving in Beijing in 1997, the parents' existence was shaped by a relentless struggle for basic material survival, motivated by a desire to finance their children, and particularly their son, through higher education. The couple were determined to realize their aims, and despite desperate hardship that would easily have pushed others to give up, they were steadfast in pursuing their goal. In so doing, they clung to principles of honesty and dignity, shored up by a deep commitment to each other as well as to their children.

When I first met Li Fuying and his wife in 2006, they lived in a small room no more than nine square meters just inside the main entrance of a big dazayuan, south of West Street. Half the room was taken up by a wooden platform they had constructed to serve as a double bed, above which they had built another smaller bunk bed–like platform for their son or daughter to sleep on when they visited. A single light bulb hung from the ceiling, revealing a floor of untreated rammed earth. Their twenty-five-year-old son was then studying graphic design at a college in Hebei; their daughter had not yet graduated from her high school in Shaanxi.

The couple managed to keep going in Beijing, moving from place to place trying to make a living, occasionally being detained and sent back to Shaanxi, until late 2015, when they decided to give up the struggle and returned to Shaanxi.

Leaving Shaanxi

Li Fuying and his wife first arrived in Beijing from a poor rural village in northern Shaanxi in 1997, after years of attempting to make a living from grain and apple cultivation. Their lives in the village were complicated by the routine violence of local gangs who would periodically turn up to steal whatever they could find. Li's complaints to the local village head fell on deaf ears because of the latter's connections with the gang members. Li owned a single sheep, and at night kept it tied up outside the door of his house. One night, the sheep was stolen, and convinced that the thief was a local man, Li went to the man's house to retrieve the animal. The culprit accused Li of maligning him but said he could help him find another sheep if Li paid. Li was unwilling to pay the price the culprit was asking, so the culprit turned to physical intimidation, beating Li up and sending a gang from another village to smash the windows of his house. Li made another complaint, but since the man had connections with the local police station, Li's concerns went unheeded. Instead he was advised to placate the man by giving him some apples and money.

At this point, Li felt like giving up. He was unable to sell his apples since they weren't good enough quality; it was totally exhausting labor; and without enough grain to keep his family going, he had to borrow. He described how he developed "a kind of hatred for apple trees." He had been planting them for nearly eight years, alongside everyone else in the village, when the decollectivization of land resulted in the local village leadership's decision to move from grain cultivation to apples. But the sheep incident was the last straw for Li. "I thought, eight years of resistance against Japan, and three more years to Liberation, that's all in the past, but it's not the same with my apple trees. . . . So I developed this feeling that I didn't want to do it any longer. Then there were the gangsters, the thieves. And I didn't have any money to invest. Lots of things, and I ended up scared. . . . I felt totally dispirited, my heart was collapsing, and I just didn't want to go on with it anymore. All because that had happened, stealing my sheep." Through a connection with a local acquaintance, Li and his wife then moved near to Xining in Qinghai with the idea of selling fruit and vegetables from a mobile cart, and leaving their two children with a maternal uncle in a village near the county town where they both attended school. Harassment from the patrol officers (*chengguan*) constantly interrupted their efforts in Qinghai, but the main difficulty was the cold.[1] No one wanted to buy frozen vegetables, and so Li turned to selling dry products—walnuts, peanuts, pumpkin seeds, dates—outside the railway station. But this brought in too little money to be able to live on.

Without access to decent food or warmth, the couple succumbed to flu. The hospital charged more than they could afford, but they were so sick that they eventually decided they had no option but to find a doctor there. Once in the hospital, they came across a kind doctor who examined them for less than half the full fee of eight hundred to one hundred yuan normally charged and exempted them from paying the three yuan registration fee charged of outpatients on every visit.

The doctor's kindness was followed by another gesture of compassion, this time from an old Shaanxi acquaintance who lived in less unforgiving conditions in the lowlands of Qinghai. This person suggested that Li and his wife move there to live in his house, rent-free. "He had electricity in his house, an electric stove; for three days, we didn't go out to sell things, so we both recovered. In fact, we were only sick because it was winter, and his house was warm, so we fully recovered. That proved it was a winter sickness."

Arriving in Beijing

Work selling vegetables in their new abode began to pick up a bit, and Li and Zhang started being able to save a few yuan each day. Li got to know another vegetable vendor whose daughter had found work as a maid in Beijing, where she earned three hundred yuan a month, along with board and lodging. Li reasoned that he would try his chances in the capital. He initially intended to go there together with his wife, leaving their two children living with their uncle while they finished their middle school education in Shaanxi. However, he was persuaded by friends and relatives to go on his own at first, because he had never been to Beijing, and apart from having little idea about whether he would, in fact, be able to make a living, he also ran the risk of being detained. So, carrying a single small bag, he took the train to Beijing, and with the aid of an old map made his way to a suburb on the northern outskirts of the city, where a young man he knew from Shaanxi had found work making television cables. The young man was hospitable and encouraging, but Li felt that he himself did not have the skills necessary to make TV cables, and so would do better trying to find a job on his own. He spent three days wandering about trying to find some of what he called the city's main "introduction agencies" (*jieshao she*) for migrant laborers, where he identified the going rate for domestic maids and opportunities for himself. He then returned home on the slow train to Xi'an, for what then was a seventy-yuan ticket, picked up his wife, and got straight back on the train to Beijing. Within a few hours of arrival there, his wife found a job as a maid working for an elderly couple who lived south of the city center.

The couple's hopes that this employment would offer them some stability were soon shattered. Most mornings, Li went to the labor market to find daily employment working on construction sites and roads, but with minimal wages and unable to afford accommodations, he had to spend the nights sleeping rough. He decided to try his luck in the famous West Station, then the largest station in Asia, where he hoped to merge with the thousands of other migrants and evade the attention of the police. The forty days he spent there were etched in his memory as an experience of danger, fear, and abject misery:

> It was really dirty, so I squeezed in onto a windowsill where it was a bit cleaner. I held my bag and went to sleep. Sometimes there were people who came to check, so I quickly jumped down, and moved over to another waiting room. Back and forth it was. It got stricter and stricter if you didn't have a pass. I couldn't go on staying there. Without a pass, you couldn't stay in the waiting room. Aiya, it was so bad. A bad time. To begin with, I didn't understand. Lots of people went to the waiting room to check, and went around stopping everyone there, one by one, blocking you in. You couldn't escape, and had to be checked, one by one. They checked us one by one, so you couldn't escape. "No pass, out." They took you outside by the door. It was winter, and outside it was very windy. When I arrived in Beijing I didn't have many clothes, and they weren't good [quality]. It was freezing outside, so I found a shop entrance I thought I could sleep in, but [they] didn't let you stay there. They didn't let you stay in the station, nor in the shop, so all you could do was sleep outside for half the night.

Meanwhile, Zhang Yuanchen's job did not turn out as planned. Although her employers had agreed to pay her three hundred yuan a month, as well as food and accommodations, they gave her no more than a small bowl of food each day, and monitored how much she drank because they said they didn't want to waste water. Li and his wife had agreed that he would call her after three days to check that she was all right, and if not he would go and fetch her. When he turned up at the house to see his wife, her employers refused to let him in. "Do you know what the old man said? 'Do you want to let him in to steal our things?'" Insulted and mistreated, Zhang left, and shortly afterward found another position with another elderly couple and their married son in Daxing County, in the far southern outskirts of the city. Here Zhang was paid three hundred yuan, even though the initial agreement with her new employers was for four hundred yuan a month. Despite her employers' complaints that she didn't know how to cook—"How could I know how to cook city food?"—and that she stole money, she stayed there for two months, until the elderly head of the family died. The son, who was manager of a small building materials factory to the north of the city, then took her to work for him for three hundred yuan a month, but the work was physically exhausting, and her employer would not let her receive phone calls from her husband, and so, again, Li went to find her to take her back to the city. The two of them found an enclosed space where they could sleep under one of the staircases in West Station, but their rest was constantly disturbed by nightly patrols with searchlights, forcing homeless migrants outside.

To begin with, Li Fuying tried to work nights loading large trucks with heavy materials such as sand to transport out of the city. The labor was back-breaking, and as one of a small group of only three or four men, he had to keep going through the night to fill the truck. To begin with he was paid fifty yuan a night, but the pay was reduced each night, and when he was paid just twenty yuan for a whole night's work, he decided to throw it in in favor of returning to the labor market to look for odd jobs. "I couldn't do anything except odd jobs, but that was no good. I just sat there, with my sign. I didn't understand much, because I'd just arrived in Beijing."

Not long after Zhang found her second job as a maid, Li found employment in a hostel where the boss was looking for someone to do odd jobs and chauffeur his clients around in a pedicab. But having initially agreed to a monthly wage of 450 yuan, he paid Li only three hundred yuan after ninety-three days' work. Li decided to leave and try to make a living driving a pedicab on his own. However, he still did not have any stable accommodations, since he could not afford hostel rents, and with his wife working for someone else, he found himself on his own. For the next five months, he ate out, and slept in his pedicab in the alleys, changing his spot every two or three days to evade the attention of the night patrol. When it rained or was cold he covered himself with a plastic sheet.

The material uncertainties Li and his wife faced during their first year in Beijing were compounded by their constant fear of being arrested and sent back home. Li was taken into detention in a "detention and repatriation shelter" (shourong suo) and repatriated back to Shaanxi on three occasions. The same happened to his wife on two occasions. One Sunday, in front of his son who was visiting his parents, Li described to me what had happened to him. He spoke at length, often having to stop to prevent himself from choking up, so overwhelming was the memory of this terrible experience. His wife listened attentively, sitting on a low stool by the door, making only occasional comments when her husband seemed too churned up to continue. His son sat on the bed, listening in silence.

Li Fuying began his account of being sent into detention by describing how not long after his arrival in Beijing, a group of policemen approached him and other fellow migrants when they were trying to find work at one of Beijing's main labor markets. The policemen insisted that they take out their ID and money in order to register their names. But instead of registering them, they confiscated everything they had and threw it on the floor, then dragged them off to a truck, then to a detention shelter in the northern suburbs.

Conditions in these shelters were inhumane: violent, squalid, and brutal in their failure to provide even the most basic rights of food and hygiene to an endless stream of migrants—many of them destitute—who now found themselves contributing to a corrupt and exploitative network of personal gain and power.[2] As he narrated this experience, Li became so caught up in the ghastly memory of it that it was if he couldn't get his words out fast enough.[3]

In retrospect, the first detention shelter Li was sent to was a shocking introduction to the ruthless realities that near destitute migrants were routinely subjected to. After being searched at the entrance for knives and other implements—including small fruit peeling knives and key chains—the guards then took all possessions away from each detainee—money, belts, leather bags—leaving only their clothes. In a show of observing the formalities, they wrote receipts for the items they confiscated. Inside the shelter, each of the classroom-like rooms held so many people that the detainees had to sleep on the floor, packed so tightly together that they could not move. There were no beds, and not enough quilts for everyone, and so squabbles and fights were routine. The food was barely enough to keep anyone going. Cornmeal buns "full of air," and cornmeal gruel, "mostly water," were the staple, which many found so distasteful they turned them down. But without any alternative, hunger pushed even the younger and stronger detainees to eat them. If hunger trumped stronger inmates' attempts at resistance, attempts to curry favor with the guards by undertaking unsavory tasks—on one occasion, carrying out the body of an elderly man who died—were no more successful, and did not result in an improvement to the diet.

The length of time detainees spent in the shelters could be anything between three days and two weeks, depending partly on where they originally came from. The trucks that transported the migrants back home had destinations in different provinces and regions, but they had to wait until they were full before setting off. This meant that inmates being returned to Henan and Sichuan, for example, generally left sooner than the others, because so many of the migrants being repatriated came from these two provinces. But there were fewer people from the northwest, from Shaanxi, Gansu, Xinjiang, or Ningxia. Li therefore found himself being detained for a rather longer time than many others.

Guard violence against inmates was routine, starting when they first arrived and were beaten at the merest hesitation when they were told to empty their pockets and take their money out. Any mild misdemeanor, in the form of answering a guard back or not keeping quiet when told to, could result in a further beating, along with a torrent of verbal abuse. Extortion was a way of life. When it came to deciding who could leave the shelter, the guards operated on a system of favoring those who could pay them the most. Detainees who had no money were shut up inside again, and without the means to leave were regularly approached by middlemen recruiting manual labor for work on construction sites and the like—bricklayers, plasterers, and so on. Such "bosses" (*laoban*) would appear in the shelter yard and announce that those willing to sign up for construction work would be released after working for a few days. The implication was that in return for agreeing to work without wages or benefits, detainees could expect to be released in good time. However, such terms were rarely respected, and detainees were invariably asked to work for much longer, to the point that some started to think of ways to escape.

On one occasion at a detention shelter in Shijiazhuang, when Li didn't have any money to pay for the trip back to Xi'an, he was kept shut up in a small room alongside several dozen other people. The room had a couple of bunk beds, both crammed full of men. But there was little space to sit, let alone to lie down to sleep, so most people had to sleep standing up. Instead of a toilet, there was a plastic bucket "full of shit and piss" in the corner of the room. Inmates were not allowed to go outside, and with only a small window beside the upper tier of a bunk bed, the stench inside was unbearable. "It was so bad that you didn't know what to do." Crowded, filthy, and suffocating, the conditions in this room could literally lead to death, as Li described when he discovered an elderly man motionless on one of the bunk beds. At first he thought the man was asleep, but when it became clear that the man wasn't moving, Li called out to the guard, who dismissed his concerns and told him to mind his own business. However, a supervisor eventually turned up and instructed four younger and stronger inmates to carry the corpse out.

One of the few interjections Zhang Yuanchen made during the ten minutes or so Li spent describing these events was a proud reminder about how her husband had managed to hide some money she had sewn into his pocket. Had he declared his money, he would not have been able to pay for the trip back to Beijing to rejoin his wife, so he preferred to feign total pennilessness, for which he had to go without food for five days. On another occasion, this time without any need for prompting from his wife, Li told us he had hidden thirty yuan in an opening he had cut in the cloth shoes he was wearing. Had the money been discovered, it would have been confiscated, even though according to regulations inmates' items were to be returned to them when they were released. Despite the charade of signing receipts, everyone knew that this rule was rarely respected; sometimes detainees were returned items that did not belong to them, and sometimes nothing was returned to them. Like the belts, Zhang reminded her husband, when only eight of the ten people released with him from the Shijiazhuang shelter had their belts returned, and so two had to leave without anything to hold their trousers up.

Returning to Beijing from the detention shelter presented new difficulties. Between the Changping and Shijiazhuang shelters, Li had struck up a friendship with a younger man, a "kid," he said, from "our Shaanxi," whose money had been taken off him by the guards so he had nothing at all. With only thirty yuan, Li did not have enough to eat as well as pay for two fares, each twenty-one yuan, back to Beijing. Nevertheless, they were famished, so decided they had to eat before trying to obtain the train tickets. Having finished big bowls of noodles at a nearby street stall, they then tried to make up the money they needed for their tickets back to Beijing by selling the few items they had—a plastic water cup and a woolen jumper. But no one wanted to buy them: "Maybe they suspected we were dirty and unhygienic." As a last resort, Li suggested going to the train station and hanging around to look for someone who looked as if he might lend them the money they needed to buy their tickets. Eventually, Li saw someone "who looked very clean and nice," who when the couple approached him just gave them the money they asked for, no questions asked.

Back in Beijing, Li returned to night work, loading sand onto trucks for twenty or thirty yuan a shift, and occasionally came across good-hearted folks from his home in Shaanxi who would let him eat for free in their restaurants. But he had to endure two further repatriations, one of which was all the way back to Xi'an, the nearest dropping off station for returnee migrants from the northwest. His account gave a glimpse of the extreme psychological and emotional strain on those subjected to the brutality of detention. His wife reminded him about a woman from Gansu who had been in the shelter a long time. She was unusually tall, and beautiful, but spent her time swearing and singing, totally out of control, and shouting that she wanted to go home to see her child. She even hurled away the food she was given, so she was literally starving herself. The detention shelter's walls were covered with obscenities scrawled by inmates. "Everyone wrote them," was Li's comment. "That's what it's like. For people who come to Beijing to work, who've been detained . . . it's difficult to forget. You just hate this society [*dui zheige shehui jiu hen*], you just hate it. It makes you crazy. And they beat you up."

Li's account of the second time he was detained described the cruel futility of what he called a stupid system that just wasted money—"sending you back, only for you to return to Beijing." In late 2007, as stringent urban regulations to clean up the capital in time for the Olympics were put in place, Li was picked up one morning by two plainclothes policemen not far from Qianmen for driving his pedicab without a license. His wife had already left for work in Daxing County. Together with another pedicab driver, Li was pushed into a car in which the doors were locked and the windows shut, "So you couldn't get away, could you?" He was kept there all day until early evening, without anything to eat or drink, and then taken off to Changping in the north of the city. It was only the next day, when his wife was selling little red flags in Tian'anmen Square, that someone told her that her husband had been detained. She was detained on the same day, without Li knowing, since he had already been taken to Changping.

After a few days, Li was moved to Shijiazhuang in a truck for male migrants. On arrival at the shelter there, the back of the truck was opened to let the men out. As he waited his turn to jump down, Li saw his wife getting off another truck, alongside his own, full of female migrants. He had no idea that she was being repatriated, and just collapsed in tears when he saw her. As he recalled his heartache at this episode, Li's voice began to break, and it was clear he was doing his best to keep back his tears, but he went on, vehemently, to say that it was the psychological pressure of detention that was far worse than the simple fact of being detained, or being fined, or even having little to eat. "It's no big deal to have to be detained and eat cornmeal buns. Right? You just eat them for a few days and then leave. But the real point is that it's mentally unbearable. Ah, you lose your mental balance inside, ah. Some people inside totally lost it."

The psychological pressure sometimes built up and exploded into violence. On one occasion, a large group of migrants retaliated against a security guard who had been laying into them for not queuing up properly. Other guards and the police turned up to find out what was going on, but because there were so many people watching, they refrained from beating them up and instead gave them a good talking to and let them go.

Li and his wife were put on the same train from Shijiazhuang back to Xi'an, but in separate compartments, on different tiers. One of the guards eventually allowed Li to go to the upper tier of the carriage to see his wife, but then on arrival at Xi'an they were sent to another detention shelter, outside the city, which was even worse than the previous ones. "Some homecoming," was Zhang Yuanchen's comment. The guards had large watchdogs they let out to intimidate the migrants at the merest sign of disobedience. Instead of toilets as in the Beijing shelter, here all they had was a small pot. The noodles they were given to eat were more water than noodles, without salt and with only a few vegetables—"You know, those wild vegetables that grow at the roadside"—and each inmate was given just one chopstick. "What use is one chopstick?"

A system of divide-and-rule backed up the security guards' use of violence and extortion to keep control in these shelters. On one occasion, Li found himself appointed monitor, tasked with keeping his fellow inmates in order. His approach was to tell everyone that they could talk quietly when the guards weren't around but to stop talking as soon as they turned up. Another inmate then picked a fight with him, accusing him of not keeping proper order. The guard appeared and accused Li of failing to keep good order, turned angry, and decided to stop Li from going outside for a week. Things then turned really nasty. "When I saw I wasn't going to be let out, I got so angry I lost control, so I bashed the door, twice." No one responded when the guard asked who had been bashing the door, but Li's expression gave him away. The guard then ordered some of the inmates to drag Li out and beat him up. "Several men laid into me. They beat me up and said they didn't want me to be the monitor anymore. I said I didn't want to be either. That was it, they just beat me up."

As I've already noted, release from the shelter depended on detainees' capacity to pay their way out, initially masked by a pretense of registering the IDs of the detainees. Then the guards indicated to the detainees where the phone was, and told them to tell their families to send "ransom money"—several hundred yuan—as a condition of their release. When Li and his wife arrived back in Xi'an and were instructed to make such a phone call, they thought that no one would be at home, since the children were out at school. And in any case, they didn't want their children to know that they had been sent back. Finally, however, Li decided he had no option, and so called his son, then studying at the Xi'an Light Industry Technical School. At first, he tried to pretend to his son that he had been unable to find work in Beijing, and so had returned to Xi'an to establish contact with someone who might give him work, but he didn't have his phone number. Could his son find it for him? But his son put two and two together, asked for leave from school, and found his way to the detention shelter, where "he saw me inside the window looking out on the yard. I crawled up to the opening in the window to see him. Ahh, he was outside looking at me, and I was inside looking at him, but they didn't let him speak to me, they didn't let my son speak to me. My son said he wanted to see me, and I said my son has come and I want to see him, but they didn't let me." Realizing that the guards would not let him speak to his parents, Young Li returned to his school, where two of his teachers gave him five hundred yuan to pay for his parents' release.

Outside the shelter, Young Li insisted that they first go to eat a bowl of noodles before going to rest at his school.

> As soon as we got to the school we first washed our faces, and he made the two of us sit on his bed, and washed our feet. He first washed mine, and then his mother's. Ah. I didn't want him to wash my feet, but he insisted. His mother didn't want him to either, but he insisted as well. And after he washed our feet, we rested. And we felt so good, right? Our son was studying in technical college, and was mature and sensible, but still understood about bathing the feet of his parents. I've told lots of people about this. This college student, a technical college student, is something . . . it's a difficult thing, washing the feet of your mother and father when they are so dirty.

After one night in their son's school, Li and Zhang returned to Beijing. The few possessions they owned were in Beijing, and even though making a livelihood in the capital was as precarious as it was tough, they reasoned that their chances there were better than in the northwest.

Pedicabs and Patrol Officers

Li started working around Dashalar as a pedicab cyclist in 2000, when he and his wife moved into the dazayuan where I first met them. The couple had endless stories to tell about their hassles with the law, many of routine harassment and aggression by local patrol officers keen to exploit any opportunity to make a bit of money. Overall, these stories described an environment of relentless uncertainty and anxiety throughout the years Li worked his pedicab. Some indicated the heightened vulnerability created by increasingly stringent government regulations about where and when pedicab drivers could ply their trade during the government's program of urban beautification in the lead-up to the 2008 Olympics. Many told of such violence and intimidation that I couldn't help but wonder why the couple persisted in staying in the capital rather than returning to Shaanxi.

In the early 1950s, Beijing's "traditional" hand-pulled rickshaws had given way to three-wheeled pedicabs and pedicarts, many of them used to carry goods. The pedicabs used to transport people were banned during the Cultural

Revolution, reappearing only in the 1980s. Registered pedicab drivers were allowed to trade in central tourist districts, including Tian'anmen Square, where many used their pedicabs to carry wounded protesters during the bloody events of June 4, 1989. By the 1980s and 1990s, they became omnipresent in old Beijing neighborhoods for transporting goods and tourists, since they were cheaper and more convenient than taxis for negotiating the warren of tiny alleys and lanes. However, as the demolition and transformation of Beijing's South City got under way in the mid-1990s, new regulations were introduced, limiting the areas where pedicab cyclists could operate. Those who lived and worked in Dashalar were prohibited from going north of Qianmen. At the same time, the arrival in Dashalar of huge numbers of migrants attracted by cheap accommodations and access to ad hoc, small-scale commercial activities such as selling Beijing trinkets to tourists swelled the ranks of unlicensed pedicab cyclists. Hardworking and honest people like Li Fuying and his wife were constantly vulnerable to the predatory interests of the patrol officers whose thuggish methods turned the couple's attempts to make a living into a grim struggle for survival.

The confiscation of pedicabs and the imposition of fines mounted noticeably before important national occasions such as National Day or Party Congresses. On such occasions, cyclists found it difficult to go out without encountering either the patrol officers or their "hired soldiers," as Li described them. Night raids were common in areas of the neighborhood where drivers used to gather to rest. Small groups of chengguan would stand in wait for drivers to emerge onto the main street from the small lanes running into it. If a cyclist said the patrol was approaching, the cyclists would all ride off into the obscurity of the hutong as quickly as they could, or would just leave their pedicabs and rush off on foot. To lose a poor-quality pedicab without a canopy could be preferable to a fine, which could easily mount to five thousand yuan. "The chengguan fall over each other to fine you. When they arrest you, they come in a big line, the public security at the front, then the officials sitting in cars, then the security vehicles and the minivans. Then right at the back is the truck that takes the pedicabs away. Lots of people, a whole line of them. And motorbikes as well. You can't run off, because if you try, the motorbikes will come after you."

In the run-up to the Olympics, the ranks of the patrol officers swelled as they linked forces with the various bodies associated with urban management—the defense, health, and communications units, and the street office—in what Li wryly called "uniting to uphold the law." Their methods were routinely violent, and they beat those who resisted their attempts to impose fines or kicked them to the ground. Pedicab cyclists' clients could sometimes behave with equal aggression. "There are many who don't give you any money at all. But you have to get it from them, because if you don't, the next time you ask them for money, they'll beat you up and swear at you. It's really wrong. Pedicab drivers all come across things like this, getting beaten up when people don't want to pay you, especially if you're older. I'd rather save myself from getting beaten up than go after five or six kuai." Li reckoned that during his first year driving pedicabs he lost some three thousand yuan to fines and fees charged to retrieve his confiscated vehicle. In one year, so his wife recalled, it was confiscated six times.

One notable occasion that Li and Zhang heatedly recounted was when a patrol officer on a motorbike ran into Li's pedicab, overturning it so that it crashed into a truck parked at the side of the road. Li ran off but was pursued by a posse of patrol officers, all on motorbikes. They caught up with him and dragged him back to the truck, where they started beating him up. At this point, Li's wife, the truck driver, and a number of onlookers, including tourists, started shouting at the patrol officers to leave Li alone. They had confiscated his pedicab, including the removable seat cover, so why did they still want to beat him up? Pushed to the brink of desperation, Li's wife started screaming at the patrol officers, "You don't let us pedal our bikes, or sell things, and you deport us back home, right? And now you want to beat him to death. What will I do if you kill him? Better kill me."

One name stood out in the couple's accounts of officials' harassment: Yang Wei—Great and Glorious Yang—a "corrupt thug," in Li's terms, who was well known in the neighborhood for his "specialty" of hounding pedicab drivers, particularly those from outside Beijing, and demanding money and cigarettes as the condition for returning a confiscated pedicab to its owner. He worked together with a neighborhood defense boss nicknamed Big Hero Li. The two would lie in wait in Dashalar's alleys, waiting for a pedicab driver to pass by, and would then rush out, detain him, and confiscate his bike. They would release it only once the driver had paid a fine, and if a driver had no money, Yang Wei would confiscate any other possessions he had on him. He thought nothing of damaging people's possessions or of physically hurting them. On one occasion, when Li was mending a broken spoke on his pedicab in West Street, Yang Wei went up to him, pushed him to one side, and overturned the pedicab so that it smashed into Li's leg, putting him out of work for a month. But even with a wounded leg, Li was determined not to give in without resisting. Even though his pedicab had been confiscated, every day he went over to Yang Wei's house near Hepingmen to shame him into giving it back. He stood in front of his window demanding his pedicab back; he had two children who were studying and needed the income it brought. A fine would be preferable to permanent confiscation. But when Li asked him to fine him instead, Yang took to insultingly mocking him, just to prove who was the big man around town, and told Li to give him 200,000 yuan there and then. Angry, humiliated, and powerless, Li had little option but to leave.

Zhang Yuanchen's gender did not protect her from physical brutality, either. On one occasion, she was beaten so badly that she lost her hearing. One of the times Great and Glorious Yang arrested her was when she was selling small items—hair clips, hair bands, and the like—on Dashalar's West Street. Li reckoned that Yang Wei's motive was pure vindictiveness; he had a reputation for harboring a particular dislike of Shaanxi people. It was midnight when Yang Wei arrived with Zhang Yuanchen at the detention shelter office, and the guards were not at all happy to see him. That day Yang Wei had sent more than fifty detainees to the detention shelter, and even though the guards stood to make material gain out of their detainees, they did not want to accept any more. Only a carton of good cigarettes persuaded them to accept Zhang. Yang Wei's reward was the vindictive delight of confiscating Zhang Yuanchen's goods and throwing them away as rubbish. But he was to get his comeuppance later, when an investigation revealed his involvement with a corrupt circle of local policemen, patrol officers, and prostitutes. He was removed from his position in Dashalar and transferred to another station, where, Li and Zhang heard, he was beaten up. This gave them little cause for delight but rather for further reflection on how their treatment by the likes of Yang Wei had pushed them to the brink. The emotional strain on Li and his wife was so unbearable that Zhang Yuanchen was driven to imagine the worst. But she also imagined finding a way to tell the world of the injustices she and her husband had had to endure. "If I could take photographs, I would show [the world] what kind of things you do, to what people, what you get up to. This is how you treat ordinary people. Ai, you don't know Chinese society! If you complain or whatever, they send you off in the night. . . . There's no harmony in the harmonious society!"

Outsiders

Li's and Zhang's accounts of living in the capital tacked back and forth between different incidents at unspecified dates since 2000, but a recurring theme concerned their status as outsiders (*waidiren*), the disdain Beijingers demonstrated toward them, and the mixture of camaraderie and conflict between migrants from different regions. Some outsiders, notably the northeasterners, had a reputation for being tough and outspoken, and for using methods that mirrored those of the chengguan when it came to protecting their own. One occasion Li and his wife recalled was when a northeasterner's pedicab was confiscated, and his fellow countrymen overturned the patrol officer's sidecar and punched the patrol officer so badly that his head was covered in blood. But if the patrol officers did not dare pick on the hard guys from the northeast, then "mountain people, ordinary honest people like us," Li commented, were another matter. "They only pick on honest folk, and as soon as they see you are a good guy, they grab you while everyone else runs off. That's how it is. I tell you, the chengguan are really lacking in morals."

Li used to work with two other pedicab drivers, both from Henan. They were known as the "gang of three." One of the three, Old Wei, kept getting into trouble while driving his pedicab, but since he knew someone in the local police office, when it was confiscated he generally found a way to retrieve it. On one occasion, however, he disappeared after his bike was confiscated. Li eventually heard the story sometime later. Apparently, when Old Wei turned up at the police station to get his pedicab back, the patrol officers had taken him inside and beaten him so badly that he had all sorts of internal injuries. He was in the hospital for a long time, where the bill mounted to thirty thousand yuan. Fortunately, an uncle of his from Henan agreed to pay the bill. But the money ran out, so Old Wei had to leave the hospital before he had fully recovered. His uncle filed a complaint and insisted that the chengguan office pay compensation. The matter was partially resolved, but the chengguan paid only for the medicine. They didn't compensate Old Wei for loss of work or anything else. According to Zhang Yuanchen, the authorities claimed they couldn't arrest the chengguan because they'd covered their heads when they beat Old Wei up, and so they weren't able to identify who was responsible. As a result of this brutality, Old Wei had become "unrecognizable." By the time Li saw him again, he was reduced to skin and bones, and was not able to walk properly. Li was sure that if it had been him, given his age and physical weakness, he would have been beaten to death. In fact, throughout Li's account of this incident, Zhang repeatedly interjected, "They would have beaten him [Li] to death."

Li's and Zhang's first experience of renting a room in Dashalar lasted no more than a month because the landlord charged an exorbitant amount for the electricity. The room had only one light bulb, and no electrical appliances. When the landlord attempted to charge them nearly forty yuan for a month's electricity—more than the standard rate then charged to Beijing tenants—Li "had a few things to say to him," whereupon the landlord told him to leave, there and then. After a bit of haggling, Li and his wife were permitted to stay on for another couple of days while they found somewhere else to live—the dazayuan room they lived in when I first got to know them. When they first moved in, it was bare and filthy. The landlord—a long-term local resident of Dashalar, and with a reputation as a minor racketeer—didn't lift a finger to make the room livable.

There was little social contact between the residents of this dazayuan, and over the eight years Li and Zhang lived there, their contact with the landlord, who lived in the same dazayuan, was limited to the brief moments when he collected the rent. Li was disparaging about the landlord's failure to treat his tenants with even the minimum human respect. To begin with, in 2003, Li's rent was four hundred yuan a month, and together with the rent from the other migrant tenants in the same property, the landlord made quite a sizeable sum. This did not stop him from pushing Li's rent up, despite the fact that he made no contribution to repairing or decorating their small room. At best, Li thought he was unhelpful, but behind his unresponsiveness to Li's occasional requests for assistance lay a sullen contempt of outsiders. Even though the landlord was familiar with the local patrol officers, he refused to intervene to pressure them to return Li's pedicab on the occasions they confiscated it. On the contrary, he used to support the officers from the neighborhood committee when they periodically decided to tow migrants' pedicabs away, particularly during the cleanup policy before the Olympics. Li's scorn of his landlord's behavior extended to the landlord's wife, who would be all smiles and politeness when she needed help with something, such as returning a heavy gas cylinder to the local store. On other occasions, however, she would pass Li by without even acknowledging his existence. Li could not refrain from taking a mild delight in refusing her requests to give her a lift in his pedicab, even when she said she would pay if it was confiscated again.

In all, Li's experience of local Beijingers, both in his dazayuan and in the neighborhood, provided bitter evidence of Beijingers' total contempt for rural migrants, even those who had some money.

> If you are from somewhere else, you can never do right, they always think you are doing something wrong. It's never them who are wrong. When they are in your pedicab they are nice to you, but when they are not they bully you. As soon as they see a pedicab is from outside Beijing, they try to rip you off. When they see you're an outsider, even if you are in the right, they say you are not. Or they just confiscate your pedicab. No matter whether you are in the right or not, it always ends badly. That's my experience. Big

officials engage in big corruption, small officials in small corruption. But for people at the bottom of the pile, doing small business, driving pedicabs, you're not allowed to live. Is it surprising that people aren't happy?

In early 2009, worn down by the physical and emotional exhaustion of trying to make ends meet, withstanding abuse and discrimination, and being relentlessly targeted by predatory patrol officers, Li and his wife welcomed the opportunity to leave Dashalar. Through an acquaintance, the couple found jobs as rubbish collectors—euphemistically titled "hygiene personnel" (*weisheng gongyuan*). A perk of the job was rent-free accommodations in a cramped underground storeroom at one end of a pedestrian underpass near the Temple of Heaven. The room was even smaller than their Dashalar accommodations, but for Li and his wife, it was much cleaner and "less chaotic" than Dashalar, and it was adjacent to a boiler room, so the hot air kept them warm in winter. In warm weather, they could move their small table and stools to eat outside in the shelter of the underpass, and no one hassled Li to keep moving his pedicab when he parked it outside his door. They received a monthly wage of eighteen hundred yuan between them, and even though they had to work every day, they enjoyed a relatively flexible arrangement with their employer. As long as they called him in advance, they could take time off, and they did not have to start work too early. More than anything, however, they felt relieved to be free of the daily impositions of prejudiced neighbors. Their new neighbors living under the underpass were all migrants, none of whom stayed for any length of time, but they all got on well enough. In a different environment, Zhang Yuanchen could now articulate her relief to be away from Dashalar: "Beijingers are cold. They don't have feelings . . . in their hearts they look down on you . . . they think you should be nice to them. They think you are there for them to take advantage of. That's what they think. They think, 'You're from outside Beijing, so you should serve me,' that's how they think. Especially in Dashalar. People who are educated are not like that. I tell you, here people are usually considerate, so if they have a dog and the dog wants to pee, they take it off to pee. They don't just let it pee in your doorway." For three years or so, Li and his wife seemed relatively content with their improved circumstances. They managed to save a bit of money, and maintained regular contact with their children. They were uncertain about whether they would eventually return to their village. Since arriving in Beijing, they had returned to their Shaanxi home only once, for Spring Festival. But Li hoped to return permanently once their son married and moved back to Xi'an. Li had kept hold of their village house, imagining that retirement, a married son, and a grandchild back home would offer him some respite and comfort after his long years of hardship in the capital. His wife, however, had a different view. For her, no matter how tough their life in Beijing had been, it was much worse in their home village.

It's full of gangs of thieves and ruffians. Huh, they want everything, even the good luck charms hanging from your waist. They want everything, at least everything they can turn into money. If there's nothing for them to steal, they steal your grain at night. Every household has grain, so that's what they steal. That's what it's like. No one in control. . . . If you want a sheep, I'll give you a sheep. You want a cow, I'll give you a cow. If you resist, they just beat you up. . . . And trying to talk reason is no good when it's up against money. They'll take whatever you have, three hundred or five hundred. That's what it's like.

Listening to this, Li could not respond positively about the prospects of returning home but concurred that "people at the bottom of society [zui xiaceng ren] have no real way to live. Everyone is after you, fining you, arresting you, and they don't even tell you why."

Hopes and Heartache

The first time I met Li Fuying and Zhang Yuanchen in their tiny room in Dashalar in January 2006 was also the first time I met their son. Young Li was then twenty-five, studying graphic design in Shijiazhuang, Hebei Province. Li's pride in his son was evident from the outset: when he introduced his son to me, he announced that his son was taller than he himself was. Tall and very handsome, Young Li sat quietly on the bed and listened as his father told me about his first years in Beijing, occasionally getting up to pour me water and offer me fruit. I then knew nothing about either him or his family's circumstances, but a strong bond of affection and respect between the son and his parents was evident. This was later affirmed by Li's moving description, mentioned above, of how his son had washed his feet when he and his wife were deported back to Xi'an.

It was only later, long after Young Li's parents had told me about how difficult life had been for them since arriving in Beijing, that they revealed to me their concerns about their children, and their son in particular. The occasion was the summer of 2011, when we were sitting outside their small room eating watermelon and chatting in the shade of the underpass near the Temple of Heaven.

Li's and Zhang's decision to leave Shaanxi was primarily motivated by their aspirations for the education of their children, particularly their son, for which they needed to make more money than cultivating apples could bring them. They were incredibly frugal; they didn't smoke, or drink, or gamble, and they ate the cheapest food they could find. They had to borrow money to finance their children's studies, but obtaining a loan or credit was far from easy, despite regulations enabling poor families to access financial support. When their son started college, he had two to three thousand yuan, partly earned, partly supplemented by his parents' savings, but this wasn't enough, and so he applied to the college authorities for support. Turned down by them, he then went back to his home village government, but they too refused to support him, whereupon he decided to go directly to the college director, insisting that the college help him, since this is what the college had initially committed to when he obtained a place there.

If it was difficult for their son, it was worse for their daughter, some four years their son's junior. She had no money to take to college. Before I met her, she had passed the exams for the People's Liberation Army Communications University in Xi'an. Li approached the university to ask for credit to help his daughter, but his request was turned down. Disappointed and humiliated, his daughter decided not to pursue higher education, and told her parents that she was taking up military training in Xi'an. After no communication from her for several months, her parents finally managed to discover that she had, in fact, been staying with a friend in Xi'an. Her parents then persuaded her to return with them to Beijing, where she started selling small tourist trinkets alongside her mother in Tian'anmen Square, sometimes also helping her father with the pedicab. She spent about a year in Beijing, studying part-time on her own, and eventually revisiting the idea of going to university. She obtained a place in a university in Hainan, in the far south, but between her parents' sense that it was too far away and the prohibitive cost of the travel to get there she decided not to take it up. Finally, after much arguing with her parents about what she wanted to do, she decided to apply to a university in Ningxia, where the fees were far less than elsewhere, and where she embarked on a sociology degree.

Even so, the fact that both his children managed to succeed in going to university was not enough to calm Li's anxieties about their future. Neither his son nor his daughter, in his view, was young anymore, so he could not stop being anxious because, as he put it, "they still have to marry and have children." When, in 2010, I expressed surprise that he should be worried about his son, he said: "Huh, he was born in 1981, so I'm just worried about how he will find a wife." Li's tight laugh as he made this comment was a barely hidden indication of his concerns for his son's—and his own—future.

Young Li had had an on-off relationship with a girlfriend since 2008, but his parents were far from enthusiastic about his choice. They felt that she was not really sincere, that she was resentful of the time her boyfriend spent with his parents and sister, and that she was attempting to drive a wedge between their son and his family. Li Fuying was particularly vocal in expressing his views. He felt that the young woman was more interested in Young Li's good looks and prospects than anything else, and that if someone else came along with better prospects, she would go off with him. "The only good thing to say for her is that she's tall," was Li's grudging comment. By January 2010, Young Li had split up with this girlfriend. Repeated arguments and short-term separations, alongside his parents' disapproval, convinced him that he should return to Xi'an to buy a flat with which he could settle down and find a more suitable partner. He was already twenty-eight years old by this time, much older than the standard age at which men from their village married. Now into their midfifties and uncertain about what their future held for them, Li and his wife were troubled about their son's situation, not only on his behalf but just as importantly on their own.

Young Li's decision to leave his girlfriend did not last for long, however, and the two reunited in 2012. His parents had previously insisted that their main concerns were about family unity, but by now it was apparent that they were worried that their son's wife would not be filial and would refuse to care for them when they could no longer work and bring in an income. The difference between parents and son seemed irreconcilable, and when I left Beijing in the autumn of 2012, Li Fuying and his wife were facing what they imagined would be total estrangement from their son.

Imagine my surprise, then, when I returned to Beijing in the autumn of 2013 and called Li to arrange to meet, and he told me that his son had married his girlfriend, and she had given birth to a baby boy. Li said all was fine now, and he and his wife were living with their son and grandson in an apartment in the far north of the city. I anticipated a joyful reunion with Li, Zhang, and their son. But as soon as Li arrived at the station in the northern suburbs where we had arranged to meet, I realized that something was terribly wrong. He explained that he was not living with his son as he had said on the phone, because it hadn't worked out. But he still insisted on taking me to his son's place, saying that Zhang Yuanchen would join us as we walked there. Apparently, the plan had been to go out to eat.

We walked slowly along the road to his son's apartment, and tears rolled down Li's face as he told me what had happened over the previous eighteen months. His despair was unbearable, so we had to keep stopping while he collected himself. Zhang Yuanchen eventually joined us, and walked silently at her husband's side with a look of utter misery on her face. It transpired that their son had returned to Beijing and decided to marry his former girlfriend and move with his wife into an apartment he rented in the far northern suburbs of the city. He initially invited his parents to live with him, so they left their underground accommodations by the Temple of Heaven to take up their new role as grandparents. Soon after the birth of the baby, however, their relationship with their daughter-in-law soured. She would not let them touch her small son, did not talk to them, and demanded her husband's assistance with this and that as soon as he turned his attention to his parents. Li and his wife felt she treated them like "filthy scum" who were too uneducated and uncivilized to care for her son.

Life became so intolerable that Li and his wife decided to move out, and they found independent accommodations not too far from their son's flat. But their hopes that spatial and physical distance from their son and daughter-in-law would help were to little avail. Whenever they went to their son's apartment—to pick something up, as Zhang put it—their daughter-in-law would not let them even see their grandson, let alone pick him up and cuddle him, nor did she leave them alone to spend any time with their son.

The parents' sorrow and humiliation were painfully exposed when, in response to their urging, and despite my suggestion that they change their plan, I went with them to see their son. It was one of the most awkward and miserable encounters imaginable. The flat was quite spacious, but with nothing but bare walls and a stained concrete floor, and plastic bags all over the place, it felt cold and unwelcoming. Young Li looked very different from the healthy, good-looking young man I remembered. He was exhausted and unkempt; later his parents shared with me the sense of shame they felt about his appearance. Li, Zhang, and I sat there in the large living room as their son kept rushing to and from the bedroom, where his wife was trying to stop the baby from crying. It was a scene of total abjection. Through the hour we spent there, not only did Young Li's wife not emerge with the baby to greet us, but she did not even pass on a message of apology to her husband to convey to us. If Li had hoped that my presence might encourage at least the veneer of some familiar contact with their daughter-in-law and grandson, the result was the reverse. His son was clearly at his wits' end, attempting to mediate between his wife, his parents, and me. So as soon as I could, I suggested that we leave on the pretext that I had another engagement.

The next day, I went to visit Li and Zhang in their new accommodations. I was not prepared for what I saw: the only way I can describe it is as a slum—a chaotic and filthy zone of development in a rural suburb not far from their son's apartment, where farmers were turning their land over to build single-story rooms to rent out to migrant laborers.[4] The scene was desolate: half-built buildings all over the place, unpaved roads covered with deep ruts of thick dried mud, row after row of windowless, boxlike concrete-walled rooms facing open ditches full of waste and rubbish. Li's room ran alongside a wide ditch that served as an open sewer, and even in the early cold of autumn, the low wall that separated the walkway from the ditch could not keep the stench away from their room. The shared toilet was at the end of the walkway—an open hole in the ground surrounded by wooden boards. A single public tap with cold water was the only evidence of any plumbing.

The couple's small room was sparsely furnished with a double bed, an old dresser, and a few pots and pans. It had basic electricity for light and a single stove burner to cook on. There was no TV, just a small DVD viewer. Chrysanthemums growing in pots outside the room gave evidence of an attempt to cheer up the otherwise dismal surroundings. Li Fuying was in a state of extreme distress at his son's behavior: "A first grandson should be a happy occasion, but we cried when we heard he was born. . . . I even thought of going to see a lawyer to demand thirty years of expenses back from my son, the expenses for having brought him up. We are no longer a family. When we visited a couple of days ago, the daughter-in-law didn't even come out to say hello to us . . . she didn't let her parents-in-law into the room to see the child."

Li went on to describe how his son hadn't wanted him, his father, to give a speech at his wedding party in a restaurant in Beijing. He, the father, had painstakingly written out the speech beforehand, imagining a ceremony in Shaanxi. As he read it to me, tears rolled down his cheeks. He and his wife kept repeating how their daughter-in-law was relentless in pushing their son to do as she wished, insisting that he bring her this and that when his parents were talking to him. She had some mental problem, they said. They also described how when they were living in their son's apartment, their son would unpredictably explode in anger at his father . . . throwing things around then hitting his own face with shame, sometimes in front of his own wife. Li was overwhelmed with anxiety at the thought that his daughter-in-law was pushing his son to the brink. How could they go on living like this? Nor did he know how to respond to the situation. If he and his wife didn't go to visit their son's home, they were accused of not caring for their grandson, but if they did, they were ignored and not allowed even to see the little baby.

Li's daughter was another worry, since she showed no signs of wanting to marry. After graduating from Ningxia University with a degree in sociology, she found a job with a nongovernmental agency based in Xi'an, working on poverty relief programs in poor villages.[5] After some time in Xi'an, she went to Fujian to work with the elderly, and rode back to Beijing on a motorbike. According to her father, the trip took five days, and she stayed in small hotels along the way. She lost one small bag during her trip, but received a phone call from someone who had picked it up, and so was able to retrieve it. She didn't tell her parents that she was riding back to Beijing but suddenly turned up at her parents' place with her bike. Her parents were too shocked to be able to greet her back properly.

Behind her parents' concern that their daughter was not married lay other unspoken and maybe unspeakable fears. She had refused all the introductions her parents had facilitated. "Does she not want to have any children?" her father asked. "Or is she now unmarriageable?" I tried to convince him that at thirty years old she was far from being unmarriageable, but Li was not convinced.

Young Li always featured more prominently in Li's narratives than his daughter, even though she visited them as much if not more than her brother when they lived in Dashalar. However, until 2013, Li's vision of his future in old age rested on the idea that his married son would be living in Xi'an, not far from their family home in the countryside. Li and his wife would be living back in their single-story red brick house in the village they left in the 1990s, Zhang would be making cloth shoes, and Li would be growing flowers to sell, with an income topped up by their old age insurance.

In the event, Li and his wife moved back to the Shaanxi countryside sometime in late 2015, heartbroken at their estrangement from their son and their inability to realize any benefits from having struggled for so long.

Interlude 4

Li Fuying's initial motivation in leaving his village was to establish a more secure livelihood than he had growing apples. By the time I met him and his wife in 2006, ten years after they had arrived in Beijing, they clearly acknowledged that their main reason for enduring life in the capital despite huge setbacks, including forcible repatriations, was to be able to finance their children, and particularly their son, through higher education. Li Fuying was explicit in articulating his desire and expectation that his son would eventually marry, have a child, and support him and his wife in their old age once they themselves were no longer able to work.

Li's and Zhang's story highlights many issues common to the experience of migrant workers all over the country. The capital's program of mass eviction of the "low-end" migrant population from Beijing's suburbs is but the most recent exposition of the desperate conditions migrant workers from all over the country are willing to endure in order to secure a basic livelihood.[1] The story I have narrated in this chapter compels us to look beyond my largely urban focus on precarity to consider rural/urban contrasts in analyzing the relationship between indigents and law enforcement. In Li's Shaanxi village, the network of complicity between gangs and local cadres created conditions of relentless physical and material insecurity that threatened even the possibility of sustaining a basic livelihood. With no end to such conditions in sight, the lawlessness of village life made existence so intolerable that Li and Zhang fled in search of alternative means of making a living. In the city, however, they confronted a different face of authority. Their attempts to make a living as labor migrants, whose status as such was condoned by and effectively encouraged by the state, repeatedly exposed them to the violent and corrupt practices of local law enforcement officers, with traumatic psychological and emotional effects. Nevertheless, thoughts of the everyday lawlessness back home did not give them the luxury of imagining a realistic possibility of return, at least while they were still physically able to work, and as long as they imagined that in their future as elderly people they would be able to depend on a filial son. Their unshakable belief in such a future sustained their enactment of agency as a capacity to endure unspeakable suffering, inflicted on them by the hostile environment they inhabited in Beijing.

Another important point that emerges from this story is a corrective to much public commentary on the Chinese state's efforts to establish an effective legal system. While in recent years the Chinese government has gone to great lengths to strengthen its legal system by underwriting the rule of law, critics have repeatedly pointed to the inefficacy of such attempts as long as they are not backed up by adequate structures of implementation.[2] Li's and Zhang's experience of the law provides a glimpse into a related but bigger and more general issue, of relevance far beyond China's borders, namely that state policy oriented to improving the legal system through the enactment of laws does not in itself lead to greater regularization of social and economic practices. On the contrary, from the perspective of this couple's experiences, irregularity, corruption, and the arbitrary abuse of power emerged as such predictable aspects of the legal structure as it was being practiced at the local level that they became associated with the legal system itself. Beyond the experience of these migrants from Shaanxi, it is this view of the limits of the law in everyday practice that explains the widespread popular cynicism in Dashalar about the capacity of the law to stand up for ordinary people's rights.[3]

The massive exploitation of migrant labor in Beijing and elsewhere in the construction of China's "economic miracle" is the effect of a strategic policy shift that has been taking shape since the mid-1990s. Yet despite the extent, scale, and character of internal migration as part of a policy shift away from industrialization toward urbanization, the movement of rural workers from all over the country to Beijing in search of a means of survival and labor is not in itself a recent phenomenon. As I have noted above, much of the earlier movement was informal and was the response of impoverished peasants to peak moments of pressure on rural resources. It was arguably only when the administrative and spatial controls on physical movement and travel were at their most restrictive between the late 1960s and the mid-1970s that this kind of informal movement into the neighborhood came to a standstill. It is also worth recalling that spatially situated between the inner city and the vast expanses of countryside outside the outer city walls, Dashalar had long been a melting pot of people from different classes, religions, and ethnicities, trading or begging and sampling the delights of the neighborhood's small eateries and leisure pursuits. As the survey published in 2005 on Beijing's "street corners" put it, Dashalar was traditionally a classic example of an externally oriented neighborhood (*dianxing de waixiangxing diqu*).[4]

However, with the new wave of labor migration, encouraged by the post-Mao governments, the official estimate in 1990 of what was then called the "floating population" (*liudong renkou*) living temporarily in Dashalar was 300,000. In addition, more than a further 100,000 were estimated to go to Dashalar on a daily basis, either to sell goods or as consumers and tourists.[5] Among the people I knew in Dashalar, one local man and his wife from the northeast ran a tiny shop selling daily essentials out of their small single-room home when I first met them in 2007. A couple of years later, they decided to rent this space out to migrants wanting cheap temporary accommodations, reasoning that they could make more money in this way than by selling goods. Over the next decade the demographic character of the neighborhood shifted noticeably, with teams of migrant workers being transported in on a daily basis to work on the reconstruction of Qianmen dajie. The general estimate now, voiced by local people, is that some 80 percent of Dashalar's resident population is from outside Beijing. The popular character of small businesses, affordable rents, services, and cheap consumer items, all available in Dashalar, is particularly appealing to unskilled migrant laborers such as Li Fuying and his wife. Moreover, the social mix and spatial layout of the neighborhood offer ample opportunities for those attracted by the flexible practices of the informal gray sector. In the terms of the official survey of 2005, noted above, Dashalar's revived status as a popular destination for "outsiders" at a time of social and demographic change fed into the neighborhood's reputation for "pornographic salons, trafficking of fake goods, and cheating."[6]

The image created in such use of language is the equivalent of a localized version of the prevalent incitement to prejudice in general that has characterized dominant media representations of migrant workers in recent decades, now culminating in the discriminatory language of "low-end labor power" (*diduan laodongli*). Moreover, seen from the perspective of disadvantaged local Beijingers, such as Zhao

Yong and Hua Meiling, people like Li and his wife who lived on the informal boundaries between legal and illegal activities exemplified the despised figure of the uneducated, unhygienic, and unproductive migrant. The fact that Zhao and Hua themselves depended on exploiting the same boundaries in order to survive did not disturb their resentment of "outsiders."[7]

However, told in their own words, Li's and Zhang's story reveals an experience that is entirely at odds with this, and that begins with the desperate conditions frequently faced by poor farmers unable over time to benefit from the state's decollectivization of land ownership and the privatization of the rural market. As time went on, it became clear to Li and Zhang that however humiliating and tough, working in Beijing at least allowed them to imagine being able to finance their children, particularly their son, through college. On a human level, however, their everyday existence was defined by a basic and often violent abuse not experienced by their Beijing neighbors, not because they were uneducated riffraff or thieves and pimps, as dominant media and local views might imply, but because, without resources, connections, or household registration, and therefore without formal rights to residence or services, they were easy targets of the venal ruthlessness of the local law enforcement agents. In Beijing, their status as vulnerable outsiders exposed them to horrendous abuses of power in the form of physical and psychological violence by those bodies tasked with upholding the law. While violence in the form of street brawls and slanging matches was an everyday occurrence in Dashalar, the character of the violence narrated by Li and his wife was on a different scale. Li's and Zhang's structural status as migrants exposed them to a relentless incidence of arbitrary harassment and physical violence that was not shared by ordinary local Beijing residents. Outright discrimination, rooted in long-embedded dispositions of a social habitus historically shaped by values associated with region and native place, offers one explanation. Another, clearly, is that the law enforcement officers, themselves poorly paid and among the least respected of urban professional categories, saw abuse of vulnerable outsiders as a way to assert their power in order to extort money and goods.[8] In turn this spawned interest networks, such as between Great and Glorious Yang and Big Hero Li, the maintenance of which effectively depended on the use of violence and corruption. In a social and political system in which money and connections count more than law, it was only in situations when the abuse of power was excessive that individuals such as Yang were held responsible and removed from their posts.[9]

The discrimination Li and his family had to endure in Beijing further brings to mind Emily Honig's classic work on native place identity as a marker of ethnic difference. Elaborated some time ago with reference to attitudes toward Subei people in Shanghai, this work argues that the boundaries of regional and native place identity in their intersection with class *among* the Han population in China are widely and historically enmeshed with deeply embedded structures and attitudes of inequality and disdain.[10] One effect of this potentially engenders the contempt associated with the racialized character of ethnic discrimination. However, native place identity is also fundamental to commonly held ideas about self and community, across China, granting the possibility of material and emotional support. This more positive gloss on regional difference was reinforced, in Li's story, by the geographical and spatial boundaries informing decisions about detention and repatriation. It contributed to a sense of solidarity with other migrants shored up by common experiences of discrimination, and to buttressing Li in his efforts to keep going, despite local Beijingers' disdain.

Looked down on by their neighbors in Dashalar as dirty and uncivilized outsiders of "low quality" (*suzhi di*),[11] and routinely brutalized by the state's law enforcement bodies, Li's and Zhang's narrative stands out among the others I have recorded from Dashalar for its evidence of the inhumanity of a social and political system that in significant measure has depended on migrants' labor for its economic achievements. Whether in its literal or symbolic form as the spatial center of an oppressive and violent policing system, or as the home of unscrupulous and avaricious landlords, "Beijing," for Li and his wife, came to signify a desperate struggle to survive in a corrupt and violent system, which occasionally reduced Zhang Yuanchen to the limits of her endurance when all she had left was to scream out in total despair, "Just kill me!" If the seeds of the couple's righteous anger against the system were already sown in Shaanxi before they left in search of making a living elsewhere, the hope they invested in their children, and particularly their son, just about sustained them through the years of hardship that they spent in Beijing.

Indeed, the single most evident thread of hope that kept Li and Zhang going through their toughest times in Beijing was that they would see their son married and setting up his own home with a child. Their expectation was explicit: that when they were too old to be able to work, their son and daughter-in-law would support them. In this, their expectations exemplified the anthropologist Steven Sangren's argument that Chinese patriliny is a culturally particular process of the production of institutions and desire, including the pervasive values of filial piety.[12] This "instituted fantasy" may take different forms, and its failure can be tragic, as in Li's case, when it became apparent that his sense of self that was bound up with his desire for his son's filial reciprocity collapsed in the face of his son's rejection.[13] Up until this moment, his capacity, even desire, to exercise agency in continuing his existence as a migrant laborer was sustained by the intersection between this "instituted fantasy" as subjective interiority and its exterior character as discursive norm. I would also argue that the desire for his son's filial reciprocity was so interwoven into Li Fuying's sense of himself as a father and as a man that it was a constituent part of it. The agonized shame that Li expressed when describing his reluctance to tell his son that he had been unsuccessful in finding work when he was repatriated to Xi'an, and his muted pride when describing how his son washed his parents' feet, or, then again, his later shame when unable to tell me on the phone that he was not living with his son—and then telling me how bad he felt about his son's appearance when we visited him and his small baby in his Beijing apartment in 2013—may all be understood in the same way. When the son appears as part of the father's own person/self, the father's pride in or shame about the son's behavior emerges as a kind of self-shame or self-pride. In this sense, the shame refers to much more than the ethical work of filial piety, since it involves the making/remaking of the moral self.[14] As such, filial piety is much more than an expectation of a patrilineal process of cultural production involving a reciprocal ethical obligation. Rather, it becomes an inseparable part of the sense of self. As a dimension of patrilineal expectations, the "instituted fantasy," therefore, is a fantasy about another's behavior as an aspect of the self. The expectation of the son's filial piety as an integral aspect of Li's sense of himself thus became the principal motor of Li's exercise of agency in finding ways to survive unspeakable difficulties. It was only when Li and Zhang finally lost all hope that their expectations of their son would be fulfilled that they decided to return to Shaanxi. Li Fuying's tears and despair in front of me, a stranger to his predicament, conveyed the anguished erosion of his capacity to sustain his former agency by a shattered sense of self. If it was his assumption of a set of norms of filial behavior as part of his self-identification that had sustained the enactment of a particular modality of agency, the assault on that self signified by his son's alienation altered his articulation of agency.

Li's attachment to the desire for his son as filial support was deeply embedded in his interior sense of self. It was this that explained his, and his wife's, conviction that his son's estrangement was attributable to their daughter-in-law. By the same token, it may have explained the impossibility of their confronting their son's estrangement for what it was. It is conceivable that in refusing to let her in-laws look after her baby, the young woman was doing little more than asserting her authority as mother and wife to establish the terms of her young child's upbringing. That she was doing this in what seemed to be rather extreme and hurtful ways may well have been the case. In this sense, the clash between her position and that of the parents can be thought of as a particularly gendered dimension of the tragedy of Sangren's "instituted fantasy."[15]

The end to Li's and Zhang's lives in Beijing was a heartbreaking demonstration of the extent and intensity of the generational and gendered changes in the relationship between parents and children that have been taking shape in recent decades.[16] Yan Yunxiang has argued that the postmillennial emergence of the individual self in Chinese society intensifies shifts in personhood engendered since the early days of the PRC, when laws concerning land ownership, labor, and social legitimacy, combined with others legalizing monogamous free-choice marriage, loosened the individual person's ties of dependence on and loyalty to the kinship group and sought to replace them with ties to the collective and the state. This process was extremely patchy and was often defined more by discursive assertion than by everyday practice, but nevertheless over time it signified a gradual dismantling of the kin and gender hierarchies associated with conventional patrilineal structures.[17]

The arrival of the market economy in the 1980s accelerated the individualized orientation of such shifts, with radical effects on the gendered and generational organization of authority. Young women were among the main beneficiaries of these shifts; better educated, better employed, and recipients of independent incomes in a cultural and discursive environment that attached increasing value to the realization of individual desires and aspirations, young women have become increasingly assertive in making decisions about their own futures. Whether as employees, daughters, intimate partners, or mothers, the formation of the individual, gendered self that is emerging in this process is radically at odds with the expectations and hopes of their parents' generation. At the heart of this shift is an increasing divergence, even conflictual divergence, between younger people's sense of self and that of their parents. From Li's and Zhang's point of view, their daughter-in-law's behavior was an offense against all they held valuable and desirable in their understanding of themselves as ethical persons. Objectively speaking, from their daughter-in-law's perspective, by not coming out to greet her parents-in-law and by not letting them care for her child in the ways they thought appropriate, she was asserting her own sense of self, and enacting agency in distinction to and against normative expectations of filial behavior.[18] Alongside Meiling's daughter, her performance demonstrates another instantiation of Yan Yunxiang's argument about the effect of recent socioeconomic transformation on the modalities of young women's agency.[19]

I write this not long after vast numbers of poor, unskilled migrant workers—precisely "low-end" migrant workers such as Li Fuying and Zhang Yuanchen—were forcibly evicted from their miserable dwellings in the outskirts of Beijing in repeated instances of a pitiless government crackdown between 2017 and 2018 supposedly to deal with dangerous conditions initially highlighted in late 2017 by a tenement fire that killed nineteen people in the city's southern suburbs. The Chinese term officially used to describe this process is *qingli* (to clean). "Social cleansing" of the already disadvantaged migrant population has become official policy of Xi Jinping's government. After years of being exploited as a source of cheap labor used to construct the wonders of the global metropolis, migrant workers are now being told that they are totally expendable. The government's bid to "beautify" the capital and free up land for property developers has become a humanitarian issue.

6

Zhang Huiming

Zhang Huiming lives with her husband, Wang Wenli, and their grown-up son in a dazayuan off West Street. Huiming's family history in this courtyard dates back more than a hundred years to when it was a native-place association lodge for students and businessmen from a county in Jiangxi Province. Many of its former residents dealt in fine lacquerware, including Huiming's maternal great-grandparents and grandparents, who lived there throughout the tumultuous upheavals of the 1930s and 1940s and into the new People's Republic. Zhang Huiming has lived there all her life, since 1954, when she was born. Her husband moved there when he married Huiming in 1979. Throughout their working lives, both Huiming and her husband were employees of small local enterprises, and as such were not eligible for better-serviced housing provided by the larger state-run work units.

When I first visited Huiming and her husband in 2007, their dazayuan was in a state of considerable disrepair. The chaotic jumble of single shack-like structures inside the courtyard obscured all evidence of its original form. The lane outside the courtyard was a mess, with old and dangerous wiring presenting a constant fire hazard. At the back of their dazayuan was a nine-meter-deep underground shelter—a leftover from Mao's underground defenses against nuclear attack from the Soviet Union—over which grew a large tree, and when it rained, water used to rise up through the exposed roots of the tree, through the cracked concrete floor, and into their living space.

Inside, Huiming, her husband, and their adult son occupied a single room of less than twenty-four square meters that abutted the back outer northern wall of the courtyard. It was divided into two by a large redwood veneer cabinet-dresser and a curtain to make an inner bedroom where the couple slept and an outer room that served as the living space and their son's bedroom. A small stove burner, a washstand, a fridge, and a television stood along one wall just inside the door, and to the left of the door were a small table and

Fig. 6.1 Inside Huiming's dazayuan, 2010.

chairs and a single bed-cum-sofa. The room was extremely tidy, and the books on the cabinet gave evidence of an interest in poetry, calligraphy, and Beijing's history. Although damp and very basic, it offered a tranquil relief from the noise and incessant movement on West Street.

Huiming had contracted polio when she was a small child, and was officially registered as a disabled person. When I first visited her home, she and her husband were waiting for news from the local government about the relocation of low-income households in their neighborhood. Given Huiming's disabled status, they thought that the government might relocate them to an apartment inside the third ring road, considerably closer to central Beijing than most local residents could anticipate moving to. Huiming also understood that every person living in less than ten square meters could apply for public housing (*jingji shiyong fang*), and with three people in her home of less than thirty square meters, she was eligible to apply. Nevertheless, neither she nor her husband wanted to move, and Wang was skeptical about the amount of compensation they would receive. The local government then decided to undertake repairs to their home rather than relocate them; Huiming's disability classified her as a priority in the local government's local refurbishments. By the summer of 2010, their entire home, including the roof and floor, had been repaired and redecorated. Huiming had bought a bright yellow cover for the single bed in the living room, and the place looked much brighter and more comfortable than when I had first visited. The only thing they didn't have, Wang noted, was a bathroom.

Wang initially seemed retiring and unassertive, but as time passed, he began to reveal an evident entrepreneurial flair. Employed as a state-licensed pedicab cyclist who took tourists on guided tours round the old parts of the inner city, he was able to recite the facts and figures of "old Beijing's" history without any difficulty. He was also a good amateur calligrapher who did not hesitate to demonstrate his skill to his clients. Between his regular income as a pedicab cyclist and the extra money he made selling his calligraphy, he was able to benefit from local tourism in ways that were qualitatively different from most others I knew in Dashalar. In so doing he was able to sustain a relatively decent life for himself and his wife. Ironically, however, as the Old City was transformed by grand heritage constructions, this local tourist economy came to threaten the couple's livelihood stability, since the destruction of the hutong—the literal erasure of place—undermined the very possibility of Wang's capacity to make an income that depended on their material existence.

Income Strategies and Material Interests

Huiming and her husband were far from well off but enjoyed a relatively stable, if still very basic, income—rather more, they both acknowledged, than most of their neighbors. Huiming used to work in a state-run sock factory before it amalgamated with a textile factory manufacturing garments for export. However, this factory did not do well, and sold off one of its workshops to a state restaurant, resulting in redundancy (*xiagang*) for many of its largely female workforce. Some found work elsewhere, but others, including Huiming, whose polio had left her paralyzed in one leg, "returned home" in 1996.[1] Four years later, when she was fifty-five, she officially retired from her former factory job. She then found work as a cashier in a private enterprise in Dashalar where she got on well with the boss, but she had rheumatism and often ran a high temperature, and her husband insisted that she stop working. "He got angry and said, 'If you go out to work, then I won't.'" By 2007 the combination of her pension and disability allowance brought in nine hundred yuan a month. She was not displeased with this, but hoped it would increase, in line with what she described as the then president Wen Jiabao's commitment that everyone should benefit from economic reform.

Wang worked for many years in the design department of the famous Dashalar shoe shop, Nei Lian Sheng, first established in the 1850s to make handmade cloth-soled shoes, which have long since become a commercialized emblem of "old Beijing." In the late 1980s, Wang left this job to work in a small local factory, but by 1994 was laid off when the government restructured factories to "reduce employees and increase profits," as Wang put it. This factory was initially a cooperative venture with Hong Kong, but before the contract for the joint venture had even been signed, the factory buildings were demolished and the workers were told to return home. They were promised that they would be able to take up new jobs there after a year. The result, however, as Wang cynically put it, was that "we went home for many years, and didn't return." He and his fellow workers were given a basic subsistence payment, and limited unemployment benefit, but no pension, because formal retirement age for men was sixty, and in any case, as he pointed out, the new owners of the rebuilt factory had no responsibility for the former workers. He and his fellow workers were left to decide for themselves what to do.

Unemployed, Wang decided to ask the government for a license to drive a pedicab, even though they were difficult to obtain. Huiming's disability status proved extremely helpful. In return for the relevant officials' support in processing Wang's license, Huiming suggested sending them a gift of thanks. "But they said they didn't want anything. They didn't take a single cent. They said it was fine to see us working to make some money, so Wang was happy." Wang charged ten yuan a ride, and in one day could make at least forty to fifty yuan, which in the early 1990s was not bad. By the time I met him, his monthly income came to more than five hundred yuan. Together with Huiming's pension and disability allowance of nine hundred yuan a month, between them, they had enough money for their son's education. "We felt quite easy about life," as Huiming put it. Wang's work as a licensed pedicab driver working for the official tourist agency incorporated him into state-sponsored tourist "hutong tours" around the famous sites and residences of Beijing.[2] He would start work at eight in the morning, and finish around four in the afternoon, or later if he wanted to earn overtime pay. He was also able to turn this work to his advantage.

The books on the shelves in Wang's home indicated an interest that went far beyond the requirements of his job. He used his spare time to write calligraphy, often to Huiming's annoyance, practicing on newspaper spread out on the floor of his home, then writing on calligraphy paper to sell to clients. Wang used to lose no opportunity to display his knowledge of Dashalar's history. He was locally known as the "Old Professor" (Lao Jiaoshou). The first time I met him in early 2007 he needed little prompting to launch into a description of the history of his home and neighborhood, perhaps memorized, in part at least, for the benefit of his hutong tour clients.

> The South City was the Outer City, divided into two, Xuanwu and Chongwen. The place where I live is the Guanyin Temple District of Dashalar. Its old name just used to be the Guanyin Temple, which was built at the intersection of two roads. It hasn't yet been destroyed. To its north is Cherry Lane, to its south is Li Tieguai. . . . The opera singers were all concentrated in Baishun Alley, Widow Wang Alley, Dali and Shamao Alleys. Mei Lanfeng lived very near to us here. Our place here used to be a native-place association lodge for Jiangxi. . . . In the Republican period, people from Jiangxi would come here to live in the lodge for free. If a student didn't pass his exams, the lodge helped out. If he did pass, then he would contribute to the upkeep of the lodge and continue to support the interests of his home place. Like when Lin Zexu acquired fame and lived in the Fuzhou Lodge at Hufang Bridge.[3]

Once Wang began his monologues about local history, he did not like being interrupted, and on many occasions he silenced his wife when she tried to join in. When she attempted to interject a comment into Wang's reference to the famous commissioner, Lin Zexu, sent to Canton by the emperor in 1839 to burn the supplies of opium stored in Britain's fleet of ships anchored off the south coast, her husband responded with evident annoyance: "No, you don't understand, just don't interrupt, you just make me confused when you interrupt." Then, ignoring his wife, he continued his monologue, ending with a reference to the courtyard where he and Huiming lived as an example of Beijing's traditional domestic architecture.

I knew that Wang was a keen calligrapher from early on in my research in Dashalar. In explaining to me why Wang had earned himself the local nickname of Old Professor, Zhao Tielin referred to his knowledge of the neighborhood's history as well as his skill as a calligrapher. Wang also loved talking about calligraphy. However, it was several years after I first met him and Huiming that I became aware that I was expected to purchase some of his work. This coincided with a time when my visits to their home were brought to the attention of the neighborhood authorities, making the couple reluctant to host me. When after several months they agreed to my requests to renew my visits, Wang began to regularly show me examples of his calligraphy, which he kept rolled up in categories according to style in a large bag under the bed at the back of the room. He had written a vast quantity of items, some just short couplets, some long poems, in a range of styles and sizes. He also demonstrated how he liked practicing different styles using big brushes, water, and newspaper spread out on the floor. On these occasions, Huiming looked on, from time to time praising her husband for his talents. I made an initial purchase of a small piece for two hundred yuan.

A few visits later, Wang started telling me about a pedicab client of his who had commissioned him to write a copy of the *Thousand Character Classic* (*Qian zi wen*) which had taken him the better part of a week to finish. The version he had copied was the one made famous by the Song emperor Gaozong (1107–87). He had only just finished it, and did I want to see it? He unrolled the scroll, and it was indeed spectacular: fluid, with variations between thickness, thinness, and length of stroke. It was an extremely accomplished copy. When Wang started pointing to the sections he was particularly proud of, I realized that I had made it difficult for myself not to follow up by asking him to write another copy for me. Having agreed to ask him to do so, I then asked him how much it would be. Although I was somewhat surprised at the amount he quoted—1,500 yuan, only slightly less than his household's monthly income—I did not feel that I could refuse. When the following week I returned to pay him and pick it up, Wang then asked me if I would like him to arrange for it to be mounted on silk at a nearby shop in Liulichang where he knew the manager.

This time, I felt no compunction in saying that I would be happy to arrange for this myself. Once I had paid for and picked up this piece of calligraphy, Wang made no further attempts on subsequent occasions to show me his work.

I did not have the opportunity to find out how much, on average, Wang made from selling his calligraphy, but I recall from my notes that during my last visit to see them in 2013, they had a new washstand and a new small refrigerator. Wang's access to boosting his income from selling his calligraphy added to his cultural and social capital. Moreover, as a licensed pedicab driver he had secure and guaranteed access to a range of domestic and foreign tourists, giving him and his wife a further advantage over his local neighbors.

Dazayuan Life under Mao

During the Republican period, Huiming's great-grandfather and grandfather were both businessmen at the nearby Nei Lian Sheng. Earlier ancestors included officials working for the Qing government. Huiming spoke with some pride about her forbears. "Before Liberation, they were people with considerable status, capitalists, small entrepreneurs. They were all businessmen, and the smallest was a small entrepreneur. They were all traders of lacquer goods, for use in the imperial household. Yes, lacquer bowls, boxes, and coffins with lacquer on the inside and outside. Only wealthy people could afford to use them. They used to get shinier the more you used them. Very beautiful." Her parents, Huiming said, "were cultured people, and like people abroad, they were quite equal, and each had their own money so could buy what they liked."

Huiming lived with her grandparents in their courtyard in Dashalar throughout her childhood. She repeatedly talked about her grandmother as her main caregiver during her childhood, and later of her son, when he was still small. Her parents moved into the courtyard only in the late 1950s, when the single-story building where they lived east of Tian'anmen Square was demolished during the construction of the Great Hall of the People. Huiming was only three or so when polio paralyzed her left leg, and she didn't start walking until she was given crutches at the age of six.

> Before then I used to get around on a wooden board, moving around by using my arms. The crutches came from the hospital in Jishuitan, where I stayed for a week. Conditions at home were quite good then, and my father earned quite a lot of money. He worked in the locomotive factory and often had meetings in the Railways Ministry. They also gave me a brace when I was six, so that my leg looked like a proper leg. My father bought it with a bonus he was given. It probably cost about one hundred

yuan, more than most people could afford. But I didn't use it because my granny said that I would keep falling down with it so I shouldn't use it. . . . I just left it under the bed, where it stayed for many years right up until I married, and then we sold it.

Despite her disability, Huiming recalled her early childhood in the 1950s as the happiest time of her life. "The first six years were the happiest. There were lots of children in the courtyard and we used to play a lot. I had lots of toys, and I loved to be the leader, and the other children were always around looking at my books because they didn't have any."

In 1958, as the Great Leap Forward's call to women to leave the household and engage in social labor took effect, three rooms of Huiming's grandparents' courtyard were taken over to use as a kindergarten. Many women in the neighborhood went out to work in small local factories or attend literacy classes. Her grandmother became a teacher in the kindergarten, and Huiming had a ready-made cohort of children more or less of her own age to play with. "They cleared everyone out to set up the kindergarten and our family was just left with a small room. Two rooms. The women all went out to work, and children who had no one to care for them all came here. . . . My grandmother became a teacher in the kindergarten. It was the big houses they cleared to set up nurseries and kindergartens, and the children who attended them were all around my age, some a bit older, children who were born in the first years [after Liberation]." The courtyard became increasingly crowded after the Great Leap as its rooms were subdivided to accommodate new residents, and by the time Huiming was five or six, there were about eight families in her dazayuan. Her family's property was subsequently confiscated during the Cultural Revolution, due to their class status as former entrepreneurs, and their living space was further reduced to a single room. By the early 1970s, most of Huiming's childhood neighbors had left, either because under the state distribution of employment they were allocated work elsewhere, or through informal exchanges to move into newer work unit apartment blocks. When Huiming's grandfather died in 1974, her grandmother initially thought that she would also move to better accommodations but eventually decided to stay, perhaps, Huiming reflected, because she didn't want to live in an apartment block. Eventually, Huiming decided to urge the local government to reallocate her family some of its former space. "When I gave birth to my son, I went to the government and said that we didn't have [our own place] to live. I took my child with me. Eventually they said that they would rent us a small place. . . . And then in 1981, I went again, and they rented us another small area . . . and the third time they rented us what we now have. According to them, we were emancipated [*fanshenle*], so they were unwilling to give us more." To this, her husband added with his customary cynicism, "What they wanted was to make sure that we remained downtrodden."

Well into the reform era, the distrust and suspicion between neighbors that had developed particularly during the Cultural Revolution years continued to leave their mark on dazayuan relationships. An elderly woman who lived in the same dazayuan as Huiming and Wang, and who during the Cultural Revolution reported on household activities to the local neighborhood committee, still kept a watchful eye on the comings and goings of her immediate neighbors. On one occasion, she apparently reported my visits to Huiming and her husband to the neighborhood committee, who then questioned Wang about the nature of my contact with them. Following this it was quite some time before the couple felt relaxed enough to be able to meet me again. However, despite the tensions of the Cultural Revolution years, it was during the reform years that the social atmosphere of the dazayuan really changed for the worse, in Huiming's view. As more new people moved in and former neighbors moved out, she felt that social relationships became distant and cold (*shuyuan*). She tried to keep alive what she called the "old atmosphere of courtyard life" by inviting her neighbors to eat sticky rice wrapped in bamboo leaves when she made it, or dropping in on neighbors' houses at New Year, but she still felt that local social relations were very superficial.

Nevertheless, Huiming and her husband continued to prefer dazayuan life to the alternative in an apartment block. Huiming mentioned a TV report she had seen about someone who had been hurt by a glass window breaking in his apartment and was suing the families living above him. Having referred to this, she reasserted that even though Dashalar was in a dilapidated state, "it's still lovely and airy. Like last night we didn't shut the window and felt really comfortable just with a quilt covering us. We still don't want to live in a block. From the health point of view, it's better to live in a single-story house."

Huiming was a cheerful person, who despite her disability and frugal living conditions had an optimistic outlook on life. Her memories of the treatment meted out to her family during the Cultural Revolution ran deep, however, and she rarely talked about it. When she did it was to recall her terror.

You were lucky just to be able to stay alive! If you haven't experienced all that it's impossible to understand. From when I was twelve years old, any small thing was enough to make me frightened. Particularly political matters. It's still as if I could see it in front of my eyes now. During the

Cultural Revolution, I was so frightened that I started shaking and having heart problems . . . and I was bullied at school. My heart used to beat so fast, and at night I couldn't sleep; I always took medicine. I didn't go down to the countryside, I still went to school, but because things at home were so difficult, I always felt really anxious and scared. I was only twelve, and at school I just couldn't concentrate. And then I had to go back home to find it so messed up. Everyone everywhere was involved in political struggle, at school and here at home. Everyone walked around with Mao's quotations in their hands, and Red Guards were everywhere brandishing big sticks and leather belts, running around shouting. In the square there were deafening loudspeakers and loud music every day. We are so near we could hear everything, just like June 4. . . . The Red Guards didn't understand anything, and all I remember was their belts and their military uniforms. I don't understand too much about these early things. Nowadays, people don't talk too much about things like these, and we don't ask too much.

The violence Huiming's family endured at the hands of the Red Guards was directly associated with her grandparents' background as small entrepreneurs. Their background also prevented her from acquiring political and social status by joining the Communist Youth League, even though she aspired to membership. Wang was even more reluctant to talk about his natal family's experiences during the Cultural Revolution; he quietly recalled how some people were beaten to death in front of a store at the end of the lane near Qianmen where he lived with his family. He was invited to join the Communist Youth League after he had demonstrated his political credentials when he contributed to an exhibition for the "Criticize Lin Biao, Criticize Confucius" campaign.[4] Years after the event, however, he was scathing in his view of the influence of the Cultural Revolution on creating a generation of cultural illiterates. "The influence of the Cultural Revolution continues to this day, and kids of twenty or so still don't study. They don't do anything." With evident sarcasm, he commented, "This is China's national essence [guoqing], and no matter what you say or how often you say it, you can't do anything about it."

Fears of a repeat of the violent tactics used during the Cultural Revolution had their effect on Wang's family's choices years afterward. Wang's parents lived in a small house on a lane facing the grain depot near Qianmen, where his father ran a restaurant before it was nationalized during the 1950s. As reform got under way in the 1980s, the government announced that local houses on the lane could be converted into shops. Wang's parents were now eligible for a license to open a new business but were nervous about taking up the government's offer, partly because by this time their five children were all working, but also, Huiming added, because they were scared that they would become new targets of attack, as in the Cultural Revolution. As Huiming put it, "Open-door reform had already started, but we were still quite conservatively minded, and didn't have the courage to resign from our jobs and go into business." By the early 1990s, Wang's parents had managed to save a bit of money, and decided to move out of their small house, because with a floor space of forty square meters they could move into a two-bedroom apartment not too far away. Their decision to move was made on the grounds that it would become more difficult to do so in the future, but even this was a calculated risk, which in retrospect Huiming felt had not been worth taking, "because it was like giving away a golden bowl to someone who then used it to make money."

Marital Compromises

Huiming and Wang had known each other for only six months when they married in 1979. He was twenty-four, and she was twenty-five, two years apart according to the lunar calendar. They met by chance. Wang was working as a craftsman in the shoe store Nei Lian Sheng, known locally for its attractive window displays and advertisements. Huiming had an artistic flair, and so used to go there with a friend, one of her former classmates. At twenty-five, Huiming had reached the age when most women would be married, or at least looking for husbands, and yet she was aware that, because of her disability, finding a partner would not be easy. "I didn't want to be introduced to someone who was not in good physical shape, and I didn't want to find someone who was really ugly. But if someone was really good, his family wouldn't agree. At that time, the way I thought was that if I could find someone who I could just get on with and who was in good health, then it didn't matter if their conditions weren't so good."

On one occasion, when Huiming visited the shoe store with her friend, Wang Wenli overheard them chatting about Huiming's desire to find a partner. Eventually Wang approached the friend and asked her to introduce him to Huiming. Huiming's friend told him to stop joking because she thought he was just making fun of Huiming. She told him that Huiming was an honest and sincere person. In response, Wang said he was totally serious, and so Huiming agreed to meet him. She was initially unenthusiastic, since he came from a large working-class family, and Huiming felt that "his manner didn't suit me terribly well." However, her grandmother advised her to persevere since he was healthy and strong, and had many cultural interests and hobbies. Huiming had previously considered two other young men, "both fit and well and intelligent," but they did not strike her as being sincere. She eventually overcame her reluctance to consider Wang Wenli when it became clear that not only was he serious, but he went out of his way to help her grandmother, even when she, Huiming, was out. The couple talked through Huiming's health issues, which helped convince Huiming of his character. He then wrote a letter to Huiming's mother, with a writing brush, in which he started by saying that he was sincere in his feelings for Huiming and that it wasn't a sudden impulse. When Huiming's mother responded doubtfully, on the grounds that marrying Huiming would hold up his future development, he responded by saying that a fully able person would not necessarily be better than Huiming.

However, Huiming's grandmother did not want Huiming to marry out, so the next step was to confirm that Wang would be willing to move into their courtyard. As the third of five sons in a family of limited means, and as someone who got on well with Huiming's grandmother, Wang was totally willing to accept this condition.

Huiming and Wang celebrated their marriage with a modest "banquet" (*yanhui*) in a local restaurant chosen by Huiming's grandmother. Wang's father took care of all the arrangements and expenses, including the cars to transport guests to the restaurant. Huiming's family gave the couple a black and white Peony TV, and Wang's family gave them some bed linen.[5] After he moved in, Huiming said, "he was very hardworking and I was really happy. I felt that we had another help around. He knew how to cook because his father was a chef. He used to take me to work and bring me home after work."

Huiming's only child, a boy, was born by caesarean section in 1980. Huiming recalled that the doctors took good care of her because of her physical weakness, and that one of the doctors wondered what kind of diet she ate, since she looked so "good and healthy." Her husband brought her food every day because the hospital didn't allow him to stay with her. But when, after four days of being confined to her bed, Huiming began to develop bedsores, Wang began to get anxious and accused the doctors of neither allowing him to stay with his wife nor of giving her proper care.

> [Wang] started swearing at them. He said they weren't feeding the baby properly, because the baby developed a kind of dysentery. They said there was nothing to worry about and everything would be fine once we got back home. But when we got back home the baby was in the same state, so we called the ambulance to take him to the pediatric hospital, where

they gave him some injection because they said he was getting dehydrated. We wanted to stay in the hospital because I wasn't very strong, and giving birth had been quite difficult, and if we went back home and something happened, we wouldn't be able to get back to the hospital in time. The hospital agreed, and we stayed there for two weeks. We were covered for everything at that time.

Huiming's grandmother helped look after the little boy for seven years, until she died, after which Wang used to take him to the kindergarten in the morning, and Huiming used to pick him up after work in the afternoon, stopping on her way to buy vegetables. He was the only child of his age in the dazayuan, and wasn't allowed out much, since, as Huiming put it, she was concerned about a child picking up bad habits from others (*pa huxiang yingxiang*). He was born shortly after the single-child policy was introduced in 1979, but for Huiming this was fine. She felt that neither her physical capacity nor her economic situation favored a larger family, although, she commented, "If you had a big house and lots of money, everyone would want more [children]." At school, her son wasn't very studious, but he liked the idea of joining the army. Despite his mother's reluctance, he insisted—"He said he knew what he was doing"—and later joined the antiaircraft artillery in Hebei Province. His mother's comment was, "At least he had a job, and it was stable. Just staying at home isn't good." By 2007, he had gotten together with a girlfriend, about whom Huiming and Wang didn't have much to say, except that she apparently liked cooking. Nor did they seem particularly anxious about whether their son was going to marry her or not, although Huiming's slightly nervous laughter when her husband said, "Let's wait and see," might have indicated greater concern than she wanted to convey. Instead, she insisted,

> He doesn't want a child. He's not worried about marrying, and I'm even less worried. It's not like before, when you married and had a child as quickly as possible. No one is worried about it now, and we don't have that much energy anymore. If he wanted to live at home, then both of us would be able to help out a bit. But he's not worried, and as long as he's not worried, that's fine . . . and in any case, he just wants to have a good time. Haven't they just reported that children born in the 1980s are one, selfish, and two, have little independent capacity? The twenty-year-olds are psychologically immature, and feel that they haven't played around enough. The younger generation don't understand things like cotton ration tickets, grain ration tickets, or food and cotton shortages.

Huiming's implied criticism of her son, however, was tempered by a pragmatic acknowledgment of the difficulties a young man faced when thinking about marrying and having a family. "Given today's living conditions in big cities, many people don't want to have children because the responsibilities are too great. Our expenses then weren't that high. Now you have to pay more than one thousand yuan a month to send your child to a nursery, and how much do you make a month? For people of my son's age, marriage is difficult enough, let alone having a child. So even if they marry, they postpone having a child."

Added to this was the difficulty of not having an independent place to live. Wang and Huiming did not have the financial capacity to buy their son a flat, and their son was not yet in a position to buy his own flat. "He'll just have to wait. Wait until the house is demolished, when we'll be able to see whether he'll be able to move to another place." However, with repeated policy changes and shifts in the timing of Dashalar's renewal program, waiting could turn out to be for a very long, if not indefinite, period. If anything, the refurbishment of Huiming's dazayuan dwelling only added to their son's difficulties, since it meant that relocation was no longer in the cards, at least in the immediate term.

After more than thirty years of marriage, Huiming and her husband had some time to go before reaching the sixty years that Huiming's parents had celebrated—"their diamond anniversary, through wind and rain." After a long marriage, Huiming's pragmatic assessment of her experience suggested a less rosy picture than her description of their early years together. "People who aren't married imagine that being married is so wonderful, but when you are married, you know what it's like to be two people living together. Definitely not a bed of roses. Each has their own way of living, has different points of view, and there are different approaches to dealing with issues, so how can there be no conflicts?"

Wang's take on the issue was typically cynical: "Marrying is a hassle. In fact, it's so easy to agree on something, but as soon as you agree you want to back out of it." Such disparaging comments, however, masked a mutual understanding that they had made their marriage work. In Huiming's terms, "We've managed to muddle along. It's passed quickly. Bringing up our son, going to work, each day has passed really quickly." True to form, Wang put it in more skeptical terms: "We've had a bit of a rough ride, but it's not been too bad. By the time you are fifty, you know what your fate is. You've basically lived your life, and by sixty you've already reached the beginning of old age." Despite their differences, the couple shared the view that they had managed to make their marriage work because of a mutual tolerance rooted in a respect of the important things. As

Huiming put it, "As long as you both respect the basic, important things, just getting by with the other things doesn't matter too much. . . . Young people today just don't give way. As long as they think everything's okay, they don't [need to] make any concessions to anyone else. [But] when they discover something they don't like in their partner, they divorce. People should be tolerant of small problems. You have to focus on the big things."

Wang added, "[It] is precisely because people don't think of the bigger framework. There are two main reasons for divorce nowadays. Some [men] leave to find a girl, and don't come back. It's called 'Liking the new and disdaining the old.' The people who introduce them don't care, and don't bother to find out, so if they don't get on, they just divorce. If you snore when you sleep, that's grounds for divorce, so they just go ahead and divorce, and pay whatever it takes."

While the couple seemed keen to demonstrate the solid basis to their marriage, Huiming showed little reserve in acknowledging the conflicts that sometimes erupted between them. When on one occasion Zhao Tielin asked her whether she and Wang had ever quarreled, she immediately answered, in a loud voice, "Of course we have. He's bad-tempered . . . Sometimes after we quarrel, and I say something to him, he starts all over again, or just refuses to speak. He doesn't come round very easily. Huh . . . it's his personality. It's closely linked to family environment. Ever since he was little he was never subject to any kind of constraint, so he says whatever he wants."

Many of our conversations were punctuated with Wang's impatience at Huiming's attempts to offer her own opinion on matters about which he felt he knew more, and he often told her that she didn't know what she was talking about, or just told her to shut up. In a heated argument about the age at which women were eligible for retirement pensions, Wang insisted that the government was going to grant pensions to women at the age of fifty-five, not sixty, as Huiming thought: "All . . . this . . . they've announced this, but you wouldn't know that, would you? You really are. . . . It's that even if you don't work, the government will still give you a pension even if you haven't reached sixty."

Huiming tended to back down and defer to her husband when such differences occurred, at least in my presence. When she had the chance, however, she expressed views about women that implied another position. "Chinese women are amazing today; they don't just hold up half the sky, they hold up much more." In her view, women's domestic responsibilities invariably meant that women shoulder more than men; the burden was particularly heavy for women whose husbands were unemployed, and for women who had to bring their children up on their own, and she was grateful that Wang's wages were enough to buy a washing machine and another TV when their son was still very little. Even so, Huiming found her domestic responsibilities demanding. Her son did very little to help. Her husband, so she claimed, did not help much either. "Ask him to do something and he gets really annoyed." "He uses his free time to do calligraphy, without even clearing the table. He prefers to write calligraphy and to read. By the evening you've been so busy that you can't keep your eyes open. The room's a mess, no time to tidy it up, the kid is crying, it's all chaotic, and you have to put the alarm clock on to get to work on time in the morning."

This did not, however, give Huiming cause to challenge her husband. On the contrary, it was her belief that a wife should be respectful of her husband, even if he was unemployed. Women who gave up on their husbands and followed their own independent interests away from home "are never honest and straightforward. A woman like that definitely has another man, and sometimes brings him home, and her husband doesn't dare say anything. In the thinking of old Beijing, this would be terrible, enough to make someone die of shame."

Huiming's commitment to the bigger framework of her marriage was thus underpinned by a fundamental sense of moral obligation and responsibility that far outweighed the importance of her awareness of the gender imbalance in her domestic arrangements. The relevant conversations we had made it clear that under no circumstances—at least when I was around—would she allow her differences with her husband to spill over into hostile criticism. From time to time, she clearly decided to suppress her annoyance at his domineering attitude toward her, and she may have complained about her husband taking over the floor space to practice his calligraphy. Yet she was proud of his cultural attainments, and given that they boosted their income, accommodating her husband's gender foibles was not an unacceptable compromise. Wang, in turn, acknowledged the cultural cachet that her family's history in the courtyard gave to his claims to knowledge about the history of "old Beijing" and his knowledge of local history. In this sense, it was almost as if there were an unspoken exchange between them that served to boost their cultural capital. It was not without reason that they were known in the neighborhood as being rather more cultured than their neighbors.

The couple's mutual commitment to each other was further shored up by shared interests in social and political matters beyond the framework of their immediate surroundings. Huiming often commented on news items she read in the newspaper or saw on TV programs and documentary films, and she was well informed about a wide range of issues, from the difficulties young women faced in finding employment to the need for an effective system of medical insurance in rural areas to curb the numbers of migrants moving to urban areas to the injustices of big property developers who bought up land only to sell it again for vastly inflated profits. She had a critical, realistic, but generally supportive view of the government's attempts to develop policies to deal with the nation's complex social difficulties, and often referred positively to government announcements about new laws—for example, to tackle the issue of maternity leave, or to introduce a balanced approach to welfare covering rural as well as urban areas. Her open gratitude to the government for the material benefits her disability registration brought her—a monthly allowance and preferential treatment in housing repairs and even in obtaining Wang's permit as a licensed pedicab driver—predisposed her to a benign and measured acceptance of the authorities' policy pronouncements on social issues.

Wang was similarly attentive to social and political issues but was invariably more cynical about the government's policies than his wife. One typical instance of this was in a conversation about the government's attempts to deal with Beijing's pollution by replacing coal with electricity for domestic heating. Wang described how he welcomed the government's decision to subsidize costs for a night storage heater, but once installed it was so effective that it retained warmth during the daytime, making their home too hot, and increasing the number of pests around. Or again, after a heated argument, Wang had to agree with his wife that the government was trying to relieve pressures on women by increasing their pensions, but he still had to have the last negative word with "but the farmers don't have anything." In response, when Huiming observed that she had heard on the TV that farmers now also received a pension, Wang retorted "TV! That's just the bias of the news. They always tell you what's good and never what's bad. . . . If you are only an ordinary person, they don't pay any attention to you!"

Interlude 5

Zhang Huiming and her husband enjoyed living conditions that could be described as basic but relatively comfortable and secure in comparison with those of their Dashalar neighbors whose lives I have already described. Huiming's disability allowance and pension brought in a regular basic income, but it was Wang's earnings plus the extras that came from his engagement with the official heritage tourism of "old Beijing" that were largely responsible for their modest advantage. I do not know how much, if anything, the adult son contributed to the household budget. However, in so far as Wang's earnings depended on tourist commerce in the Old City, a question mark hung over the future of the couple's material welfare, given the transformation of the traditional hutong into bijou restaurants and shops. Huiming's and Wang's story illustrates the contradiction in Wang's position as both beneficiary of and hostage to local heritage tourism. The same commercial opportunities that enabled Wang's relative success also threatened its sustainability.

One expression of this contradiction in recent years is the "Dashilar Project," an initiative launched in conjunction with the state-sponsored Beijing Design Week to inject new ideas into proposals for community development that are respectful of the neighborhood's cultural heritage. A visit I made in 2013 to the displays and designs in a hutong just north of Dashalar's West Street revealed a series of pop-up exhibitions of postcards, art, and environmentally friendly architectural designs for the reconstruction of the neighborhood's dazayuan. Many of these efforts were launched by young Western entrepreneurs and artists wanting a platform for their work, and foreign academics and professionals from prestigious institutions in the United Kingdom and elsewhere were involved as expert consultants in such matters as product design, restoration, and digital crafting. Not one of the local Dashalar residents I knew had heard anything about this initiative, despite its claimed intention to invite local community participation.[1]

The encroaching gentrification of Dashalar under initiatives such as Beijing Design Week has seen the opening of cafés, restaurants, and shopping centers catering to young urban and foreign interests with the resources to afford prices way beyond the capacity of Huiming and her husband, let alone the others whose stories I have narrated here. The cultural heritage tourist industry that enabled Wang's income was thus at most a mixed blessing. If it temporarily facilitated a kind of success that his near neighbors could not access, in the form of the Dashilar Project it threatened to overwhelm him with interests with which he could not hope to compete. Even if in the short term, therefore, he and his wife could benefit from commercial heritage tourism, the benefits could not be more than short-lived. Maybe Wang's increasing investment of time in his calligraphy and his increasingly close links with entrepreneurs in Liulichang presaged the direction of his future.

Huiming's and Wang's lives clearly focused on their material livelihood, yet their cultural interests situated this within a broader frame of reference that potentially touched on worlds of desires and experiences far beyond their immediate circumstances. The couple displayed a kind of cultural capital that was distinct from the other households I knew in the neighborhood. Boosted by Huiming's evident pride in the cultural standing and achievements of her natal family, she and her husband enjoyed a modest cultural status that was locally acknowledged, as evidenced in Wang's neighborhood nickname. They were not snobs, and did not use their cultural interests to assert any kind of superiority over their neighbors, nor, as far as I could tell, did Dashalar locals who knew them indicate any envy of them. Apart from Jia Yong, whose story I narrate in the next chapter, Zhao Yong, from chapter 3, was the only other local person I knew who shared an interest in realms of thought and imagination beyond his immediate existence, but due to his social marginalization and lack of access to the material stability that Huiming and her husband enjoyed, he could not display it as cultural capital.

Huiming's memories of her childhood contained an element of nostalgia for the cultural delights of her past that I did not encounter elsewhere in Dashalar. After their home was refurbished in 2010, the couple's everyday life exemplified a modest enjoyment of dazayuan life rather than a relentless slog to keep going. Huiming and her husband also demonstrated a mutual tolerance, affection, and willingness to compromise with each other. Of course, I have only a limited understanding of the circumstances that facilitated what seemed to be a less fraught relationship than the others I knew in the neighborhood. However, as I've already noted, the material circumstances of their lives facilitated a modest pleasure in cultural activities, all the more so when they generated income, that was conducive to mutual tolerance.

Another feature distinguishing Huiming and her husband from the others I knew was their more benign attitude toward the state. Wang's cynicism did not obscure the fact that their household had benefited from the state in ways that Huiming was explicit in acknowledging. A substantial part of their income derived from her disability allowance, and it was because of her disability that they were given preferential treatment in household repairs and redecorating. While some of their comments about political and social matters implied an equivocal response to state policy, they had been able to turn the limited opportunities available to them, including Wang's work as a pedicab driver for the official tourist agency, to their own modest advantage. Overall, this predisposed them to a view of the state not as the source of constraint and control, as Young Gao and Zhao Yong implied, but fundamentally as supportive of their material interests. By the same token, this sustained a performance of agency that, in contrast to others I have already discussed, indicated an uneven but basically affirmative participation in activities facilitated by the state. To draw on the terms used by the anthropologist Hans Steinmüller, they participated in a complicity with the state's terms that simultaneously permitted them the possibility of maintaining a distance from it, apparent in Wang's many sarcastic jibes at the authorities.[2] That the couple wanted to preserve their position of relative advantage vis-à-vis the state was evident in their concern that my presence in their house might cause them difficulties with the local authorities. Although far from wealthy, and although their future is far from clear, the couple's conditions of existence were not precarious. Indeed, again in contrast to most of the others in the neighborhood I knew, there was an implicit acknowledgment of the benefits market reform had brought to their lives. They did not talk about the implications of the commercial gentrification of the neighborhood on their lives.

The couple's account of their marriage and the exchanges between them that I witnessed further distinguished them from the others I knew. This was a marriage contracted in ways that combined respect for the older generation with individual choice, covering the "free choice" principle of the time and the then standard practices of peer introduction and parental approval. Huiming's initial agreement to marriage was based on her understanding of need in a social and economic environment in which not marrying was not an option. Wang was not forthcoming about his willingness to marry into his wife's home, but given that he was the third son of a lowly working-class family, it is reasonable to suppose that his material considerations outweighed the potential social disdain of entering into an uxorilocal marriage. Whatever the nature of the initial exchange, Huiming's account of their early years and her later tolerance of her husband's whims further contribute to a description of their marriage as a process of growing compromise as well as affection. While Wang's domineering attitude toward his wife clearly irritated her, she did not let this shake her insistence on concentrating on the pluses of their marriage. Their criticisms of the younger generation were rooted in the same set of moral principles that they described as underpinning their marriage. Frustration with small, insignificant differences, generated by being brought up in conditions of relative material ease, enabled young people to indulge in a view of intimate relationships that had little to do with the sense of responsibility that Huiming and Wang claimed to exemplify.

If their moral outlook enabled them to weather their differences, the social and cultural habitus the couple inhabited produced gendered dispositions that were as embedded in "old Beijing" practices of gender behavior as were Zhao Yong's. As the male head of the household able to display a cultural capital that was clearly a source of pride to both himself and his wife, and as a man proudly associated with "old Beijing" customs, Wang exemplified another version of what I have described as the "thick masculinity" associated with the customary characteristics of Beijing men. His mode of demonstrating this was as performative as Zhao Yong's: loud, disdainful of his wife, convinced of the authority of his own opinion, and claiming an entitlement to speak without interruption. In contrast with Zhao Yong, however, and boosted by his work as an official tour guide, he could indulge in lengthy monologues about old Beijing's history. This was his version of talking about "big things" and his assumption of the right to pontificate about nondomestic matters. Even when proven to be mistaken by his wife, his sense of gendered authority, also acknowledged by his wife, invariably privileged him with the last word.

The timing of Wang's interest in showing me his calligraphy suggested a tactical move to obtain certain benefits from my presence in his dazayuan, maybe even on a certain level to compensate for the anxiety my visits had apparently caused him and his wife. His implicit pressure on me to share my resources with him could thus be seen as a manifestation of a culturally embedded notion of reciprocity and exchange that was part of Wang's understanding of appropriate social relationships as much as it was instrumental. That I was the more privileged and wealthy partner in our relationship potentially facilitated a tacit expectation on his part that I would share my resources with him. In terms of the local culture of reciprocity and exchange, this was neither manipulative nor exploitative.

Finally, this story illustrates the tragedy of the demolition of Beijing's hutong neighborhoods. Huiming's formally registered status as a person with disabilities enabled her and her husband to enjoy a quality of life in their dazayuan that was unique among the other local residents I knew in the neighborhood. Both she and Wang, moreover, were clear in their preference for this kind of accommodation. The final total demolition of the old dazayuan in Dashalar can only be a matter of time. However, Huiming's and Wang's attachment to the dazayuan lifestyle invites us to reflect on how local domestic, architectural, and social characteristics of "old Beijing" could, theoretically, have been preserved in a modified and partially "modernized" way.[3]

7

Jia Yong

The only significantly successful individual I came across in Dashalar was Jia Yong. A local lad born and brought up in the neighborhood, he made good through a combination of hard work, wit, intelligence, and humanity, all evidenced in his business and social skills and enfolded into another version of the "thick masculinity" I have already described. He was a beneficiary of the relative privileges accorded the industrial working class during the Mao era, when he was growing up, and of the commercial opportunities afforded by the marketization of the economy. He was also a nonconformist individualist committed to pursuing his personal passion for photography, and a canny operator, skilled in manipulating relationships with authority figures to turn them to his advantage. His photography evidenced a deep attachment to Dashalar that focused on recording the lives of his disadvantaged neighbors as testimony to a disappearing popular culture being engulfed by global commercial competition. Jia Yong exemplifies a complex mix of commercial and political savvy, loyalty to his neighborhood class origins, personal talents and people skills, and the success of the party-state across time in molding individual people as its loyal subjects.

The first time I met Jia Yong was in 2004 when I went with Zhao Tielin and Huang Mingfang to have a meal in the restaurant he owned in Dashalar. He was loud, very welcoming, and extremely funny. His powerful physique also gave him a dominating presence. Within about an hour after meeting him, tears rolled down my face as he recounted hilarious anecdotes about the people and events in his restaurant. This first encounter pointed to what I came to learn over the years were key aspects of his character and commercial success.

Jia Yong was born and brought up in Dashalar in a dazayuan off West Street. He speaks in the local slang, and has a raucous sense of humor that makes ample use of the rich repertoire of puns of Beijing's popular dialect. He seems to know everyone in the neighborhood, and has many connections in higher places, in film, TV, the art world, and journalism, as well as in local politics. He enjoys a local reputation for being good at renji guanxi (interpersonal relations). In his own terms, he would describe himself as an example of Beijing's traditional, heavily masculinist "old master culture" (*ye wenhua*). From a more elite perspective, he would be looked down on as a "small-time hood" (*hutong chuanzi*).[1] His main income-generating business is a popular "old Beijing"–style restaurant in Dashalar. This was a single high-ceilinged space with a balcony area set against the back wall and overlooking the main downstairs dining room, which he later expanded to incorporate another dining room in a building opposite. The atmosphere of the restaurant when I first went there was dingy: dark wood paneling around the lower half of the walls, and peeling paint yellowed with age covering the upper half. Framed black-and-white photographs of "old Beijingers" lined all the walls. Flies and cockroaches didn't seem to worry anyone. At the back of the main dining room was a counter on which stood a huge medicinal demijohn filled with what looked like very aged liquid. A motley bunch of waiters, mostly young men, some seemingly no more than fifteen or so, dressed in grubby white cotton jackets, stood around chatting and moving between the kitchen at the back and the dining area. At the front of the restaurant between the two entrance doors was a single washbasin, with a big flat screen above it that used to run loops of popular Beijing opera. At the back of the restaurant, across a small unpaved courtyard and up some rickety stairs was a small room that Jia Yong called his office, where he sometimes slept and where he kept large quantities of his unframed photographs, along with objects salvaged from local demolition sites.

The restaurant was immediately opposite the tiny alley where Jia Yong grew up in a dazayuan and where the migrant workers he employed in his restaurant lived. It was also opposite one of his many former business ventures, a photography and print shop, which he closed down sometime in 2011 in order to make it into a second dining room for the restaurant. Around the same time, he converted another nearby space into a bar serving Western-style espresso, wine, and liqueurs. When I first knew Jia Yong, he lived with his wife and son in a large apartment in one of the huge gated communities that now dominate Beijing's urban landscape, in a district to the south of the city. By 2014, his son had married and had a son, and so the daughter-in-law and young grandson also lived in the family apartment. Most days, Jia Yong used to arrive in Dashalar in a black four-by-four—sometimes driven by his wife—and spent his time in meetings with fellow businessmen, or chatting to customers.

During the early years of my research in Dashalar, Jia Yong's restaurant was managed by his wife's sister, and he had ten or so mainly young male migrants working as sous-chefs, waiters, and kitchen assistants. When he closed his photography and print shop, the latter's manager, also a migrant but married and settled with his family in Beijing, took over a share in the management of the restaurant. The restaurant was a thriving business: at lunchtime and dinnertime it was invariably packed with customers, including the odd backpacking foreigner. Then, as Jia Yong was expanding into his new bar to the side of the restaurant, he decided to "modernize" his restaurant facilities by replacing the single squatting toilet at the back of the main dining area with a new Western-style toilet in a newly constructed room with a washbasin and a tiled floor, at the back of the yard behind the restaurant and beyond the kitchens.

Jia Yong's powerful physical and social presence aside, the most striking feature of his restaurant were the many black-framed black-and-white photographs of "old Beijing" scenes and people hanging side by side on the walls of the dining areas. These were the restaurant's signature feature, all taken by Jia Yong, of people, places, and activities in this neighborhood where he grew up. The photographs had an evocative appeal to their audiences. On many occasions when I was sitting there, customers came in through the main doors and before sitting down at a table went straight to look at the photographs: the old guy sitting on his stool in the shade of a dazayuan doorway fanning himself to thwart the humid heat of summer; the young girl peeping out through the barely opened outer doors of a local dazayuan; young children playing in the hutong. Such images spoke of Jia Yong's familiarity with Dashalar, and of his nostalgic desire to record the local everyday culture that had molded his interests and talents. He was not averse to making a bit of money out of selling his photographs, and so if a customer indicated interest in his work, he sometimes disappeared into his office and reemerged with large portfolios of unframed photographs displaying the broader range of his work. However, he did not put much energy into publicizing his photography commercially, nor did he depend on it to make a living. Rather, photography was a passion he had nurtured ever since he was a teenager, and which he was able to draw on to his social advantage.

People from all different walks of life used to come and go in Jia Yong's restaurant—families, couples, businessmen and cadres, local patrol officers, artists and students, backpackers and tourists. All were welcome, and many became regular customers, drawn to the sense of local history and nostalgia that his photographs conveyed. The video footage of the demolition and reconstruction of the neighborhood that he used to show on the restaurant flat screen drew particular attention from his customers, who would sometimes congratulate him on recording scenes to which few photographers

Fig. 7.1 Through the main entrance to a dazayuan, 2007. Courtesy of Jia Yong.

had access. Not infrequently he entered into animated conversations with people who wanted to know more about his photographs or his film work, much of which challenged the veracity of footage of similar scenes available on mainstream TV.

Learning the Trade and Family Life

Jia Yong was born in 1958. He was adopted out to a couple who lived in Dashalar in the dazayuan where he grew up, opposite his restaurant. He hadn't known that he was adopted, although in 2010 he told me that he'd always had the feeling that something was a bit different about him. A woman he called his "auntie" (*yi*) periodically used to go to see him when he was a child, and he recalled resisting her attempts to pick him up. These visits apparently came to an end in the 1970s; it was then not until 1997 that, approaching middle age, he met his birth mother for the first time. He had happened to come across a photograph of himself as a child alongside two other boys who looked quite like him, and decided to try to find out more about his background. His (adoptive) mother then revealed to him the biological facts of his parentage. He eventually decided to try to find his birth mother; he didn't know her name, and the only small detail about her that he recalled was that she had a severed finger—apparently the result of an industrial accident. So, with no more to go on than the general area where he thought she lived, he went from factory to factory asking people if they remembered a woman who had a severed finger. He eventually found her, and over time came to discover more about his biological lineage.

Jia Yong's mother had three sons, born between 1958 and 1962, all with the same father. She never married him, since he remained married to another woman with whom he had five children. In 2010, reflecting on his adult reencounter with his birth mother, Jia Yong said he had found it difficult to acknowledge her as his mother, but now, in his middle age, he felt the time had come to be filial. Indeed, the occasion prompting Jia Yong's conversation with me about his birth mother was a visit she was going to make to stay with him and his wife, for which he, Jia Yong, had agreed to go and pick her up. It was clear, however, that being filial to his mother was not too burdensome a task, since she was well supported by Jia Yong's second brother, and lived in a decent apartment in a respectable residential area of Beijing.

If by 2010 Jia Yong had accepted his birth mother as someone to whom he had a moral obligation, his story about his father was very different. It turned out that his adoptive parents were friends of a fellow worker of his father's and it was through this connection that he—Jia Yong—had been adopted out at four months old. His biological father had been a workmate of the father of a well-known local restaurateur who later became Jia Yong's mentor. It was through this latter connection that Jia Yong decided to track his father down. He eventually turned up at a given address, where he was given short shrift by an elderly man who did not respond warmly to his enquiry about the whereabouts of his father. Jia Yong recounted how he then saw another elderly man seated inside at the back of the room, who seemed terrified at the sight of him. In response, Jia Yong backed off, saying, "Don't worry, I don't want to hurt you, I just wanted to see where you were."

Jia Yong's parents were both workers in a state factory, so they could depend on reasonable incomes. By 1976 his father earned sixty-five yuan a month, and his mother thirty-four; as state workers, they had access to basic medical care and good enough food at a time, Jia Yong noted, when many people did not have enough. At school, Jia Yong was not enthusiastic about academic subjects, and as a kid, he used to play a lot outside in the alleys of the neighborhood. In his late teenage years and early twenties, he was no more diligent, and rather than studying preferred hanging out with his mates, sauntering around in his bell-bottom jeans with his guitar and boom box. To buy the latter, he borrowed money from his father, who in turn had to borrow it from his work unit. His mother seems to have been an upstanding member of the local community. Between 1960 and 1982, along with two of her friends, she acted as a security officer on the local neighborhood committee. The three remained friends throughout their lives.

As a teenager, Jia Yong demonstrated two particular talents. At school, he developed what became an abiding love of photography and spent long hours in the darkroom of one of his teachers. He also had an evident entrepreneurial flare. He used to hang around a restaurant in Dashalar, opposite where he lived, that was then owned and managed by a man he described as his mentor—his "elder brother" (da ge)—who, realizing that the young lad was quick to learn, took him under his wing. Very early in the mornings, before daybreak, Jia Yong would ride his pedicart out to the suburbs of the city to buy vegetables for the restaurant. Under his mentor's tutelage, he learned the ropes of restaurant management and budgeting, and later on put this training to excellent use when his mentor moved off into the cement industry, leaving the restaurant under Jia Yong's management, to become what it was when I met him. The two made a blood pact swearing eternal loyalty. "Elder brother" consistently appeared as a key figure inspiring Jia Yong to make something of his life.

Due to his artistic interests and background, Jia Yong was assigned to work in the Beijing Enamel Factory and started taking photographs of everyday life in the lanes and alleys of his neighborhood around 1984. He was also a keen sportsman and used to train in a local sports college, where he met the young woman who later became his wife. She was tall, very beautiful, and, like her husband, completely unabashed about speaking her mind. One episode I witnessed stands out particularly clearly. It was in 2007, when the local government had issued orders to local shopkeepers to put up new shop fronts and signage and to clear their wares from the street in front of their shops. Jia Yong and a man who ran a small restaurant adjacent to his own got into a spat about the boundary between their two properties, and the man lashed out and punched Jia Yong. A small crowd quickly gathered around to watch Jia Yong, now sitting on the ground cradling his head, apparently waiting for the police to turn up. Hearing a kerfuffle outside the restaurant, Jia Yong's wife went out onto the street and started yelling at the man, telling him that he deserved to be arrested for abusing her husband.

As I got to know Jia Yong better, I came to understand—in a way that eluded me when I first met him—that family was *the* crucial anchoring feature of his life. I knew that some of his most dependable employees were relatives. His sister-in-law stopped managing the restaurant only when she had to give up work to care for her aging father-in-law. Jia Yong was keen for his son, Junxi, to acquire some knowledge of the hospitality industry. When I first met him, Junxi was a lithe and handsome teenager, with aspirations to become a hip-hop dancer. Indeed, he was apparently quite talented and had a number of paid gigs. A couple of years later, by 2011, however, things had changed: he had a girlfriend and at his father's behest was working as manager of the new bar Jia Yong had opened. Junxi did not seem at all enthusiastic about this job. By the spring of 2013, Junxi was married, and by October of the same year, his wife had given birth to their first baby, a boy. Junxi had put on a lot of weight, the result, he said, of having a wife who cooked for him. The three of them lived with Junxi's parents, although Jia Yong said he was putting money aside to buy the young couple a flat to move into once the baby had passed his first year. Meantime, Jia Yong said that life at home was very pleasurable since his wife, Meiyan, got on really well with their daughter-in-law, going out shopping together like friends.

In all, Jia Yong was the entrepreneurial and patriarchal pillar on whom his family and employees depended. He was the center of the world of his restaurant, and this was the literal physical and social site of convergence of his diverse aspirations, interests, and ambitions, which in time took him out of Dashalar.

Photographs, Nostalgia, Historical Responsibility, and Reclaiming the Past

Over the years I used to visit Dashalar, Jia Yong occupied himself with making changes to expand his restaurant and improve its facilities, but the photographs on the walls of his restaurant remained fixed in place. Strikingly displayed in strong black frames, these black-and-white portraits of Dashalar's "old Beijingers" had a powerful presence. They told a story of local people whose relationships and everyday activities acquired meaning—came to life, as it were—in the lanes and alleys of their neighborhood, but whose place-based association with the "old Beijing" that preexisted the arrival of global capital in the 1990s was being dislodged by the encroachments of property developers and commercial consumer culture. The "vision" of China's future on which Beijing's urban planners have been setting their sights is a future of national prosperity and power sustained by the global political economy that materially, spatially, and socially, consigns the present to the "dustbin of history" for all those unable or unwilling to welcome its promises. In this vision, Beijing's rich and diverse history is now all but invisible except in spectacular heritage sites, such as the Forbidden City. Tourist websites bemoan the loss of the hutong and encourage visitors to take photographs of them before they disappear, but at the same time explain that their destruction is necessary in order to raise people's living standards. The Beijing Capital Museum's display in 2010 of "old Beijing" customs, featuring a replica of an "old Beijing" courtyard with models, images, and descriptions of marriage and birth customs and family life was a clichéd travesty of the lives of those who claim "old Beijing" as their own. But Jia Yong's images tell a story not of a neighborhood consigned by this vision to a distant past but of a diverse and vibrant mix of people, buildings, and spaces whose disappearing material and spatial history leaves unmistakable traces in their present realities—in the rubble and chaos around them, in a look in their eyes, a certain kind of body language associated with local cultural practices, or in the commercial advertisements announcing the rebuilding of their neighborhood. His photographs constitute his subjects not as passive observers of practices beyond their control but as active agents asserting their recalcitrant presence in the processes of change of which they are part. As they look out of their frames, they silently affirm their ownership of the places and spaces they inhabit, and of the activities that absorb their energies and that claim our attention as their observers.

A visitor to Dashalar today would have to look hard for evidence of these different versions of "old Beijing." As I noted at the beginning of this book, most of the neighborhood's long-term residents have moved out, leaving those who remain and its newcomer "outsiders" to make a living through the service and tourist opportunities its transformation offers. Its untidy lanes have been replaced by widened roads and walkways, and its ramshackle street stalls have been taken over by neatly renovated shop fronts, uniformly painted in the cold gray of Beijing's architectural tradition. Its former eateries, commercial outlets, theaters, guesthouses, and brothels now house downmarket restaurants and shops, catering to popular domestic tourism rather than the local Beijing population. Further east, in nearby Qianmen dajie, big global fashion retailers such as H&M, Zara, and Gap jostle with newly gentrified coffee bars and restaurants targeting the young elite, with names such as Meeting Someone.

Fig. 7.2 Elderly man staying cool in high summer, Dashalar, 2008. Courtesy of Jia Yong.

Against this background, a bittersweet mood of nostalgia for an "authentic" past appears as a key theme in Jia Yong's photography. The effect of his photographs is to evoke what observers might associate with the quiet emotions and gestures of retro authenticity.[2] But this is not the only or even most important aspect of his photography; nostalgia for a lost past is not as important here as a sense of the past in the present as a shared memory of everyday life asserting locals' cultural ownership of the neighborhood in the face of its accelerating engulfment by an uncertainly unfolding future. Jia Yong's eye for the changing aura of his neighborhood also tells of his abiding commitment to keeping a historical record that would otherwise be missing. He directs his lens to the same places, time and time again; lanes are widened, shop fronts change, courtyard rooftops are replaced by the straight lines of residential and office blocks; the seasons come and go; neither time nor space stands still. These photographs thus evoke much more than the picturesque images of "old Beijing" courtyards and hutongs of the tourist guidebooks. They are not of a neighborhood frozen in time in nostalgic displays of the capital's rich cultural and commercial history.[3] The mood they evoke through their sensitivity to the unspectacular and the everyday creates a feeling of temporality, place, and space—the lived rhythms, patterns, and places of neighborhood life over time—that few "outsider" lenses would be able to capture. The affective appreciation of neighborhood life contained within the frame of these photographs can be understood as a form of embedded local knowledge derived from an easy familiarity with everyday social and cultural practices. Today, the visitor to Qianmen Dajie and Dashalar is invited to experience a display of "old Beijing's" cultural heritage that bears little resemblance to the neighborhood of Jia Yong's childhood. In contrast with official appropriations of the heritage of "old Beijing," displayed, for example, in the Capital Museum, Jia Yong's photographs situate Dashalar's history among the local residents to whom it belongs but whose ownership of that history is being displaced by another temporality and social existence heralded by the unattainable promises of global capitalism. They are also a moving record of the loss of his neighborhood. "Without the buildings, there's nothing left," Jia Yong once commented, "so what you have to do is keep a record of those buildings, otherwise no one will know that there was once an old Beijing."[4] For years predating my acquaintance with him, Jia Yong regularly used to go out with his German Leica to photograph local people, places, and processes: demolition and reconstruction of lanes and buildings, including former brothels, temples and native-place associations, rooftops and temple remains, as well as local residents, dignitaries, shopkeepers, pedicab drivers, migrant workers, and children.

Fig. 7.3 Reconstruction of Qianmen dajie, 2007. Courtesy of Jia Yong.

Then, with new technology, he began to use a digital camera to make short films. By the time I got to know him he had many hours of extraordinary footage charting the physical, social, and political processes of the transformation of his neighborhood.

Jia Yong's imagery offers compelling visual evidence of the inseparable interconnectedness of place, space, and time that gives meaning to the everyday history of his neighborhood. History is not stilled here in a slice of time within the photographic frame, nor through the depiction of place as a fixed locus of meaning. The juxtaposition of face, person, place, object, and activity in his photographs explicitly evokes the past in the present. At the same time, the temporal quality of his photographs is inflected by reminders of another temporal reality depicted in images of scaffolding sustaining constructions of the future, now the new present of his neighborhood. The "totemic resonance" of place acquires meaning in these photographs as the locus—physical and symbolic—of recognition of the past and present in the lives of those disadvantaged people caught up in and overwhelmed by the construction of a future from which they are excluded.[5]

Stashed away in random boxes in his office, Jia Yong has collected numerous roof tiles, finials, old mirrors, dresser handles, and small carved wooden window screens, all salvaged from local demolition sites. Through his camera and his collection, his identification with his neighborhood thus acquires a sense of historical responsibility as a way of dealing with his loss. It is a daring project. His wife chides him for spending his time courting potential problems. Seen from this perspective, his project may indeed be interpreted as an unsettling exposure of the chaos, negligence, and often-arbitrary exercise of power that for so many local people characterize the plans and policies of the developers. Jia Yong, however, insists on giving his project another emphasis, which is not so much a critique of "them up there" as a recognition of local subaltern existences disdained and discarded by the authorities. In time, his camerawork and collection may eventually contribute to a public commemoration of the lives of those whom mainstream history does not record.

Trading between State and Market

One particularly poignant episode captured on Jia Yong's camera revealed the tension in his position as, on the one hand, the local lad-made-good attached to the place of his childhood, and, on the other, the successful entrepreneur and political operator. It was October 1, 2009, when the nation was celebrating its sixtieth anniversary—a key date in China's cosmological system.[6] Excavation to widen Dashalar's West Street and reroute its service cables had begun in 2008, exposing a tangled mess of open cables and rubble in the tiny pedestrian margins left at the sides of the street. Everyday mobility for local residents was severely hampered for many months while hutongs were resurfaced. Picking one's way along the narrow walkways involved a laborious process of walking single-file over boards covering perilously large gaps, ducking to avoid the overhanging cables, and waiting for pedestrians coming from the opposite direction to pass by before being able to move ahead. By the summer of 2009, access from Meishi Street to the nearest subway station at Qianmen was completely blocked off in a general "lockdown" on residents' mobility as preparations for the National Day celebrations got under way.[7] The refurbishment of Dashalar's West Street was officially completed and formally announced on October 1, but local residents were ordered to stay in their houses as the official celebrations took place in the nearby Tian'anmen Square. Video footage Jia Yong took that day revealed an eerily empty West Street stilled into lifelessness by spotlessly clean buildings neatly aligned behind new gray facades. The only movement was Jia Yong's small dog; the only color relieving the dull flatness of the gray was a little spot of the bright orange of an artificial geranium in a flowerpot placed on the newly paved pedestrian lane. Jia Yong's camera then panned up the side of the buildings facing north to reveal a number of people sprawled over the rooftops watching the parades in the Square. Jia Yong, skilled operator that he was, knew that he would not be penalized for going outside his restaurant in order to take this video footage—his relationship with the local authorities afforded him a protection few others in the neighborhood enjoyed—but he also wanted to record how his fellow locals subverted the constraints on their mobility.

Jia Yong's lens sheds light on the mundane ways in which local people negotiate the familiar places, spaces, and temporalities of social life in an environment of constraint and uncertainty. This often inflects his images with an apparent refusal to bow down to the authorities. In a short film he took of the official opening of Qianmen dajie on August 7, 2008—the eve of the opening of the Olympics—after a number of long official speeches celebrating the opening, local residents were unequivocal in their views: "What are those white lamps supposed to be? They're not like old Beijing—what's the idea? To build another fancy shopping street?" The sole remaining occupant of a courtyard mostly reduced to rubble appears as a staunch defender of his rights to retain his space of the present in preference to accepting the compensation offered him to move. However, to read subversion into such an image obscures an important dimension of the interests of the individuals and households involved, namely, to hold out against the authorities for as long as possible in order to maximize the compensation they can receive from them. There is thus a fitting parallel between the stories that Jia Yong's lens tells, his personal interests spanning his photography, his commercial and political connections, and the concerns that these obscure.

Alongside his historical project, Jia Yong the entrepreneur is also involved in reinventing a Beijing tradition that is lucratively inscribed in the city's future as it takes shape in his neighborhood. The tourists who delight in his restaurant photographs also delight in the restored buildings of the new "old Beijing" in Qianmen dajie. International backpackers linger over their food as they watch his "subversive" film footage on the screen at the front of the restaurant, and sample his espresso coffee in the bar next door. And they return, repeatedly, becoming Jia Yong's friends, sharing a common language of enjoyment not in words—few of the backpackers I have seen in the restaurant speak Chinese, and Jia Yong does not speak English—but in the space of "old Beijing" that his restaurant represents. The social interests and interactions that converge in the "old Beijing" space of the display of his photography and film thus also suggest an investment in the commercialization of "old Beijing."

Jia Yong was often commissioned to film events, including the opening of new enterprises, private viewings of exhibitions, and wedding banquets. For the opening of his new bar in 2011, he held a large party to which he invited many local dignitaries, artists, and academics. He later announced that he wanted to use the bar as the base for a new photographic enterprise he was setting up—a photographers' association linked to a US photographers' association. Two years later, he wanted to link up with the local street committee office that had started facilitating annual exhibitions in the neighborhood, including those of the Beijing Design Week, noted in the last chapter. Building on his official connections, in the autumn of 2012, long after the date when local businesses were informed they were no longer allowed to display their wares on the street, Jia Yong obtained official permission to mount an exhibition of photographs on old wooden screens placed on a red carpet in front of his restaurant. That the photographers in question were mostly foreign and had little or nothing to do with Dashalar was beside the point. Celebrating the opening of the exhibition, various officials stood in front of a big banner announcing the event, and gave formal speeches congratulating Jia Yong for curating it. Each of the participating photographers then had to walk the length of the red carpet, toward the main banner at the end, followed by local journalists and photographers. The efforts Jia Yong put into convincing local officials to allow the exhibition to take place clearly paid off when they allowed him to extend the exhibition over five days.

This exhibition was the most spectacular public event organized by Jia Yong that I witnessed, but he was also highly skilled at turning ad hoc opportunities to his advantage. On one occasion in the summer of 2010, two Dutch tourists, neither of whom spoke Chinese, turned up at Jia Yong's restaurant. Via much gesturing and sign language, they explained that they were professional chefs with friends who knew Jia Yong. He then invited them to demonstrate their cooking on the street in front of his restaurant and prepared a large makeshift wok burner for them, and they set to, attracting large crowds curious about the culinary skills of two very evidently *lao wai* (old foreigners).

Jia Yong's skills also extended to being invited to participate in lengthy trips organized by local officials and acquaintances in the entrepreneurial and cultural worlds. He went to Xinjiang in 2009, and in 2012 he joined a delegation of local officials and artists invited to visit France and Switzerland to promote cultural collaboration. His interests in hanging out with officials came to occupy an increasingly prominent place in his everyday activities. As official constraints on local entrepreneurial activities grew, so, it seemed, did Jia Yong's efforts to court the local government's approval. The last time I tried to see him in May 2017, he was in Berlin as a member of a Beijing cultural delegation.

Although Jia Yong did not see his interest in photography principally as a source of income generation, he was not averse to promoting it in order to develop his connections with local officials. Here again, however, his ambitions were by no means oriented toward obtaining recognition as a member of the establishment (*tizhi nei*). Rather, as a successful individual "outside the establishment" (*tizhi wai*), accommodating those "inside," he could enjoy a measure of protection for activities that simultaneously boosted the local economy *and* his own interests. The only time I know of when his activities transgressed acceptable boundaries was on June 4, 2009, when he was arrested for screening in his restaurant an uncut version of a CCTV documentary about China's twentieth-century transformation that featured scenes of the protests in Tian'anmen Square in May and June 1989. The story he told me was that the violent events of June 4, 1989, appeared on the flat screen in his restaurant just as a policeman entered. He then had to spend five days in a detention center. Even there, though, his people skills put him in good stead, and he spent five days eating well and playing cards with other detainees. A photograph of him and his wife when she went to pick him up on his release showed him in triumphant mood, standing and laughing outside the detention center.

There is thus a correspondence between Jia Yong's personal interests and the political and commercial impulses producing the heritage reinvention of "old Beijing." Both suggest not so much a celebration of locals' subversion or the preservation of a disappearing past, as a place-based accommodation of dominant state/political interests. Jia Yong's photography has involved elaborate public and official activities to cement his social and cultural status; his photography thus operates as a key element of his cultural and social capital, and as such it is an indispensable tool facilitating the expansion of his entrepreneurial interests and his own social and cultural mobility. Instead of a choice between "them" and "us," between support for the planners' future or solidarity with its resisters, his photography and individual positioning demonstrate a trading of sentiments and interests in repeated negotiations between and across this divide. Alongside his accommodation of political and entrepreneurial interests, Jia Yong's implicitly subversive activities in filming what mainstream media regarded as sensitive issues, including the demolition of local buildings, thus need to be understood as an indication of a complex political and social positioning, defined by an intermingling of affection for the place and culture that nurtured his success, and an entrepreneurial flare for turning that to his advantage.

Jia Yong's story, therefore, is strikingly different from the others I have told; his is the success story of someone who has been able to build on the relative advantage of his working-class background during the Mao years to explore the commercial and entrepreneurial opportunities offered him by China's engagement with global capitalism. If his attachment to place is no less explicit than the other "old Beijing" residents' in the previous chapters, it differs from them in that he has transformed it into an affective as well as commercial project that gives him a mobility others did not enjoy.

Notwithstanding all this, however, Jia Yong remains almost viscerally attached to a sense of his own, and the capital's, past. His commitment to recording and collecting the past of Dashalar is not principally to make commercial gain but to preserve traces of a particular local history. At the same time, and in part because of the privileges he manages to gain from his political and commercial dealings, he can display scenes, most notably through his video footage, that speak of a profound unease with the government's process of urban redevelopment and that attract people to his restaurant for its display of an alternative narrative obscured by the polished constructions of global architectural design.

Patriarch and Patron

As a family man, Jia Yong is a less paradoxical figure. He has been successful enough to buy a large apartment in a gated community and a large four-by-four vehicle. It is his satisfaction in providing for his wife, son, and grandchild that anchors his political, cultural, and entrepreneurial ambitions. His wife, as I've mentioned, has no qualms in speaking her mind, but never, in my presence, at least, in ways that challenged her husband's claims to patriarchal authority. His indulgence of his son during the latter's teenage years gave way to his decision to instruct his son to learn a profession in order to support his future wife and family, leading to responsibilities for managing the bar Jia Yong opened at the side of his main restaurant. The son had little choice but to obey his father's instructions, though, as I've mentioned, without much enthusiasm. Then, when he married and had a son, he gave up working entirely, and settled back into comfortable dependence on his father.

Jia Yong extended his role as family patriarch and restaurant patron to many contexts in which he could display the authority of his knowledge and connections. He could be extremely, if selectively, generous. From time to time he used his car to help young aspiring photographers he knew to transport large objects, such as tables and photographic stands, from one place to another. He took particular delight in advising young photographers about equipment and technique, displaying the wealth of his own experience and knowledge as a self-made photographer. On one occasion, when I told him I needed to buy a new camera, he spent most of one day driving me out to the western suburbs to a huge retail park specializing in all kinds of photographic equipment, new and old, where he assured me that he could get an excellent deal for me through a friend of his who had a business there.

Jia Yong did not need to display his authority in any particular way to convince his audience of his qualities. His authority was manifest for all to see in his entrepreneurial and cultural success. It was also manifest in his assumption of the "old master" (*laoye*) qualities of Beijing's "tradition" of masculine authority, face, and patronage—his loquaciousness, his self-interest, and his sense of entitlement to give voice to his opinions. His "old master" character was on full display in the dinners for friends and acquaintances he used to host in his restaurant. Sitting at the head of a number of tables put together to make one long dining table, he used to loudly hold forth telling stories, cracking jokes while eating, drinking and smoking, and generally lording over his guests as their beneficent patron. Alongside the odd foreigner, his guests invariably included at least one or two long-term friends of his—his *gemenr* (bros), as he called them—artists and businessmen who played supporting roles to his lead. If clients came into the restaurant to eat while Jia Yong was eating with his friends, he would invariably invite them to join us, particularly if they were foreign. He was the true patron of his restaurant.

Interlude 6

That Jia Yong's story is radically different from the others in this book is self-evident. His social status, authority, relative wealth, and personal passions gave him the opportunity to explore interests outside the material and social frameworks of his immediate needs and interests in Dashalar, which could potentially contribute to documenting a record of the neighborhood long after its final demolition.

Jia Yong's status as a successful entrepreneur was well known in the neighborhood. It is possible that before I arrived there other successful individuals from Dashalar had left for other parts of Beijing or elsewhere. In Dashalar, however, Jia Yong was unique among those I knew as a local success story.

Furthermore, apart from Jia Yong, all the other restaurateurs and shop owners I came across in the neighborhood were "outsiders" from other provinces cashing in on the popular tourism of South City. One of the two exceptions I knew was a famous tripe restaurant nearer Qianmen, an establishment that had been in the same family for several generations and thus could boast an "old Beijing" lineage. The other was a young bookseller whose family courtyard in the neighborhood was demolished in the early 2000s, and who started up a small bookshop devoted to items about Beijing. His motivation in launching this was to commemorate his family's ancestral ownership of the courtyard in Dashalar where he had been brought up. Prior to the courtyard's demolition, this young bookseller spent long hours taking detailed photographs of its furniture, domestic items, and design features, which he told me he wanted to keep as a record to preserve the memory of a disappearing history. Over the following years, his business expanded, incorporating "old Beijing" trinkets such as small figurines of Beijing opera characters, fans, and writing brushes. He also became a frequent visitor to Jia Yong's restaurant, where Jia Yong was happy to advise him on his business strategy. By 2017 this young bookseller had moved out of the neighborhood into an old state-owned courtyard near Drum Tower, and on social media referred to himself as proud to be a "small master" (*xiaoye*) from Beijing, hence subscribing to the "thick masculinist" emphasis of popular Beijing culture. When I met him in this courtyard in May 2017, I was unprepared for what seemed to be his total transformation from a committed independent bookseller to an entrepreneur wanting to adopt the performative habits of the "traditional" old Beijing patriarch and increasingly reliant on patronage from political authorities.

Jia Yong's entrepreneurial and social flair was locally acknowledged, though not without some measure of envy. His disdain of others, including Zhao Yong's family, for being unable to make anything of their lives was mirrored in Zhao Yong's muted criticism of Jia Yong's pursuit of his own self-interest, and of his moral failure to bring up his son as a person with integrity, able to focus on more than his own self-centered concerns. While Jia Yong enjoyed good social relations with local law enforcers and government personnel— which allowed Jia Yong a mobility and access to use of public space not enjoyed by other local entrepreneurs—he did not have much to do with the local people I have written about in this book. Not once did I see any of these people enter his restaurant to eat or drink there. It is also significant that he did not attend the two "big local events" that took place in the neighborhood during the years of my research there: Young Gao's daughter's wedding, and Young Gao's funeral.

His absence from these events and social distance from those he grew up with in the neighborhood demonstrated a very different kind of agency from that of the others I have narrated in this book, implying a desire for a different kind of recognition. This can be summarized as his embrace of a narrative that foregrounded his initiative in managing to escape from poverty and hardship. His contempt for those such as Zhao Yong who found themselves imprisoned by poverty was the flipside of an ideological position, embedded in Beijing's engagement with global capitalism, that in many ways corresponded with the discursive privileging of the competitive individual able to improve his life chances by relying on his own initiative. However, when I first knew him, his commitment to recording the disappearing past of his childhood obscured his identification with the interests promoting this main orientation of his agency. Li Fuying's enactment of agency took a radical and unanticipated turn when he was confronted with circumstances beyond his control. Jia Yong's implicit celebration of his autonomous agency in being able to reap the rewards of engaging with the market and state emerged increasingly assertively across the years of my research in conjunction with the changing economic and political environment. Both individuals, in their very different ways, exemplify how the enactment of agency does not follow a predictable or linear path.

Jia Yong's fundamental commitments to his family and relatives as male head of his household were reiterated in the authority he claimed and was given as boss and patron of his restaurant, and in the personalized advice he extended to young people, such as the young bookseller I mentioned above. This latter instance was just one I witnessed in which Jia Yong was potentially outside his comfort zone. However, he dealt with the young man's greater expertise in his area of specialty by adopting the mantle of the confident older and experienced entrepreneur. As with the stereotypical male patron—or the "old master" (*laoye*) of "old Beijing" tradition—Jia Yong's sense of entitlement was evident as much in the attention he demanded from others as in his assumption of his right to have his voice heard as boss of his restaurant and family. In his family, professional, and social life, Jia Yong's status thus derived from and boosted a gendered authority that he openly claimed and that others recognized.

As industrial workers and stalwart subjects of the state, Jia Yong's parents were solidly positioned as beneficiaries of Mao's socialism. Jia Yong grew up as a cherished son, accustomed to having his way; we might recall his father's willingness to borrow money to purchase the boom box he wanted. In explaining the differences between his own personal history and that of others in the neighborhood, Jia Yong was explicit in acknowledging the security his upbringing had given him, which he could then use to his advantage in the changed environment of commercial competition. In this, his personal history sheds important light on our understanding of the roots and reasons facilitating commercial success in China's cities, transcending the simplistic distinction between the Mao and post-Mao eras. A combination of family opportunities—framed by class positioning, assisted by personal intelligence and individual agency, and buttressed by a network of male bonds—established the foundations enabling Jia Yong to make the most of his relations with both market and the state when the collective era of state ownership that had favored his background came to an end.

Just as Jia Yong's success does not fit into a neat division between the Mao era of full state ownership and the post-Mao era of individual opportunities and market competition, his interest in recording Dashalar's history cannot simply be characterized as subversive. Much of his photographic activities, including his filming of the demolition of Qianmen dajien, and his screening of sometimes highly sensitive video material in his restaurant, might imply a deliberate transgression of official boundaries. However, a few years later his curation of a photography exhibition outside his restaurant with the approval of the local authorities at a time when other entrepreneurs were prohibited from commercial activity outside the interior walls of their premises suggests a complicity with the state. Over time, his photographic project thus encapsulated a range of competing and conflictive attitudes and interests, opening up a space of collective memory for those who looked for it, while largely accommodating the status quo. The complicity with the state that he manifested thus allowed for *both* identification with the establishment *and* a critical distance from it.[1]

Jia Yong's photographs of his neighborhood's people, places, and customs revealed a deep sadness at its disappearance. As time went by, however, and the commercial reinvention of "old Beijing" began to take shape in West Street, these same photographs could seamlessly transmute into artifacts of the nostalgia industry, attracting punters looking for the authentic experience of "old Beijing." A desire to preserve a disappearing record coexisted with an interest in making commercial gain out of it. Jia Yong's photographic recognition of the significance of place as a means of acknowledging local lives excluded from the written record was not necessarily incompatible with his participation in the commercialized projects implied by the state-sponsored reconstruction of Qianmen dajie. His photography thus emerges as a reminder of *both* the persistent recalcitrance of popular and local feeling vis-à-vis the state's authority *and* the hegemonic forces of the market that are integral to the state.

When I first got to know Jia Yong, at a time when civil activities and individual enterprise in Beijing, and across China as a whole, were beginning to suggest the possibility of critical debate and contestation removed from direct state intervention, his restaurant seemed to offer a social and cultural space for different opinions to come together in nonantagonistic encounter. However, as official control of local entrepreneurial activity became increasingly stringent around the time of the Olympics and afterward, Jia Yong's interests became increasingly overlaid with the need to comply with local government regulations in order to maintain his own freedom of activity. In the process, the apparently critical edge I had initially associated with the space of his restaurant gave way to a growing emphasis on instrumental exchange with the authorities facilitating commercial advantage in forms that corresponded with the changing consumer mood of cultural authenticity and heritage tourism.

Neither Jia Yong's photography nor the social space of his restaurant correspond with the oppositional tropes of subversion of *or* accommodation to the designs of the state in the form of the local urban government and developers. The stories and images of his photographs can be understood as the stilled point of convergence between many others' stories, memories, and experiences, including those for whom the physical and spatial destruction of the neighborhood signifies the disappearance of the familiar rhythms and forms of everyday life. While everything changes outside his restaurant, its unchanged internal décor acquires new meanings, enabling Jia Yong to lucratively participate in the heritage reinvention of the place in which he was born. His restaurant emerges as a space of his personal commitments and intersecting discourses, traversed by people from different walks of life and with radically different opinions about Beijing's transformation.

These shifting meanings and intersections aside, Jia Yong's story is profoundly place-based. For most of those who appear in this book, being place-based meant being pinned to place and unable to move, whether they liked it or not. In contrast, Jia Yong's place-based work and activities gave him the possibility of social and spatial mobility. Echoing Stephan Feuchtwang's theorization of the making and remaking of place as a process of centering, Jia Yong's literal "centeredness" in the physicality and visuality of Dashalar gave him the resources to be able to leave it physically and socially before the last traces of the "old Beijing" it stood for were entirely erased from material and spatial existence.[2]

If place in Jia Yong's work and life signified attachments pulling in different directions, his gendered status and identity as patriarch and patron were less complex and ambiguous. Jia Yong the family patriarch and Jia Yong the entrepreneurial patron were two sides of the same coin. His claim to authority as male head and patriarch of his household, acknowledged by his wife, his affinal kin, and his son and daughter-in-law, was echoed by his status as boss (*laoban*) of his employees, benevolent patron of young entrepreneurs, and generous host of guests and friends. In terms of the moral domain of "human feeling" (*renqing*) and "interpersonal relations" (*renji guanxi*), and the kind of exchanges with others his position as "old master" (*laoye*) set up, these two highly gendered roles converged in embodied and social form in the person of a single, physically large, authoritative and masculine man whose sense of self-worth was inseparably bound up with what, for him, was the naturalized indispensability of his role as local "old master." Seen from the perspective of renqing ethics discussed by Yan Yunxiang, Jia Yong's position of authority, acknowledged by all in the local community, imposed on him an obligation to help and support others.[3] Moreover, his sense of face—of being seen to be true to this role—was fundamental to his capacity to fulfill such an obligation.

The spectacularly gendered quality of this aspect of renqing ethics does not appear in Yan's analysis. Jia Yong's position as patriarch and patron depended on his status not simply as a *person* of local distinction but also as a *man* whose masculinity was culturally and socially constituted in characteristically local ways. His loquaciousness—and his evident enjoyment in his ability to captivate his audiences with stories, anecdotes, jokes, and so on—was sustained by an evident sense of entitlement to talk to, and instruct, his audiences, implicitly exacted in exchange for his benevolence. His audiences, in the form of his guests, were also gendered. Few of the gatherings he hosted for dinner in his restaurant had more than a couple of women. These gatherings drew on the structured networks of male sociality (*gemenr*) that boosted Jia Yong's claims to authority.

The members of the networks Jia Yong invited to his restaurant, or chose to socialize with, were exclusive. While everyone acknowledged his local standing, local people did not frequent his restaurant, even though its prices were as reasonable as others in the neighborhood. It was as if there were an unspoken distance between him and the others I knew. This was a distance that cannot be explained by referring to success alone. His assumption of the roles of patriarch and patron formed the core of his self-identification in the world, spanning family and social networks, in terms that Zhao Yong (and maybe others) recognized and would have welcomed for themselves. Despite his attachment to the place of his childhood and the place-based largesse he liked to demonstrate, Jia Yong had little sympathy for those local residents who, for whatever reason, had not been able to pull themselves out of poverty and benefit from the system. Thus, despite his attachment to place, his complicity with the system functioned to shore up his distance from it through piling on the benefits of official recognition, constituted and performed through structures of male networks. This constituted a modality of agency that clearly set him apart from the others, despite his profound attachment to the neighborhood.

This study of how Beijing's poorest long-term residents have experienced the changes transforming their lives in recent decades provides evidence of how the subaltern, incompletely accessed through oral narratives, archival research, and participant observation, is analytically crucial to our historical understanding. Far from being illustrative adjuncts to a disappearing past, these stories of life in Dashalar have to be incorporated into the analytical core of what we understand as history. They are as much part of Beijing's recent history as other narratives. Indeed, it is the inconsistencies and contradictions between these Dashalar stories and other, more familiar ones that reveal the complexities of history.

It goes without saying that our understanding of history is shaped, inter alia, by the historiographical analyses to which we have access. In turn, the broad factors explaining what becomes mainstream history are necessarily dependent on the historian's particular focus. They are also imbued with considerations of power, especially in a political and educational environment in which tight controls govern what can be published and said. The historiography of Beijing's processes of transformation through the socialist period and since has been dominated by official accounts from which the capital's subalterns have been largely absent. In treating Dashalar people's memories as properly historical material, this book offers a historiographical narrative that largely departs from the main events and timelines of dominant history. In concluding this book, I summarize the main themes in which this becomes apparent.

Temporalities of Neighborhood Life

Between the 1930s and 1949, local people's everyday lives in Dashalar, as elsewhere in the capital, were framed by the turbulent uncertainties of civil war, gang thuggery, street violence, corruption, drug abuse, high child mortality, sickness, and destitution. The year 1949 brought an end to civil war and military violence, but the effects of these conditions could not be resolved overnight.

Throughout the early years of the PRC, the living conditions of Dashalar residents were characterized by chronic overcrowding and material deprivation. Local government intentions to improve neighborhood conditions had little effect. On the contrary, in conditions of poverty and political constraint, exacerbated by the periodic arrival of large numbers of migrants from the countryside, local residents had to plead with the local authorities to protect what they considered their right to accommodations.

Into the post-Mao years of market reform, and despite successive plans for the neighborhood's regeneration, nothing much really changed in Dashalar until the layoffs of the mid-1990s, when many local people found themselves unemployed and increasingly dependent on informal resources to make ends meet. Many younger people and those with social and economic resources began to move out for better accommodations and jobs elsewhere, leaving mostly the oldest, most unskilled, and poorest residents in dazayuan that had remained virtually unchanged since the late 1950s.

Then, after 2008, following the refurbishment of Qianmen dajie, the encroaching chaiqian already under way in adjacent districts finally reached Dashalar. The pace of change accelerated, with immediate effects on local lives. Now that local residents were prevented from street vending and even denied access to local subway stations, their sense of having been neglected, abandoned, and left out took expression in attitudes that veered between fatalism, anger, and escapism.

Few of those I knew during my research in the neighborhood now remain: their lives of deprivation, hardship, and social exclusion in a neighborhood they claimed as theirs are finally being engulfed by the powerful nexus of the state, the market, and global capital, as evident in the rapid gentrification of the neighborhood. After decades of neglect, the marriage between the Chinese state and global capital has impelled the final demise of the Dashalar I knew, along with the way of life of its old, long-term Beijing residents.

Decades-long experiences of scarcity, hardship, increasing precarity, and final engulfment have, as we have seen, produced diverse narratives that moved in and out of acknowledgment of and engagement with the concerns of official history, but were far from replicating it. Crucially, local narratives did not correspond with the notion of rupture around which key events of China's late twentieth-century historiography cohere. For the Mao years, it is noticeable that neither Old Mrs. Gao nor Old Mrs. Zhao, both of whom recalled life before Liberation, even mentioned 1949. In their later years, it did not feature as a memorable date. Nor did 1949 feature in the accounts of their children's generation. Given the age of these people, growing up in the 1950s and 1960s, this may not be surprising. Yet they were educated at a time and under a political system that gave the year 1949 extraordinary prominence as a liberating moment of progressive departure from the past. However, in contrast with the key dates of the official historiography of the Mao years, the narratives of this middle-aged generation focused mainly on moments of shortage and violence. The most notable of these was the Great Leap Forward and the "three bad years," when, as famine devastated many regions of the country, Beijing's poor population was forced to fall back on family efforts to scavenge whatever edible plants could be found in the rural outskirts of the city. Then, the Cultural Revolution, largely associated in Dashalar with the activities of the Red Guards, was recalled mainly as a terrifying episode of brutality and chaos that had long-lasting psychological, social, and cultural effects. Even so, the Cultural Revolution by no means featured uniformly as the tragic state of victimization and suffering characteristic of elite intellectual accounts. Young Gao, along with others, regretted the closure of schools and the missed opportunity to benefit from a decent education. The Old Professor condemned the Cultural Revolution's legacy of dulling people's minds and consolidating the rule of the single leader. It was also remembered as a time when young boys were free to play without having to obey adult supervision and could build up street cred among their peers for their fighting skills. Memories of the Cultural Revolution thus evoked a jumble of emotions, including a sense of pleasure and pride in having been able to acquire local status, even if not in mainstream form.

Following the end of the Mao era, local people's narration of their lives traced increasing conditions of uncertainty as lack of education and dependable employment threatened their livelihoods. Had I had the opportunity to talk with them before they were laid off and pushed into dependency on the informal economy in the 1990s, they might have narrated their experiences in other terms. As it was, the themes and moments that structured their accounts of these years contrasted the potential benefits of greater consumer choice with the emphasis they gave scarcity, deprivation, and exclusion from the advantages that the market was bringing elsewhere. The key moment of rupture—the "turning point" of 1978—was no more prominent in their accounts of the post-Mao reform years than 1949 had been in their memories of the Mao era. Their silence about the historical significance of 1978 does not, of course, mean that they were unaware of its implications. They lived the gains others made from the market economy in the relentless noise and detritus of construction projects, in the glitzy reinvention of Qianmen dajie, and in the everyday constraints of existential uncertainty. Spatially, materially, socially, and affectively, they were forced to live with the demands of state-sponsored market reform and global capital in the form of chaiqian, whether they liked it or not.

The temporalities—the time frames—through which Dashalar residents narrated their lives thus shared little with the temporal stages of official history structured around the core notions of rupture and progress. The contrast between these different temporalities was also manifest in local people's use of language and terminology. Only rarely did I hear anyone use the terms of official discourse in describing their own lives, unless it was to voice a deep and potentially subversive cynicism, even despair, as when Zhang Yuanchen condemned the hypocrisy of the "harmonious society." Terms students of the history of the PRC might take for granted for their almost naturalized status in "campaign time" were simply absent. For example, the language of nannü pingdeng (gender equality) barely surfaced in any of my discussions with women or men who had grown up under Mao. With the exceptions of Old Mrs. Gao and Old Mrs. Zhao, all the other women I knew in Dashalar were beneficiaries of the CCP's policies of gender equality, enabling them to work and acquire an education as a matter of right, regardless of whether they made use of it. In their narratives, the absence of reference to gender equality as a marker of difference with the period before 1949 was thus striking. Equally striking was their silence about the benefits to poor people of market reform, given the overwhelming global media attention given to how China's post-Mao rise has successfully lifted huge numbers of the population out of poverty.

Beyond the specific content of the memory and the life story, therefore, the contrasting temporalities of different historiographical narratives themselves shed important light on the exclusions at work in what we come to understand as the authorized historical account.

Place

Dashalar's infrastructural stagnation over the past half century or so gave local lives a profound, literal, and affective attachment to place, even in circumstances in which the subjects of those lives, such as Jia Yong, no longer lived in the neighborhood. Such place-based attachments bear few echoes of the longings of the nostalgia industry that hankers after a notion of heritage best illustrated by the commercial reconstruction of "old Beijing." As we have seen, local people's attachment to the place of Dashalar was embedded, across generations, in complex social and emotional entanglements with family and neighborhood networks. It was also demarcated by the cramped physical spaces of the dazayuan that many, if not all, would have readily dispensed with had they been offered viable alternatives.

Dashalar, the place, defined the physical, spatial, and sensory qualities of the only social and emotional center of self-identification and recognition that many of my acquaintances knew. For these, never having left the neighborhood except for brief periods, Dashalar effectively became part of the self; to remove an individual from it could thus be imagined as an act of violence against the self, as Old Mrs. Gao's withdrawal from the social world, even from her family, indicated after she was moved from Dashalar. However, the desire to leave did not, in itself, indicate a denial of Dashalar's centrality in everyday life. On the contrary, the desire to leave could, for some at least, be seen as an affirmation of its centrality in everyday life. Meiling's desire to leave had to take a back seat for years while Dashalar compelled its physical presence in her life due to forces she was powerless to affect. Her response was to barricade herself in and surround herself with things and people who gave her a sense of dignity, self, and agency, thus enabling her to deal with the frustrations of her existence. The real possibility of moving began to filter into her resigned acceptance of her lot only during her brief reunion with her parents, after her mother's death, when she nursed her father through his last years. A filial daughter could anticipate inheriting some of her father's estate.

The remaking of Dashalar as "old Beijing" has involved successive stages of reinvention and the assertion of new boundaries between the elite and the local urban poor. My friends were acutely aware that the "old Beijing" being fashioned out of the popular cultural traditions of their neighborhood catered to interests far removed from their own lives, desires, and experiences. Indeed, the "heritage-ization" of Dashalar around the time of the Olympics confirmed the neighborhood's commercial reinvention as "old Beijing" as a strategy to attract external income, separating off local residents from the realistic possibility of asserting their historic claims to the neighborhood they grew up in and considered as theirs. Their derision at the formal opening of the refurbished Qianmen dajie in the summer of 2008 voiced the predictable responses of subalterns long accustomed to the predatory impositions of the state and market. In this, their responses could be summarized in terms that correspond with James Scott's, as a form of cultural resistance articulated through a noncooperation with the terms of dominance.[1]

Such derision, however, did not mean that Dashalar locals rejected the opportunity to make money out of the heritage reinvention of their neighborhood. If given the chance, they would willingly turn the new "old Beijing" to their advantage—as with pedicab cyclists conveying tourists through "old Beijing" hutong, taking advantage of foreigners' gullible impressionability to usher them into "old Beijing" houses where they would be given tea and told tales of hutong life, before being asked to make a donation to the host as a token of their appreciation. The pedicab cyclists would also introduce them to restaurants and eateries owned by their local connections, presumably for a fee.

On a different scale, and alongside his passion for recording the disappearing history of his "old Beijing," Jia Yong was professionally adept at turning the wave of "old Beijing" tourism to his benefit. The claims his restaurant made in tourist guide books rested not so much on the culinary appeal of its dishes as on its nostalgic atmosphere created by the black-and-white photographs lining its walls. The "old Beijing" of my acquaintances' self-identification was *both* a term of affection, familiarity, and nostalgia for a past certainty, however illusory that was, *and* an artifice initially created externally but available for commercial manipulation.

Affective attachment to place was thus not inconsistent with its instrumental status as a source of income, cultural and social capital, and, in Jia Yong's case, mobility. His attachment to Dashalar was additionally associated with his gratitude to his parents for having facilitated the development of his skills. Yet his residential detachment from Dashalar and his willingness to undertake projects that contributed more to the gentrification of Dashalar than to the interests of his down-at-heel neighbors demonstrate how attachment to place is not synonymous with maintaining physical and spatial ties with it. Indeed, it was Jia Yong's commitment to recording the neighborhood of his childhood in his photographs and the interior design of his restaurants that facilitated the possibility of his physical departure from it. To different degrees, both Jia Yong and Wang Wenli exemplified the apparent paradox of a deep emotional attachment to place and a complicity with the powers responsible for its destruction and replacement by a commercial heritage version of the Dashalar both knew. To put it more directly, the place that generated their income was disappearing in part under the impact of their own activities, hastening the material expiry of the spatial center of their affections.

At the same time, as long-term local residents were having to come to terms with their marginalization from a neighborhood they had long considered to be theirs, the arrival of large numbers of migrants since the 1990s further contributed to locals' sense of alienation in the place with which they were so familiar, implicitly deflecting their attention away from their frustrations with the state. The anger Dashalar locals frequently articulated toward migrants who worked the shops and restaurants of the neighborhood, alongside their willingness to make money out of them by renting rooms to them and so on, were classic responses to conditions of deprivation that find echoes in similar forms of discrimination way beyond the borders of Dashalar, and indeed beyond the borders of Beijing and China. Recent events in the United States and the United Kingdom, for example, give extensive evidence of how class, ethnic, and religious-based discrimination against the "outsider" can become a powerful mobilizer of political passions among some of the most disadvantaged of contemporary society. In the absence of media and political protection of the migrant laborer as a deserving citizen, vilification of the outsider could become a convenient local explanation for conditions of precarity and social disorder. It could also function as a means of reasserting a desire for rootedness and security in a ragingly uncertain world.

By 2017, most of the familiar places of local people's memories of Dashalar no longer survived. After a protracted, apparently haphazard, but inexorable process of encroachment and demolition, the bulldozers gradually retreated, leaving designer cafés, shops, and new commercial experiences in their wake. The distorted version of "old Beijing" that local people had seen taking shape in front of their eyes, and which they saw as a kind of assault on their sense of neighborhood belonging and ownership, finally took shape in a series of ultra-cool new small restaurants and shops vying for pride of place in the gentrified neighborhood.

Through the different stories of the people present in this book, the place of their neighborhood emerged as a resource of connectedness to a community of belonging, however illusory or nonexistent that community might be. In turn, this underpinned a desire for certainty to thwart the ravages of precarity and destitution. Fondly, sometimes nostalgically, rehearsed in naming the former temples and old streets, Dashalar was the repository of contradictory desires and experiences, metaphorically offering a lifeline sustaining the fragments of individual and family existences before they finally succumbed to the overwhelming power of capital and the state. In this, to draw on Erik Mueggler's description of a very different marginalized community light-years away from Beijing, Dashalar was a "place that, in being lived so intimately and known so well, offered its inhabitants abundant resources for engaging with the afflictions, uncertainties, and consolations of memory."[2]

Place thus was at the center of the affective lives and self-identifications of all those whose stories I tell in this book. Yet what place meant across their stories varied widely; there was an entire spectrum of meanings attached to it, from the literal and inescapable physical and social locus of everyday activities and relationships to a lucrative source of income permitting a kind of so-

Fig. C.1 Gentrified Dashalar, mid-2018. Courtesy of Luo Pan.

cial distinction and mobility detaching an individual from the neighborhood while retaining affective ties with it. Place, in this sense, doesn't stay still but is endlessly remade as a resource of emotional attachment and dignity.

Precarity and Exclusion

The individuals who feature in this book are some of Beijing's most disadvantaged and marginalized people. Throughout the years of my research in Dashalar, the main concerns framing their memories focused on the demands of survival and getting by in conditions of everyday precarity. They drew on the past not as a repository of all that was "backward" and in need of transformation, as dominant discourse would have it, but rather as a source of explanation for the difficult conditions they lived in the present, read back into the past. This past also legitimated their claims for ethical recognition as social subjects that the bigger, external world of political and economic power consistently denied them.

Most of the stories I have narrated outline poor people's efforts to assert their place in the only world they knew as it faced its final death throes. After long decades of enduring hardship in a turbulent political environment, their constant reiteration of basic everyday concerns about how to keep going in intensifying conditions of uncertainty conveyed an existential struggle to link the past with the present, and in some cases the future, through reference to children.

While each of their stories possesses the singularity of individual family circumstance and history, together they also reveal certain commonalities of experience. The 1950s through 1960s emerge as years of extreme hardship, experienced as neglect and abandonment and exacerbated by political/class categorization and social ostracism that in one case reached the point of near destitution. The massive relocation during these decades of other long-term local residents of Beijing from their hutong neighborhoods under the program to construct vast new industrial and professional work unit compounds would suggest that this experience was probably far from unique to Dashalar. Indeed, the 1950s was a period of material constraint for most of the urban working class, let alone the rural population. Nevertheless, the features that made Dashalar distinctive—the relative poverty of its district government and the density, mix, and mobility of its population—established a specific and enduring relationship between the neighborhood and the state according to which the state, in the form of the local government, repeatedly went back on or had to revise its plans about neighborhood improvements.

Added to the constraints and anxieties of material uncertainties were physical debarments that became spectacularly apparent in the accelerated pace of neighborhood regeneration around the time of the 2008 Olympics. These were not unintended exclusions but deliberate debarments, as Dashalar residents and pedicab cyclists were barred from access to their local subway station for many weeks as the capital prepared for the Olympics. They were also prohibited from leaving their homes during the National Day celebrations in 2009. Alongside such direct injunctions were the implicit prohibitions of activities and behaviors deemed unsuitable for the global consumer culture taking shape in the new shops and restaurants around the neighborhood. The gentrification of the small streets around West Street signaled new spaces welcoming an unfamiliar social elite, establishing yet more boundaries for the exclusion of the long-term local population. Indeed, in spatial terms, the proximity of Dashalar's West Street to the global dazzle of the rebuilt Qianmen dajie inscribes the discursive rupture between the Mao and post-Mao eras with evidence not of the enriching effects of marketization, as standard commentary would have it, but rather of the social exclusions of urban subalterns as a condition of the global commercialization of the capital's economy.

Family, State, and Expectations of Gender

The world described in this book, of people living in the crowded houses and narrow alleys of their neighborhood, has almost entirely disappeared. Recording memories of that world, therefore, is more than a historical project of bringing hitherto hidden experiences to light. For the historical record, what these stories reveal is that despite the centrality of the state shaping the conditions of their lives going back to 1949, through its decisions concerning housing, employment, and education, and despite the party-state's attempts enacted in various laws to shift individual subjects' focus of loyalties away from the family and household and toward the collective and the state, the family remained the bedrock of individual passions. Decisions about everyday social activities—what job to look for, what to cook and how much to pay for it, how to juggle the pressures of employment with the care of children and the elderly—entailed a bodily interaction between the individual, place, and space in conditions of relentless scarcity and uncertainty. Regardless of local differences of generation and gender, family and household stood out as the single most important site—spatial, physical, affective, and ethical—of individual loyalties and passions.

By contrast, with few exceptions, the state generally figured in the narratives of neighborhood life as a potentially ominous force lurking in the foreboding realms "above" (*shangmian*). Neither a system of institutions or laws nor an observable structure beyond the offices of the street committee, the state loomed as an aspect of a kind of social imaginary. The agencies representing the state ranged from obscurity, negligence, and apparent absence to out and out physical violence and psychological abuse, mostly perpetrated by the local patrol officers and policemen. But imagining the state as a portentous agent "above" did not make it external to the embodied concerns of daily life. It penetrated the interiority of the dazayuan in the form of the ordering (or disordering) of space; in the anxieties, struggles, and family disputes over residential security; in fundamental concerns about health and hunger; in despairing anger; in abject resignation to "fate"; and, very occasionally, in explicit protest. In extreme but by no means exceptional cases, as we have seen, it attacked the bodies as well as the minds of its subjects. In this sense, the state was a profoundly constitutive force at the heart of local people's social, bodily, and affective lives.[3] It was thus intimately terrifying in the extent of its powers.

However, the customary social and spatial distance between my acquaintances and the institutions and personnel of state facilitated exchanges, jokes, and frequently critical comments about "the system" that I have rarely come across in such concentrated form among other groups of people I have known well in Beijing. Between their very basic school education and their largely un-skilled jobs outside the standard work unit, few of the people I knew in Dasha-lar had ever found themselves in social or employment situations in which they could be interpellated as subjects of the state in the form represented in state discourse. On the contrary, their use of language and their everyday comings and goings, their cultural activities and social exchanges, suggested a desire to evade or ignore the involvement of state power in their lives, along-side their concentrated focus on the immediate issues of everyday existence.

The resilience of the family and household as the main focus of individual concerns was not synonymous with unchanging gender practices. Indeed, at the heart of the changes poor people in Dashalar have experienced over the past half century or so are gender practices and relations. Young women and men growing up in Dashalar today have potential access to opportunities for mobility, consumption, education, employment, and online networking that open up new horizons of imagination and desire and thus position them as gendered subjects who share little with their parents' and grandparents' gen-erations. At the same time, across the generations, gender practices and rela-tions echoed attitudes and assumptions that seemed oddly resistant to change and, on the contrary, were productive of activities and identifications that can be summarized as a form of reconfigured patriarchy.[4]

For women of Old Mrs. Gao's generation, class background, education, and short-term, gendered jobs under a piecework type system of largely un-skilled labor coordinated by the neighborhood committee—folding paper into pages for use in book making, washing and mending clothes, making shoes and matchboxes—were not acknowledged as social labor in the formal wage system of the state work units. The women engaged in such activities were still officially categorized as "housewife" (jiating funü) or "dependent" (jiashu). But for women of her daughter-in-law's generation, remaining a dependent "housewife" was not an option, although it was to become so through the 1980s for increasing numbers of upwardly mobile and middle-class women. Most women and men who grew up under Mao's banner worked in full-time jobs, allocated by the state, in a range of local manufacturing and repair opera-tions. The middle-aged women and men I knew in Dashalar grew up in a social and cultural environment in which they understood that as adults they would have no choice but to join the labor force, both to bring in an income and because, under the system of state allocation of jobs, not working was not an op-tion. They also understood that without access to more than a basic education, and without social connections to help them find good jobs, being employed was the necessary means to material survival; it had nothing to do with even basic enjoyment, let alone creative self-fulfillment. It was through these jobs that most of them met their future spouses.

Evident gender differences in type of employment and income-generating capacity began to reassert themselves with a vengeance in the late 1980s, and particularly after the mid 1990s, when, along with many other workers in Beijing and elsewhere, a number of my acquaintances were laid off as unprofitable factories went under. By the time I started my research in Dashalar, the commercialization of the market and labor was making its mark on local people in evidently gendered ways, notably in a reassertion of a division of labor that harked back to practices prior to the Mao era and joined forces with practices shaped by the global capitalist economy. In what was a clear tendency toward the feminization of labor in the service industry, more women became employed in low-paid casual jobs such as cleaning floors and washing up in restaurants. They were also more involved in domestic work and caring for elderly or infirm individuals.

There was also a difference in how women and men spoke about their jobs. The women were invariably more vociferous than their husbands in claiming recognition for their efforts as wage earners and domestic carers. They rarely complained, overtly, about the pressures they had to endure, but Young Gao's wife's barely veiled comments about her husband's failure to pull his weight and Zhao Yong's wife's fantasies of life in Hong Kong indicated that their reticence masked all sorts of tensions and desires to which I was not privy. In contrast, the men were less forthcoming about their jobs. Young Gao was ashamed of not being able to do what a man should, by rights, do; Zhao Yong chose not to talk about his "business affairs" in my presence; and the Old Professor focused particularly on his cultural authority by demonstrating his knowledge of local history and skill as a calligrapher.

Despite their status as main contributors to the household budget, women seemed accustomed to being put down by their husbands, who not infrequently told them that they were stupid and didn't understanding anything. In my presence, at least, women's attempts to resist their husbands' scorn generally ended in their apparent deferral to their husbands. Initially I found this perplexing because it pointed to a major contradiction with their feisty assertion of independence as wage earners. The reasons for this became clearer the better I got to know them. Even so, I still had to make sense of what to me remained puzzling. Instrumental considerations were blended into what I think of as a kind of bodily and emotional attachment to ideas about the correct gendered order of things. For Qian to confront Zhao Yong would have been to challenge the only source of authority and dignity in his social world that he could claim for himself. In return for respect of this authority, Qian obtained a basic material and emotional security for both herself and her daughter. For Xiao Xi, deference to her husband, despite his inadequacies, and filial care of her mother-in-law contained an aim to secure her own residential and material security after her mother-in-law's death. For both women, folded into their material self-interest was also an ethical sense of self, as wife and daughter-in-law of the "men's family." While both women well recognized the imbalance between themselves and their husbands as regards to what they did and what they could say, the boundaries of their gendered worlds still prioritized male interests over their own. Their ideological outlook and sense of moral duty did not allow them to threaten those interests in order to further their own.

For me, the outside observer, these apparent contradictions presented a paradox: on the one hand, a stringent and, in Meiling's case, fiercely asserted, claim to independence, and on the other, inconsistent attachments to conservative ideas about male authority. While the notion of male authority was tinged with criticism, the assumption that male support offered possibilities of welfare and protection not available from other sources was unmistakably transmitted to Meiling's daughter. Elsewhere, I have called this a kind of "patchy patriarchy," an uneven reconfiguration of ideas and practices centering on, though not limited to, assumptions about marriage, reproduction, family, kinship, and female virtue, ordered by an inextricable mix of culturally familiar gendered and generational obligations.[5] Despite reformulations over the past half century or so, these have proved resilient to radical change.

Steven Sangren has argued that Chinese patriliny can be understood as an "instituted fantasy" produced through individual desire and collective practice. While its effects manifest differently in women and men, it describes a desire in the individual for "autonomy, self-productivity or ... agency"—or imagining "being the author of one's own being."[6] Hence in women it may manifest itself, as we have seen, in assertions of determined independence, while in men, notably Zhao Yong, in an appropriation of the claims to masculine authority implicitly inherited from the father figure through obligations of filiality and reproduced in his expectations of his female subordinates. Both, in different ways, contribute to reproducing a reconfigured patriarchal social order. The notion of women's agency in this process may be conceptualized more as inhabiting conservative norms than embracing liberatory goals.[7]

Nevertheless, while the "instituted fantasy" of a reconfigured patriarchy continues to be produced through the desires and fantasies of my older and middle-aged acquaintances, evidence from the younger generation—their children's generation—suggests the radical *and* catastrophic effects of resistance to the expectations inscribed in unchallenged desires to reproduce the patrilineal order. The single most prominent expression of this I came across during my research was the decision by Li Fuying's son not to go along with his parent's expectations of filial reciprocity. Seen from his aging parents' perspective, what they saw as their daughter-in-law's refusal to let them care for their grandson was an assault on their understanding and expectation of filial care and respect. Their son was clearly conflicted, rushing between his parents and me in the living room and his young wife and baby in the adjacent bedroom. From his wife's perspective, however she explained it to herself, she was objectively asserting her desire to look after her baby as *she* decided. When the father's desires for a filial heir clashed with the desires of the newly married son to forge a different kind of life to that to which his father aspired for him, the consequence for the father was heartbreaking despair.

Persecution, Class, and Human Rights

Published narratives of experiences of the Mao era, and particularly the Cultural Revolution, focus on the educated urban elite of cadres, intellectuals, professionals, and students, those for whom there are archival and biographical records of persecution and death, years spent in cadre schools and labor camps, and in the countryside as "sent-down youth." It is through the "victim literature" and its concerns with the suffering perpetrated on the nation's educated elite that the Mao era is best known both to Western audiences and to younger generations in China. In this, moreover, there is a frequent slippage between the Mao era and the Cultural Revolution, such that the Cultural Revolution effectively becomes synonymous with the Mao era as a whole.[8] The forgetting and simplification of the different stages and experiences of the Mao era in official historiography reproduces this slippage.

The urban subalterns such as those whose stories I have narrated here—the street vendor of Buddhist trinkets, the garbage collector, the public lavatory cleaner, the illiterate "housewife" and member of the household-based production group—made no claims to a privileged victimhood. They did not have any noticeable social or political stakes in debates about the legacy of the Mao era, nor did they have the educational skills or social capital to record their own, or their families', experiences. The only partial exception to this was Jia Yong. The memories of my narrators, all long-term residents of Dashalar, covered experiences of physical violence, family rupture, and local factionalism that were not at first glance totally dissimilar to those of the educated urban elite. In contrast, however, they construed the Cultural Revolution not as the tragic years of a "state of exception," as official discourse implies, but as one moment, albeit distinctive in its particularities, in a bigger history of uncertainty, neglect, and hardship predating and following the Cultural Revolution years.

That social and political disadvantage was an effect of class backgrounds inherited from previous generations was explicit in Zhao Yong's story; it may also, in part at least, have explained the local disdain he and his family had to endure. Political persecution also featured in Zhang Huiming's family history, although she did not share this with me. None of those I knew in the neighborhood sought public recognition of their suffering; the only instance of overt forms of protest that I came across there was the small handwritten petition displayed in an alley by the elderly relatives of Meiling's mother-in-law. Rather it was through interpersonal transmission of memories that the family tensions and everyday wretchedness of living with the effects of persecution and long-term precarity became apparent. From this perspective, the particular difficulties and demands of the Cultural Revolution emerged not in black-and-white terms as the worst and most tragic event of local people's lives, responsible for the political persecution and suffering of entire families, as mainstream historiography of the Mao era would have it, but as one singular episode, sandwiched within a longer history of relentless adversity and oppression. In this light, then, the Cultural Revolution confirmed the already disadvantaged status of local residents, inherited from the 1950s and sustained in different forms throughout subsequent decades, on into the polarizing effects of market reform in the 1990s and beyond. By contrast, the educated elite's access to connections and mobility enabled them to recover from the devastations of the Cultural Revolution.

Move the clock forward to the era of the full-blown commercialization of the economy, and the Cultural Revolution becomes even less like a "state of exception." Continuing narratives of state violence and the violation of rights—producing despairing and sometimes misplaced responses of injustice, hopeless rage, desires to hold people to account, and fantasies of revenge—repeatedly surfaced in my acquaintances' accounts. Zhang Yuanchen's despair was unambiguous when she told one of the policemen beating up her husband to kill her instead: "Just kill *me*! How would I survive if my husband is dead?"

Recognition and Agency

A major reason explaining my acquaintances' willingness to share their stories with me was because my interest in their lives signified a recognition of them as human subjects in a world that consistently withheld from them all that the desire for recognition implies: respect, consideration, and justice. Long years of having been denied even the basics of human respect occasionally exploded in rage and despair: in Meiling's vociferous claims to virtue, in Zhao Yong's loud accusations against the police for infringing on his human rights after a minor traffic offense, or in Li Fuying's tortured memories of police brutality, forcible separation from his wife, and finally his despair when having to face his son's decision to lead his life in ways that clashed with his sense of self as apparent in his hopes and expectations.

Interpreted through the lens of agency, these people's narrations of their experiences, memories, and longings can be thought of as expressions of desires to assert a kind of authority in their lives. Agency here appears not as a "synonym for resistance to relations of domination," as Saba Mahmood put it, but rather as a form of struggle on the part of disadvantaged people to claim a dignity in an environment that, objectively, denied it to them.[9] Understood in these terms, the expression of agency can be conceptualized as a search for recognition.

To outward appearances, Young Gao had given up hoping for recognition of any sort several years before he died. Yet one event before his death made it clear that he harbored a desire for dignity and authority in different terms. This was his daughter's marriage, which, as Young Gao described it, and as the photographs would suggest, was a highly ritualized event, carefully stage-managed to ensure proper procedure, as Young Gao understood it. He was determined to go to virtually any expense to show the world that he could hold his head high when the occasion demanded. His funeral was also a highly ritualized occasion, with professional pallbearers in full military regalia leading the procession, a band playing the funeral dirge, a military salute, and a fulsome display of big funeral wreaths. It was as if, having died a premature death, after a life of what Young Gao himself considered to be repeated failures, his family and neighborhood decided to send him off in full style, redeeming a dignity and recognition denied him during his life.

If such a search for recognition manifested a redemptive quality, it was also gendered in various ways: in Old Mrs. Gao's implicit claims to righteousness for having kept her family going through decades of hardship; in Zhao Yong's impassioned assertions of his personal philosophy, centering on his commitment to fulfill his filial and family obligations; and in Meiling's equally impassioned self-production as a virtuous mother. In contrast, Young Gao's abjection was rooted in what he considered to be his inadequacies as a son and husband, and therefore his inability to claim recognition. Li Fuying's despair voiced the deep wound to his sense of self as man and father inflicted by the failure of his expectations of his son's filial reciprocity.

In some of my relationships with Dashalar residents, the desire for recognition was unquestionably more important an impulse than the expectation of or desire for some kind of instrumental exchange. This was particularly the case for people whose depleted resources left them with virtually nothing except, in the most notable case, anguished grief. For Li Fuying and his wife, my presence and support signified recognition of their difficulties and their pain, at a moment when no one else seemed to be around to offer any comfort. Ultimately, I think they saw my attempts to understand them and my recognition of their grief as offering the hope of repair.

By "recognition" I am not referring either to a fixed notion of the human subject nor to concepts derived from identity politics that couple injury to the sense of self or the related group with misrecognition of identity. Rather, following Nancy Fraser, I mean a kind of recognition that contrasts with the customary depreciation experienced by the interlocutor, subordinating her to the impossibility of participating in social life as an equal of others. This is a kind of ethical recognition that acknowledges the subject's performance of personhood as that of a full partner in social interaction, regardless of her positioning in the hierarchies of local society and the political economy.[10]

Over the years I knew him, Li gave me repeated and detailed accounts of past experiences of suffering and despair without any indication of expecting anything in return. The only time he asked anything of me was, after many years knowing him, to help out with his son at a time of extreme distress. Far from wanting anything from me in material terms, I came to realize, Li and his wife treasured a sense of emotional comfort rooted in the recognition of their personhood that my visits seemed to give them.

The pleasure of recognition—of being recognized—was not incompatible with other, more instrumental interests. While the most obvious of these took financial form, in other instances it was more directly and simply associated with face. My presence alongside Zhao Yong, on an occasion when he probably knew he might be publicly disdained, could give evidence that he enjoyed a connection with a privileged foreigner, and thus could make claims to a social capital that the others on this occasion did not possess.

The world of my Dashalar acquaintances, living in the crowded houses and narrow alleys of their neighborhood, has all but totally disappeared. Recording memories of that world, therefore, is more than a historical project of bringing hitherto hidden experiences to light. Oral historians have long noted the enthusiasm, sense of release, and even catharsis that their interviewees bring to sharing their stories. My Dashalar friends were no exception to this, and as I got to know them better, I felt that their willingness, and in some cases evident pleasure, to talk with me, often at great length, conveyed a desire to be recognized as subjects of their own histories. Indeed, the deep sadness many of them demonstrated when they heard of Zhao Tielin's death was accompanied by an explicit regret that he would no longer be around to record and give public recognition to their lives. The people whose stories I tell in this book are fully aware that they have never appeared as people who count, either in the historical record or in the party-state's urban strategies. "They've never cared about us," "All they do is look down on us," and "They think we are the dregs of society" were some of the phrases they used to refer to the status attributed to them by the authorities. The space of articulation of memory that the oral historian offers the marginalized and disadvantaged, such as the long-term residents of Dashalar, thus invites a redemptive retrieval of the past as a claim for recognition after long decades of neglect, culminating now in demolition and relocation. My project can thus be understood as an ethical as much as a historical task of recognition. It constitutes an attempt to return to a subaltern people the recognition and authority they used to associate with belonging to a particular place, and gives evidence of recognition of the subaltern as constituting a subject position both worthy of being narrated and—at least partially—possible to narrate.

On January 13, 2019, the Planning Committee of Beijing's municipal government issued a communication about the imminent demolition of the capital's still-remaining "historic core areas," including Dashalar, involving the removal of another hundred thousand residents from their single-story buildings. According to the communication, residents were encouraged to give up their dwellings voluntarily in exchange for flats and monetary compensation.

In late March, friends in Beijing sent me photographs of the frontage of Jia Yong's main restaurant on Guanyin Temple Street—doors padlocked and chained, windows papered over, displaying a sign saying, "Historic building [*wenwu*] evacuated and returned to [*tengtui*] West District," and stamped with a large red "closed" character—along with other photographs of rebuilt and repaved lanes and alleys outside Meiling's dazayuan, and plans and diagrams for the reconstruction of the rest of the neighborhood. Meiling had left the neighborhood, without compensation, after hospitalization for a heart attack.

Preface

1   This literal translation of the term also distinguishes these low-rise structures from the dominant associations of the term "tenement" with the high-rise buildings of New York or Glasgow and of the term "slums" with their largely sprawling suburban location in Mumbai or Mexico City, for example.

Introduction

1   In 2003, Ye Guozhu was forcibly evicted from his home in Beijing to make way for Olympic Games construction projects. Soon after seeking permission in August 2004 to hold a march for other evictees in September of that year, during the annual meeting of the Communist Party Central Committee, he was arrested on "suspicion of disturbing social order" and sentenced to four years in prison. Human Rights Watch, "China's Rights Defenders."

2   Following a fire that broke out on November 18, 2017, in a three-story apartment block in Daxing district in southern Beijing, killing nineteen migrant workers, municipal authorities launched a massive campaign to evict all "low-end" (*diduan*)—migrants from the capital. Replacing the earlier discursive disdain of all migrants as dirty and uneducated, this new, derogatory term distinguishes the "outsiders" who have benefitted from market reform to become members of the property-owning middle class from those at the bottom end of the social scale, whose presence is deemed to sully the sparkling appearance of global Beijing.

3   In using the term "underclass," I do not subscribe to any particular sociological theory, let alone politically inflected theories that use the term for purposes of moral judgment. Nevertheless, as a term referring to a social sector at the bottom of the class hierarchy that is structurally integrated as a casualized service population into the high-tech economy of the capital, it is useful as a descriptive term. Thanks to Steve Smith for helping clarify this issue. Michael Meyer's *The Last Days of Old Beijing* is particularly relevant to my study. Based on several years living in Dashalar, where the author was a volunteer teacher of English in a local school, this is a closely observed description of the effects of market reform on everyday life in the neighborhood around the time of the Olympics. Qin Shao's *Shanghai Gone* is a detailed analysis of local protests against demolition. Part family memoir, part oral history of alleyway households in Shanghai, Jie Li's *Shanghai Homes* offers a bottom-up view of neighborhood life since the 1950s. For earlier periods, David Strand's *Rickshaw Beijing* narrates the lives of the urban poor in the 1920s. Hanchao Lu's *Beyond the Neon Lights* turns to how ordinary people in the alleys of Shanghai

coped with the upheavals of war and revolution. Madeleine Yue Dong's *Republican Beijing* examines the relations between popular practices of entertainment, consumption, trading, and the state, and argues that these reveal a complex intermingling of past and future, linked by a nostalgic desire for the past as an outline for the city of the future. Zhao Ma's *Runaway Wives* examines low-class women's everyday strategies to survive appalling conditions of poverty, destitution, and violence. Janet Chen's *Guilty of Indigence* turns to the homeless in Beijing and Shanghai in the first half of the twentieth century, detailing their attempts to evade eviction as well as their precarious existence, living in coffin repositories and cemeteries. More recently, in *Traffickers and Family Life in North China*, Johanna Ransmeier examines trafficking, particularly of women and children, between the late Qing and early Republican periods and argues that far from being a symptom of periodic crises of poverty and destitution, a range of transactional practices involving the exchange of people, money, and goods was fundamental to the system of domestic and reproductive labor.

4   Salaff, "Urban Communities."

5   Recalling his earliest childhood memories of Tian'anmen, Wu Hung's description of the spatial and architectural patchwork of Beijing in 1955 is telling. His father's work unit, he writes, "had just moved from central Beijing to a place in the western suburbs called Zhongguancun, where an entire City of Learning was being constructed, amid cornfields and local graveyards, to house China's Academy of Sciences, to which my father's institute belonged. My new school was in an abandoned Buddhist temple, with ruined but still colourful statues of arhats and heavenly kings lined up against the walls of the only classroom." Wu Hung, *Remaking Beijing*, 21–22.

6   For a detailed account of this conflict, covering the main political, design, administrative, and governance issues, see Wang Jun, *Cheng ji*.

7   The single-story dazayuan is a building that retained the outer walls of the original courtyard but which since the late nineteenth century had been filled in with shacklike structures to accommodate the capital's growing and impoverished population. The term is variously translated as "compound courtyard," "big messy courtyard," "big, mixed courtyard," "tenements," or "slums." I use Wu Liangyong's "big cluttered courtyard," from his *Rehabilitating the Old City of Beijing*, out of respect for an architect who designed a model for the conversion of Beijing's dazayuan into modernized structures that retained a feel of the traditional courtyard.

8   I do not have evidence of the numbers of local residents whose decision to leave was the effect of heavy pressure if not outright coercion, but Ou Ning's documentary film *Meishi jie* highlights the methods not infrequently used in the early stages of the neighborhood's reconstruction.

9   For a collection of papers analyzing China's transition from one of the most egalitarian societies in the world to one of the most unequal, see Kuruvilla et al., *Iron Rice Bowl*.

10 Hershatter, *Gender of Memory*, 22.

11 Hsing, *Great Urban Transformation*, 108–11. This book is a compelling analysis of the massive shift in China's urban economic strategy signified by the politics of land ownership and property development in recent years, and explains the logic of the state's strategy of chaiqian.

12 Maurice Halbwachs, *On Collective Memory*, quoted in Wachtel, "Introduction," 211–12.

13 Feuchtwang, *After the Event*, 14.

14 Feuchtwang, *After the Event*, 14.

15 Frisch, *Shared Authority*, 188.

16 The classic article here is Gayatri Spivak's "Can the Subaltern Speak?," originally published in 1988, when Spivak argued that the non-Western, female other is unknowable within the discursive language and practices of colonial and postcolonial regimes.

17 Prakash, "Impossibility of Subaltern History," 268, emphasis mine.

18 The term *shehui diceng* (social underclass) used by Chinese sociologists, is now so prevalent in media and official discourse that from time to time my interlocutors in Dashalar used it as a term of self-description.

19 Hershatter, *Gender of Memory*, 27. Xuanwu District was integrated into an enlarged "East District" (Dong qu) in 2011, as part of an administrative remapping of central Beijing, and announced as part of an effort to bring greater prosperity to Xuanwu. As with other official archives in Beijing, the Xuanwu District materials were organized hierarchically and according to political, departmental, and administrative distinctions. The main categories I concentrated on were health and hygiene, housing, education, commerce, the labor union, the Women's Federation, and Dashalar.

20 Ye and Esherick, *Chinese Archives*, 75.

21 Implemented in 1951, the Three Antis (against corruption, waste, and bureaucracy) mainly targeted party members, former members of the Guomindang, and bureaucrats. The Five Antis, launched in 1952, was much broader since it was directed toward private entrepreneurs and businesses throughout the country as a preparatory stage of the new government's attempts to eradicate the bourgeoisie and capitalism. Attacking bribery, theft of state property, tax evasion, cheating on government contracts, and stealing state economic information, the campaign encouraged activists to report on local business activities. It resulted in numerous arrests, incarceration in labor camps, and possibly executions, although in the absence of any accurate figures, it is impossible to make a correct estimate of the numbers involved.

22 I acknowledge that as a foreign researcher I may not have enjoyed the same access to sensitive archival material that Chinese scholars might have had at the time. However, Chinese scholars' access to archival material cannot be guaranteed since it depends on discipline, place, and the political sensitivity of their topic.

23 XWDG, 13-2-129 (March 1, 1973), 16–17.

24 XWDG, 16-1-1 (August 31, 1962), 1–8.

25 XWDG, 16-1-1 (November 30, 1962), 92–95.

26 XWDG, 13-2-156 (January–May, 1965), 1–10.

27 XWDG 13-1-34 (May 5, 1961), 4.

28 XWDG 13-1-34 (May 5, 1961), 4.

29 XWDG, 13-2-6, (September 25, 1959).

30 Scott, *Seeing Like a State*, 346.

31 This comment does not imply a generalization about the success or failure of the state's attempts to constitute other disadvantaged peoples as its subjects. Indeed, elsewhere, in rural and urban areas, the party-state was extremely successful in transforming subalterns into its willing subjects. While without having conducted a comparative analysis of the history of other hutong neighborhoods of Beijing, I cannot comment accurately on the specificity of Dashalar's history, it is worth pointing out that Zhao Tielin repeatedly emphasized that Dashalar's recent history affords a microcosmic view of urban life and change, encapsulating the entire range of issues confronting urban reconstruction since the early days of the PRC.

32 Thompson, *Voice of the Past*, 99.

33 See, in particular, Yang, *Mubei*.

34 Weller, "Salvaging Silence," argues that, by definition, silence cannot be pinned down to any single meaning.

35 Scott, *Domination*.

36 Hall, "When Was 'the Post-colonial'?"

37 The anthropologist Michael Lambek has long argued that ethics is a part of the human condition, manifest in tendencies to evaluate the ethical consequences of speaking and acting; it is "ordinary" and tacitly embedded in everyday practice, without calling attention to itself. Lambek, *Ordinary Ethics*.

38 Human Rights Watch, "Demolished."

39 A report authored by Beijing's leading social science research institute, The Chinese Academy of Social Sciences, noted that while the combination of poor environmental conditions, old housing stock, inadequate infrastructure, low per capita incomes, an aging local population, and increasing numbers of migrants featured in Xuanwu District as a whole, they were particularly acute in Dashalar. See Zhu, *Beijing chengqu*, 77.

40 Mainstream reporting of much of the chaiqian work around Dashalar was tightly controlled, and as the pace accelerated to complete reconstruction of Qianmen dajie before the Olympics opened in 2008, photographers and journalists were not allowed into the demolition sites to record the ongoing work. Government sensitivity was significantly due to the widespread international reporting of the extent of forced evictions and resulting local protests. While China's 2001 ratification of the UN's International Covenant on Economic, Social and Cultural Rights prohibited forced evictions, the Chinese state's ownership of land permitted the expropriation of urban land for the purpose of supporting the "public interest," a vague concept which nevertheless could legitimize the state's decisions on "eviction." The Chinese legislature finally implemented a new law in 2012 limiting the use of violence in forced evictions, outlawing the clearing of property at night and

during holidays, and allowing the use of violent law enforcement measures only in "emergencies." Hogg, "China Law to Limit Home Demolitions and Evictions."

41 Zhao Tielin died on May 16, 2009, without finishing his volume on Dashalar, which he provisionally called *Lao Beijing hua chengnan* (Tales of old Beijing's South City). Attempts to publish his work posthumously came to nothing. Some of his photographs are available on the English-language website https://zhaotielin .photoshelter.com/portfolio/GooooemxvRZocQhE, accessed November 25, 2018.

42 Despite anthropologists' common experience of such discomfort, it is difficult to find ethnographies that discuss the effects on the researcher of this imbalance in the research relationship. The anthropologist Erik Mueggler discusses his intense unease, even guilt, when reflecting on a fieldwork encounter with a Lolopo man in north-central Yunnan, which involved the payment of money. Mueggler, *Songs for Dead Parents*, 167–92. I refer to Mueggler's experience not because it is similar to mine, but for its rare, straightforward revelation of the kind of disquiet that fieldwork encounters can produce.

43 These observations beg many questions about the meaning of consent. Obtaining informants' consent is the first major ethical principle of all anthropological research. However, what general consent means, in circumstances when the informants have no access to understanding what the researcher does with the information obtained, is another issue. The ethical implications of this are a matter for another discussion.

44 Ou, *Meishi jie.*

45 Jie Li described almost identical approaches, along with the complex motives involved in individuals' decision to hold out in their nail houses, in *Shanghai Homes*, 195–98; 202–8. "Nail house" is a term applied to the dwellings of residents who refuse to vacate their home, despite local orders to do so. Relevant images prominently feature a lone house standing in the middle of a construction zone.

46 Shao, *Shanghai Gone.* While in the pages that follow I make reference to singular, individual efforts to contest local government demolition orders, analysis of the reasons explaining the lack of collective protest in Dashalar, in contrast to the adjacent neighborhood of Chaoyang, has to be left for others to research.

47 The writer Ba Jin famously called for the establishment of a memorial Cultural Revolution Museum "to testify what took place on this Chinese soil twenty years ago." Jie Li's forthcoming book *Utopian Ruins* takes up Ba Jin's invitation and offers a narrative exploration of film, police records, and architectural and material ruins as an example of what such a museum could be.

48 Mann, *Talented Women*, xvi. This "solution" initially emerged from conversations with Rebecca Karl. My final decision to include the "interludes" was inspired by conversations with Gail Hershatter and her PhD students in UCSC in November 2017. I thank all these for pushing me to think outside the box about Susan Mann's book.

49 Mann summarizes the critical narrative style of the great Han historian Sima Qian as a practice of keeping separate his "lively historical narratives and his personal judgments" (xvi).

Chapter 1. Dashalar

1   Inequalities have grown rapidly in the last three decades under the effects of widening urban-rural differentials and rapid urban income growth from private assets and wealth, and the current high levels of inequality in China both in comparison with the past and with other countries in similar stages of development have been widely noted, though conservatively estimated in official Chinese figures. Yu and Xiang, "Income Inequality in Today's China." See also Li and Sicular, "Distribution of Household Income."

2   The "Resolution on certain questions in the history of our party since the founding of the People's Republic of China," adopted by the Sixth Plenary Session of the Eleventh Central Committee of the Communist Party of China on June 27, 1981, was the first official evaluation of the achievements and shortcomings of the Mao era, publicly disseminated by the immediate post-Mao government led by Deng Xiaoping. Its basic periodization of the history of the People's Republic of China (PRC) revolves around the "turning point" (*zhuanzhedian*) of 1978, which marked a decisive departure from the collectively oriented policies of the previous Mao era. The attribution of a radical shift dating back to 1978 has remained a key principle of the official historiography of the PRC. Backed up by the official occlusion of the Mao years from current critical debate in China, the assumption of a rupture between the Mao era and subsequent periods has so dominated media and academic commentary on China that it has entered the realms of "common knowledge" about China.

3   Strand, *Rickshaw Beijing*.

4   In a March 2004 Human Rights Watch report, "Demolished," noted that while online protest against demolitions and forced evictions was tolerated to a certain extent, the rising tide of residents' petitioning against such moves was met with outright suppression, with the arrest and imprisonment of tenants' rights activists.

5   Zhu, *Beijing chengqu*, 77.

6   The *ba da hutong* is a term still commonly used by local residents to describe their neighborhood. The term itself refers to the eight main lanes of the neighborhood's red light district before 1949. The term "Nan cheng" (South City) is widely used as a metaphor for Beijing's "traditional" popular culture as narrated in Lao She's famous novel *Rickshaw Boy*, first published in 1937.

7   Arguably the most famous name associated with Dashalar in modern times is the extraordinary opera singer Mei Lanfang (1894–1961), widely known as one of the greatest female lead (*dan*) actors of Peking opera. For a fascinating queer analysis of how his portraits and bodily gestures transgressed standard gender boundaries, see Zou, "Cross-Dressed Nation."

8   Zhu, *Beijing chengqu*, 77.

9   Zhu, *Beijing chengqu*, 13.

10 Zhu, *Beijing chengqu*, 77.

11 Zhu, *Beijing chengqu*, 13.

12 A tourist website introduces "Dashilar Street" as "famous for all kinds of stores with an antique flavor," and states, "Many people come here to experience the relics of historic wealth." The website goes on to note that the "famous Nei Lian

Sheng shoe store was put on the list of State-Level Intangible Cultural Heritage in 2008. . . . The headquarters is at No. 34 Dashilar Street. At first, this store made only court boots. Shoes here are still popular today not only because they are made by hand, but also because they are comfortable and healthy to wear. . . . Some visitors buy them as a souvenir." "Dashilar Street," Travel China Guide, August 31, 2018, https://www.travelchinaguide.com/attraction/beijing/dashilan-street.htm.

13 The term used to refer to the famous old stores is *lao zihao* (traditional brands). The famous Chinese medicine store in Dashalar, Tong Ren Tang, is now a global brand, with at least one branch in London as well as other cities in Europe and the United States.

14 The gray bricks of the Republican-style facades in Dashalar are, in fact, not bricks at all but a thin brick veneer, of such poor quality that it started crumbling within months of having been installed. The term "faux-Republican," which is sometimes used in commentary to describe the style of the refurbished street, is thus appropriate in more ways than one. For a study of the role and status of native-place lodges in Beijing before they were condemned as "feudal remnants" by the new government in 1949, see Belsky, *Localities at the Center*.

15 This was Ou Ning's description of the street in a lecture and presentation in 2008 hosted by Tate Liverpool and Liverpool University. Ou, "Poverty and Politics."

16 By early 2018, these chess-playing emblems of "old Beijing" had been replaced by other bronze figures of men with long braids operating the early film projectors inside the coffee bar at the side of the Da Guan cinema. Thanks to Luo Pan for this information.

17 The Da Guan Hall first opened in 1905 and was China's first cinema to abolish sex-segregated seating.

18 Despite claims that the restoration of Qianmen dajie is in keeping with traditional styles, local commentators immediately pointed out that the white lanterns had nothing to do with old Beijing tradition, which to this day uses red as its celebratory color. One comment was that the newly opened street resembled an anonymous film set, and could be anywhere. I refer to the amateur video footage that captured these responses immediately after the official opening of Qianmen dajie on August 7, 2008, in chapter 7.

19 In common with dominant historiographical narratives of China's twentieth century, the style of the refurbished Qianmen dajie evokes a link between the 1930s and now, implying an erasure of the revolutionary legacy of the Mao era. For an insightful analysis of the political and ideological significance of this link, see Karl, *Magic of Concepts*.

20 The Four Olds campaign (*po si jiu*) consisted of an attack on Old Customs, Old Culture, Old Habits, and Old Ideas. Launched in the summer of 1966, it dominated many of the Red Guard activities in the first years of what now is officially designated as the ten years of the Cultural Revolution.

21 Following the refurbishment of West Street in 2009, local rumor abounded that the Bodhisattva Temple was going to be rebuilt to attract tourism to the neighborhood. By late 2014, however, this rumor had proved to be baseless.

22 Chau, "An Awful Mark." In this article, Chau argues that "chai" may be inversely associated with "modernity" since it implies a process of regeneration and a better future. While this is appropriate as a theoretical concept contextualized by the dominant narrative of progress informing urban renewal in the capital, people in Dashalar with whom I talked about this sign saw it only as a sign of negative destruction, masking promises that excluded them from the possibility of prosperity.

23 Zhang Dali is a prominent contemporary artist current living and practicing in Beijing. Born in 1963, he studied at the Central Academy of Fine Arts and Design in Beijing. His work has moved through analyses of photography and political propaganda, urban art and graffiti, and large-scale installations. He engages with the challenges of being an artist in China and pressing social issues, including the uncertainties of migration and demolition. Wu Hung, "Zhang Dali's Dialogue."

24 Ma, *Runaway Wives*, 131.

25 "As [the former courtyard] households were 'proletarianized,' the Confucian idea of four generations under one roof gave way to a new spatial arrangement that enabled dozens of families to live in the one compound house." Dutton et al., *Beijing Time*, 117. Despite the suggestion that the dazayuan date from the early years of the PRC, there is ample evidence in Strand, *Rickshaw Beijing*, and Ma, *Runaway Wives*, demonstrating that they featured in this neighborhood much earlier, from well before the Republican era, when they were graphically described by Lao She in his famous *Rickshaw Boy*.

26 *Sannian zainan* ("three years of disaster") is the term officially used to refer to what others call the Great Famine. Depending on interpretation of the data, the famine claimed the lives of between fifteen and forty million people, and resulted in a huge drop in fertility rates. After decades during which the extent of the disaster was not recognized as famine, recent years have seen a partial shift toward official acknowledgement of it, but the term is still not commonly used, either in official or popular language. Despite this, it is significant that across the categories of archival documents I consulted, extensive official attention was given to local conditions of food scarcity and sickness during these years.

27 Ou, *Meishi jie*. For graphic detail of these processes, see Shao, *Shanghai Gone*.

28 Local rumor had it that the delay was caused by corruption on the part of the responsible officials on Beijing's Municipal Committee, which subsequently turned out to be true. While I have not been able to find any precise evidence of this, it is clear that the entire project was caught up in debates and differences of opinion between officials and the real estate company, SOHO, charged with undertaking the reconstruction work. The mayor who took charge of the project was Wang Qishan, vice-premier and member of the ruling Politburo, best known for his instrumental role in president Xi Jinping's anticorruption drive. He was promoted to the position of vice-premier in 2007 before the Olympics. Under his charge, however, the reconstruction of Qianmen daijie was far from smooth, and involved heated debates about its design and possible violation of preservation regulations. Against protests from the nongovernmental China Heritage Foundation on the grounds that the proposed designs for the reconstruction of the street

did not correspond with the government's commitment to preservation, rights to develop the area were eventually given in 2006 to SOHO China, one of China's largest real estate developers, headed by the fabulously wealthy husband-and-wife team Pan Shiyi and Zhang Xin. Thanks to Luo Pan for helping me access this information. For a summary of the historical importance and recent reconstruction of the Qianmen area, see Layton, "Qianmen." See also Johnson and Leow, "Builder Soho China."

29 I describe this footage at greater length in chapter 7.

30 According to an official report, Dashalar's conditions in the mid-2000s were not dissimilar to those of the 1950s. Zhu, *Beijing chengqu*, 77–79, 213–17.

31 Of the 124 families studied in Sidney Gamble's survey of 283 families in Peiping in the mid-1920s, 44 percent lived in one room, including 41 families with five to seven people. Gamble, *How Chinese Families Live*, 129–30.

32 XWDG, 13-1-34 (August 7, 1961), 3.

33 XWDG, 10-2-17 (January 18, 1962), 7:100–2.

34 XWDG 13-1-34 (August 7, 1961), 3. Another interesting insight from this document, foreshadowing more recent evidence about urban men's marriageability in Fincher, *Leftover Women*, concerns the criteria for a desirable husband; a key condition of men's marriageability during this first decade of the Mao era was access to a home, if not home ownership.

35 Beijing Annals Editorial Committee, *Beijing zhi*, 244–45.

36 For a description of the processes involved in the planning and design of these "ten great buildings," see Wu Hung, *Remaking Beijing*, 108–26.

37 Beijing Annals Editorial Committee, *Beijing zhi*, 219.

38 The local archives contain numerous documents from this period indicating the local government's attempts to persuade peasants to return to their villages.

39 Beijing Annals Editorial Committee, *Beijing zhi*, 244.

40 Interestingly, Belsky argues that state appropriation of native place association lodges (huiguan) for use as schools, kindergartens, factories, and offices, as well as residential properties, ironically meant that "despite all the rhetoric of destroying the past to build the new" characteristic of the Mao period, the physical structures of the native-place lodges were for the most part much better preserved during that period than they have been during the subsequent decades of post-Mao reform." Belsky, *Localities at the Center*, 257.

41 Meyer, *Last Days of Old Beijing*, 46. A number of detailed policies for the protection of the old city were set out in the 2002 Conservation Plan for the Historic and Cultural City of Beijing. Local property owners have little recourse to law to uphold their opposition to demolition since the state owns all land on which property is built. A plaintiff in a case against the Xuanwu District government in 2006 prevented demolition only because he managed to unearth a legal document drawn up years beforehand identifying his dazayuan as a "cultural protection site." Personal communication with the plaintiff, January 17, 2010. For more discussion about protest against the state's claims to urban land ownership, see Hsing, *Great Transformation*, 60–72.

42 Ou, *Meishi jie.* See also Ou Ning's 2008 lecture on the plans for Dashalar, in Ou, "Poverty and Politics."

43 Broudehoux, *Making and Selling.* This policy around the Olympics echoed similar policies in preparation for National Day in 1999, when rural migrants and illegal residents were targeted by eviction campaigns designed to reduce the number of illegal migrants living and working in the capital, and residents of local neighborhoods were prevented from leaving their homes in order to "give the capital a clean, well-managed look and to ensure that crime rates stayed as low as possible." Broudehoux, *Making and Selling,* 178–88.

44 "Critics of high-rise apartment housing often point to the indifference that characterizes relations between their residents. However, in the one-story courtyard houses, close relations among the residents do not necessarily mean intimate relations. Their interaction is forced upon them by tight circumstances and entails a fundamental disruption of privacy." Wu Liangyong, *Rehabilitating,* 114.

45 Prakash and Kruse, *Spaces of the Modern City,* 13.

46 Roy argues that the "subaltern space of the slum" constitutes a vibrant source of creative "urban informalities." As such the subaltern subject acquires a recognition absent from the emphasis on urban dystopias and their effects in dispossessing urban inhabitants. Roy, "Slumdog Cities," 10.

Chapter 2. Old Mrs. Gao

Parts of chapter 2 appear in "Patriarchal Investments: Expectations of Male Authority and Support in a Poor Beijing Neighborhood," in *Transforming Patriarchy: Chinese Families in the Twenty-First Century*, edited by Gonçalo Santos and Stevan Harrell, 182–98 (Seattle: University of Washington Press, 2017) as well as in "Neglect of a Neighbourhood: Oral Accounts of Life in 'Old Beijing' since the Eve of the People's Republic," *Urban History* 41, no. 4 (2014): 686–704.

1 At the time, the family estimated that they would have to pay several thousand yuan to employ a nurse to look after Old Mrs. Gao in a hospital, and given that such nurses were generally untrained migrant women, they preferred to look after her themselves.

2 In conditions of extreme poverty and in which a preference for a son was the norm, female infanticide was common throughout the nineteenth and early twentieth centuries as a means of reducing the economic burden of raising a child who would eventually become the property of another family. An expression widely used to describe a girl was "a commodity on which money has been lost." Smith, *Village Life in China,* 326. This comment made by an older relative may thus indicate the acceptability of a response to conditions of extreme poverty such as those into which Old Mrs. Gao was born. Throughout the Republican era, the sex ratio in Beijing was consistently skewed, resulting in a surfeit of unmarried men of marriageable age. Ma, *Runaway Wives,* 255.

3 For a rich description of the everyday lives and activities of poor women in the crowded conditions of Beijing's dazayuan and hutong, see Ma, *Runaway Wives,*

particularly chapters 1 and 3. Strand's *Rickshaw Beijing* also contains graphic descriptions of the chaotic conditions of busy hutong in the 1920s.

4   In *Traffickers and Family Life*, Johanna Ransmeier argues that Chinese families at this time were invariably "transactional families" and refers to how arrivals and departures in a household, particularly of wives and concubines, involved the exchange of money or goods and the services of a broker. Her research also argues that in contrast with received wisdom, to date, there were no significant distinctions in terminology used to discuss the transactions for a wife versus those for a concubine or a maid. "Trafficking was an essential part of community-level mutual aid" (5). In this sense, the trafficking of people, particularly children and young women, was not merely a symptom of times of crisis, but was routinely tolerated and facilitated by community networks. While trafficking could implicate criminal activity, it was not seen as morally reprehensible as we now tend to think.

5   Women's active presence in the informal economy of such jobs offered them an invaluable means of survival but was disdained by social reformers as a sign of cultural and moral turpitude. It was also, however, treated as a source of stigma in popular circles. "Local customs also dictated that only families in abject poverty would send wives and daughters out to work, and this created and perpetuated a kind of social stigma despising and prohibiting married women from working outside the home." Ma, *Runaway Wives*, 40.

6   Although I do not have precise evidence, I assume that in noting this date Old Mrs. Gao was referring to the lunar calendar, still in popular use.

7   The "public amalgamation of private enterprise" (*gongsi heying*) was a term that recurred from time to time in Old Mrs. Gao's memories of the period. Given the large number of small entrepreneurs and private vendors in the neighborhood, it is plausible to speculate that her memory for this, in contrast to her rather vague recall for other campaigns, was a response to the extent of the efforts made in the mid-1950s to nationalize private enterprise. It is interesting in this context that neither she nor any other of my acquaintances in the neighborhood made any reference to the Three Anti and Five Anti campaigns of the early 1950s.

8   Eating red dates has long been considered a health tonic in Chinese medicine, and they are taken to boost blood deficiency particularly during pregnancy.

9   "Speak bitterness" (*su ku*) was the term used by the Communist Party in the early 1950s to mobilize oppressed workers and peasants to publicly recall their suffering under the feudal landlords and exploitative factory bosses as a means of collective self-empowerment. The Beijing-based anthropologist Guo Yuhua and sociologist Sun Liping referred to this model as one of the main ways in which the new party-state interpellated ordinary workers and peasants as its new subjects. Guo and Sun "Su ku." See also Anagnost, "Making History Speak." Anagnost argues that speaking bitterness was a "reworking of memory into a narrative of class antagonism . . . in a process of merging the consciousness of the party with that of the 'people,' which legitimated its claims to represent the voice of the masses" (32). Lisa Rofel sees su ku as political praxis consisting of speech *acts* conveying a rhetoric of

complaint as a "historically and culturally specific narrative practice." Rofel, *Other Modernities*, 138.

10 One might have imagined that as a woman sold as a "child-bride," she would have been drawn into the official campaigns of the early 1950s that sought to publicize the new rights of women. She may well have been, but whatever the nature of her activities in the 1950s, they no longer figured at all in her memory in 2009.

11 This may have been another confusion on Old Mrs. Gao's part, since a title of May 7 would very probably have referred to the key date of May 7, 1971, the date when Mao Zedong wrote a letter to Lin Biao, then head of the army, stating that the army should become a model of a new kind of education and that military affairs should be combined with studying politics and engaging in civilian affairs, including agriculture and industry. May 7 subsequently became the title of new "cadre schools" established throughout the country, to which all urban professionals were periodically sent for shorter or longer periods throughout the early 1970s.

12 For an early discussion about the neighborhood committee's role in administrative control and political mobilization of local populations, see Salaff, "Urban Communities." Salaff argued that women's piecework under the neighborhood committee was not seen as "productive work" commensurate with the work done in the organized work units. Since Salaff's work, the contribution of "dependent housewives" to the local economies under the auspices of the neighborhood committee is one aspect of the urban economy during the Mao years that has been woefully understudied. In one of the few studies, Wang Zheng argued that one effect of the neighborhood committee's organization of local female labor was a feminization of local space involving the blurring of the boundary between inner, domestic (*nei*) and outer, social (*wai*) spheres. Nevertheless, while "housewives" were now a significant part of urban reorganization, no longer only associated with the relegated domestic realm, they remained subordinate to the more prestigious sphere of male-dominated productive labor. Wang Zheng, "Gender and Maoist Urban Reorganization."

13 The difficulties in question concerned the neighbor's anxiety about the effects of an informal arrangement to exchange living accommodations that she had entered into during the mid-1960s: she had swapped her accommodation in Chaoyang district for her present room in Old Mrs. Gao's dazayuan, because at that stage she wanted to be nearer her natal family and friends. The man with whom she had done the swap now wanted to reclaim his property in Dashalar, but in the meantime he had sold her original place in Chaoyang district. She was desperately worried that she would be evicted and left homeless and thus wanted her friend's advice about what to do.

14 In this, Old Mrs. Gao resembles both the figure of the matriarch and women's gendered role in protecting the kin group against fragmentation and dispersal that Charles Stafford has discussed in *Separation and Reunion* and "Actually Existing Chinese Matriarchy."

15 "Poor people can't afford to fall ill" is a comment I often heard in Dashalar. Old Mrs. Gao's hospital bill for a bed and daily checkups over two weeks amounted

to several thousand yuan. This excluded routine nursing, changing her bedpan, bringing her food and water, turning her over in her bed to prevent bedsores from developing, washing her face and body, and so on, all of which duties were carried out by her relatives. At that time, those without relatives and with the resources employed migrant women at about three hundred yuan a day to undertake such tasks.

16 In 2007, the monthly basic welfare payment in Beijing was 300 to 310 yuan. It rose to 580 yuan in 2013, and 900 in 2017, the latter for individual monthly incomes of less than 1410 yuan.

17 The government's policy of local urban "beautification" in the run-up to and during the Olympics also involved blocking off local Dashalar residents' access to the nearest subway station at the C entrance to Qianmen station, meaning that to reach the subway residents would have to walk much further due east and then north. Pedicab cyclists were also prevented from going north to Tian'anmen Square.

18 According to a European source using data published by the Beijing government, average per capita income in Beijing rose from just under 20,000 yuan in December 2005 to over 35,000 in September 2014. CEIC, "China Average Income per Capita." Other sources report an average minimum in Beijing of 1,720 yuan per month in February 2018. https://checkinprice.com/average-minimum-salary -beijing-china/.

19 The campaign to popularize Zhang Tiesheng was used by the Gang of Four to launch an attack on the professional, "expert" credentials of the small urban elite. Zhang Tiesheng was appointed to the Standing Committee of the National People's Congress in 1975. He was then put on trial after the arrest of the Gang of Four in October 1976, and sentenced to fifteen years in prison. He later became a multimillionaire after the company he cofounded, Wellhope Agri-Tech, went public in July 2014.

20 In the conservative sexual environment of the time, this kind of myth was possibly widespread. Similar comments were made to me by much more educated women in the 1960s and 1970s, as I relate in *Subject of Gender*, 147–53.

21 It must have been quite difficult for Young Gao to borrow such cars at the time, given the lack of availability of individual cars. But even in conditions of extreme scarcity, Young Gao insisted on observing proper ritual, and found a way to go through with the traditional wedding ritual, albeit in modified form, of picking up the bride and carrying her to her new marital home in a sedan chair. Given the extent of traffic congestion in China's cities now, in large part the effect of private ownership of vehicles, it is almost impossible to imagine that only four decades or so ago, very few cars were privately owned. Following on from the restrictions on private ownership and car usage in the 1960s and 1970s and into the early and mid-1980s, the common form of individual transport was the bicycle. Most work units possessed at least one car for its leadership's use, supposedly on special occasions. It was only the political, bureaucratic, and military elite who had regular use of a chauffeur-driven vehicle.

22 For an analysis of the pressures on women to find marriage partners who come with an apartment, and the links between this and gender discrimination in the real estate market, see Fincher, *Leftover Women*.

23 The pejorative term *dongluan* ("turmoil," "disturbance" or "upheaval," or "chaos") is commonly used in official and media accounts and has become one of the main terms popularly used to refer to the protests.

24 Limited though it is, such details give evidence of the presence of local Beijing "citizens" (*shimin*), as the media called them, in the protests. The support Beijing shimin gave to the protesters in the form of food and water was widely noted in the English-language press, and a June 4, 1989, BBC report noted that "at a nearby children's hospital operating theatres were filled with casualties with gunshot wounds, many of them local residents who were not taking part in the protests." BBC, "On This Day."

25 Only when I visited Xiao Xi in her new home nearer to Tianqiao after her mother-in-law's death was my sense of Young Gao's sense of failure and depression confirmed by his widow. No one mentioned it, even indirectly, while he and his mother were still alive.

Interlude 1

1 Old Mrs. Gao's performance in this sense bears out the insights of Margery Wolf's argument that in a patrilineal system, women built up their own authority and status through nurturing their uterine families, and particularly their sons. Wolf, *Women and the Family in Rural Taiwan*.

2 *Rickshaw Boy* (*Luotuo Xiangzi*) was written as a social critique of the everyday life of the subalterns in what was then called Beiping, in the early years of the Japanese occupation, when the capital moved inland to Chongqing in southwestern China. It centers on a hardworking and honest lad from the countryside who works as a rickshaw puller, dreaming of making enough money to eventually own his own rickshaw. He manages to keep this dream going despite repeated setbacks, until he succumbs to illness and vagrancy. The novel was subsequently criticized by the Communist authorities, who condemned it for its failure to give oppressed laboring people hope for the future. Lao She himself was arrested and persecuted during the Cultural Revolution, and committed suicide by drowning in 1966.

3 Old Mrs. Gao's manner of talking and use of vocabulary was utterly steeped in the local cadences and rhythms of the popular culture of her neighborhood. Without Zhao Tielin's help I would have found it difficult, if not impossible, to understand her.

4 See Henrietta L. Moore's discussion of Paul Ricoeur and Hayden White in *A Passion for Difference*, 119.

5 Stafford, "Actually Existing Chinese Matriarchy."

6 Estimated on the basis of the international poverty line of $1.90 a day, World Bank figures indicate that the percentage of the population living below the international poverty line fell from 88 percent in 1981 to 6.5 percent in 2012, and to 4.1 percent in 2014; *The World Bank in China Overview*. However, a senior Chinese

official estimated in 2014 that some 30 percent of China's population was under the poverty line of $1 a day. Laccino, "China."

7 Mahmood, *Politics of Piety*.

8 Stafford, *Separation and Reunion*, 110–26.

9 Feuchtwang, *Making Place*, 25.

Chapter 3. Zhao Yong

Parts of chapter 3 appeared in "Neglect of a Neighbourhood: Oral Accounts of Life in 'Old Beijing' since the Eve of the People's Republic," *Urban History* 41, no. 4 (2014): 686–704.

1 The policy agenda of the "harmonious society" (2003–13) emphasized equitable growth, with the government introducing measures to reduce disparities, including social welfare, increasing the minimum wage, increased spending on poverty alleviation, and targeted tax reductions. Nevertheless, income inequality increased, such that by 2013, World Bank figures listed China as among the top 25 percent most unequal countries worldwide. The single most significant factor was the rapid growth of the higher-income groups, boosted by the growth of the private real estate market. See Sicular, "Challenge of High Inequality."

2 Since the concept of the "informal economy" was introduced in 1973 as part of development discourse, it was taken up by policy makers who argued that "informal economic activities could help reduce poverty and unemployment and advocated these activities as beneficial 'self-help' strategies of the urban poor." Millar, "Informal Economy," 55. By 2008, the informal sector constituted 78 percent of all nonagricultural labor in Africa, 58 percent in Latin America, and 45–85 percent in Asia, indicating that the expansion of the informal economy was no longer treated as a temporary measure enabling millions of workers to transition to the world of formal employment, as many early studies of the informal economy suggested, but had become a fixed aspect of the increasing precarity of social and economic life under the effects of global capitalism. Millar, "Informal Economy," 55–56.

3 Zhao Yong noted that this warlord was Zhang Zuolin, but Zhang Zuolin died in 1928 and was not active in Shanxi, where another warlord, Yan Xishan, held sway. This was one obvious instance in which memory was clearly at odds with the actual facts of family history.

4 *Bagua* (lit. "eight trigrams," referring to the Daoist classic the *Yi Jing* [Book of Changes]) is one of the three main martial arts schools. Defined as an "internal practice," it covers diverse schools, some of which use implements such as swords, spears, and staffs.

5 One of the few family photographs Zhao had that he proudly showed me the first time I met him was of a group of students at this school—all young men dressed in the long gowns of the time, standing in front of the building where they trained.

6 The Miyun Reservoir lies about one hundred kilometers north of Beijing. It was built in September 1960, using labor requisitioned from the recently established people's communes, and involving massive dislocation of villagers from their land. Its initial objectives were flood prevention, electricity generation, and agricultural

irrigation, but by the mid-1980s it was also used for drinking water. Covering an area of 15,788 square kilometers and with a storage capacity of more than four billion cubic meters, it is the single largest source of water for Beijing. See Wang Jian, "Remembering Miyun Reservoir."

7 At the time, a slight relaxation of the initially stringent single child policy permitted divorced but childless individuals to have a child in their second marriage, regardless of whether their new spouse already had a child or not.

8 Ci Xi (1835–1908) was the famous empress dowager of the late Qing dynasty. Although an ambivalent political figure who tried to appease and court the support of different interest groups, Chinese and foreign, depending on her interpretation of the political situation, she was and continues to be seen as a ruthless despot. She has long been a household name in China associated with the discriminatory gender stereotype that chaos is the inevitable result of women acquiring political power.

9 *Fangsheng* refers to a practice now widely associated in urban China with releasing animals from captivity, leading to some reports of urban residents buying large numbers of birds from bird sellers and then releasing them into the wild. Buddhist and Daoist practices are conflated in Zhao's account of how he became a Buddhist. *Chaodu* is more associated with the Daoist Zhong Yuan ritual that typically occurs on the fifteenth day of the seventh lunar month, to release ghosts (unappeased souls) from suffering.

Interlude 2

1 The best known of these is still Jung Chang's *Wild Swans*. First published by HarperCollins in 1991, it has had at least three editions, and has been translated into thirty-seven languages, selling more than twenty million copies. It was adapted as a stage play in London in 2012, and rights were sold to make a film in 2006. Combining biography, autobiography, and history, the book compels readers' attention through its focus on three generations of women, yet at the same time it confirms many stereotypes equating the Cultural Revolution with the suffering of China's intellectual elite. Other "eyewitness" accounts have been unable to compete with this, not due to their inferior narrative style—on the contrary—but because they have been unable to dislodge the media and academic dominance of a historical narrative of the Mao era that refuses to take it seriously as a revolutionary moment of global significance effectively lasting for more than half a century. Young Chinese students have minimal access to critical accounts of the Cultural Revolution in the national education curriculum, and commonly acquire very stereotypical ideas about the sufferings of the "sent-down youth." In the face of active discouragement by government and media to delve into the history of this "lost decade," young generations in China commonly succumb to what could be described as the officially sanctioned amnesia of this period of the Mao era.

2 One of the few histories of the Mao era that treats it seriously as a period of revolutionary transformation is Karl, *Mao Zedong and China*.

3 CCCP, "Resolution on Certain Questions."

4　Between 1978 and 1989, a series of urban-centered campaigns, beginning with the Democracy Wall Movement (1978–79) and ending with the bloody events of June 1989, sandwiched a series of largely localized protests calling for political reform of the authoritarian system of CCP rule. Many of these were spearheaded by students and young professionals, although the involvement of the working class in 1989 was arguably one of the triggers to the government's violent clampdown. Nevertheless, despite the suppression of these movements and the arrest and imprisonment of their leaders, they were not equivalent to the class-based attack on the intellectual and professional elite during the Cultural Revolution.

5　This is Doreen Massey's argument in her analysis of the "complex geometries of differential power" and spatial inequalities in London's success as a major center of finance capital under the increasing global dominance of neoliberalism since the 1980s. Massey, *World City*, 54–62.

6　Arguably the most famous relevant film was Tian Zhuangzhuang's *The Blue Kite*, made in 1993. The film's depiction of the harrowing experiences of the antirightist movement and the Cultural Revolution resulted not only in the government's decision to ban the film but also in the imposition of a ten-year ban on Tian Zhuangzhuang from filming. Outside China, the film won massive international acclaim and various awards.

7　See for example, Patel and Kleinmann, "Poverty and Common Mental Disorders."

8　Lu Hsun, *True Story of Ah Q.*

9　Davies, "The Problematic Modernity of Ah Q."

10　Yan, *Flow of Gifts*, 122–46.

Chapter 4. Hua Meiling

Parts of chapter 4 appeared in "Neglect of a Neighbourhood: Oral Accounts of Life in 'Old Beijing' since the Eve of the People's Republic," *Urban History* 41, no. 4 (2014): 686–704.

1　The short-lived campaign "against spiritual pollution" (*fan jingshen wuran*) formally originated with the 12th Party Congress in September 1982, when Deng Xiaoping's attempts to implement economic reform met with extensive conservative opposition from senior party figures who were concerned about the cultural and political effects of westernization in China. In media attacks on "bourgeois individualism," notably fashions, hairstyles, pornography, "obscene" artistic performances, and anything that fell under the vague category of illicit social and sexual behavior, the campaign reached its height in mid-November 1983. Some argue that it was an extension of the central attack on bourgeois liberalization launched in March 1979 to bring an end to the Democracy Wall movement that had called for the "Fifth modernization—democracy." Barmé, "Spiritual Pollution."

2　The system of administrative detention has long been used in China as a means of detaining people without trial for up to four years and as a source of cheap labor. It has been repeatedly condemned by human rights organizations as a system that invites the abuse of power in order to maintain public order and assert political control.

Interlude 3

1   Ou, *Meishi jie*.
2   A visit to a property developer in Chaoyang District in 2010 brought home to me the potential significance of this interest. The property developer wanted to take over an old factory unit but was unable to do so, since one of its small buildings was occupied by a long-term resident who refused to leave, not apparently out of any affection for the building but in order to force an increase in the property developer's compensation. Thanks to Luo Pan for setting up this meeting.
3   Stafford, "Actually Existing Chinese Matriarchy."
4   Wang Zheng, "Gender and Maoist Urban Reorganization." With reference to the rural sector, Ellen Judd argued long ago that there was a noticeable contradiction between women's practice as laborers contributing to the household economy and welfare, and the "pervasive devaluation" of their practice in everyday life. Judd, *Gender and Power*, 254.
5   Yan, *Private Life under Socialism*, 99.
6   For further discussion about educated, middle-class women's desires in marriage and family life, see Xie, "Embodying the Exemplary Gender Ideal"; and Fincher, *Leftover Women*.
7   Kandiyoti, "Bargaining with Patriarchy"; Judd, *Gender and Power*; Stafford, "Actually Existing Chinese Matriarchy."
8   Stafford, *Separation and Reunion*.

Chapter 5. Li Fuying

1   Situated high up on the Qinghai-Tibetan Plateau, Xining has long hours of sunshine but is bitterly cold, with temperatures falling to as much as –14 degrees Celsius between November and March.
2   For a graphic description of similar conditions in detention shelters elsewhere, see Siu, "Grounding Displacement."
3   The following account is a summary of a lengthy, impassioned description of conditions in two detention centers, one in Changping County in the northern suburbs of Beijing and the other in Shijiazhuang in Hebei Province. The Shijiazhuang center operated like a transit depot for migrants being repatriated from Beijing. Once released from the Shijiazhuang center, they had to pay for train fare or bus fares to travel back to their hometowns.
4   For similar descriptions see Siu, "Grounding Displacement."
5   Ningxia University, located in Yinchuan City, is the leading university of the Ningxia Hui Autonomous Region. As such it caters to a large intake of "ethnic minority" and rural students. In terms of educational hierarchy, it was much lower down the scale than the graphic design college Young Li had attended in Shijiazhuang.

Interlude 4

1   Chuang, "Adding Insult to Injury."
2   Diamant et al., *Engaging the Law in China*.

3   It is beyond the limits of my research to explain why certain groups of poor urban residents, such as those Qin Shao discusses in *Shanghai Gone*, are prepared to make use of the law to defend their cases against demolition and relocation. However, this issue certainly demonstrates the need for such a comparative study of the urban chaiqian program.

4   Zhu, *Beijing chengqu*, 214.

5   Beijing shi Xuanwu qu, *Dashalar jiedao zhi*, 55.

6   Zhu, *Beijing chengqu*, 214.

7   It is worth bearing in mind that this response of the Beijing residents to outsiders is by no means unique to this situation. An equivalent disdain has in recent years been the rallying cry for many disadvantaged people susceptible to the appeal of the populist far right in the United States, the United Kingdom, and elsewhere in Europe.

8   Under the Urban Management Bureau, and as employees of the local government, the chengguan in Dashalar are probably at the bottom of the patrol officers' salary scale, with a monthly income in 2017 that could be as low as twelve hundred yuan per month. In comparison, the police, under the Public Security Bureau, are formal civil servants paid according to one of the civil service pay scales, with monthly incomes ranging between three thousand and ten thousand yuan.

9   Li Fuying's reference to Great and Glorious Yang being beaten up is a version of a higher-profile case involving one Cui Yingjie, a migrant from Hebei who was working as a mobile sausage seller. When a chengguan attempted to confiscate his tricycle in 2006, Cui lost his temper and in the confrontation that followed stabbed the chengguan to death. Public support for Cui Yingjie before and during the trial in 2007 may have affected the leniency shown him in commuting his death sentence. For a report of the official narrative of the case, see Pan, "Stabbing Leads to Conviction."

10 Honig, "Native Place."

11 Kipnis, "Suzhi."

12 Sangren, "Masculine Domination."

13 Thanks to Steven Sangren for inspiring this argument.

14 Thanks to Yan Yunxiang for a brief exchange of ideas about these topics, in which he pointed out that one way of understanding why this sense of shame is not more discussed in the Chinese literature is because it is so much part of one's sense of self as to be obvious.

15 Yan, *Private Life under Socialism*.

16 I am reminded of Guo Yuhua's article on the crisis of care for the rural elderly signified by the young generation's increasing unwillingness to commit the economic and emotional resources to such care in changing social and economic conditions that give the young greater economic independence, and therefore greater authority to make their own life decisions. Guo, "Daiji guanxi zhong de gongping."

17 Yan, *Private Life under Socialism*.

18 These comments were inspired by a conversation with Judith Farquhar in a conference in Cologne in July 2017.

19 Yan, *Private Life under Socialism*.

Chapter 6. Zhang Huiming

1   This coincided with the widespread layoff of many workers, particularly middle-aged women, following the restructuring of the state industries after the mid-1990s. Of those laid off, 62.8 percent were women, even though women constituted only 39 percent of urban workers. Wang Zheng, "Gender, Employment and Women's Resistance," 65.

2   A multilingual flyer of the time titled "Hello Beijing" advertised such tours as "lovely strolling through the old alley" past famous buildings and markets, along with booking arrangements, times of tours, and instructions on how to avoid the "wrong pedicabs."

3   Lin Zexu (1785–1850) is a household name in China, known for his moral rectitude as a Confucian official and his firm stance against Britain's opium trade in China. He was sent as imperial commissioner to Guangdong in 1838, empowered to bring an end to the opium trade then flourishing through the auspices of the East India Company and private merchants. He confiscated vast quantities of opium and arrested many dealers in moves that became the catalyst for imperial Britain's invasion of China in the First Opium War (1839–42). Wang's implicit comparison between the history of the former native-place association where he lived and Lin Zexu was an evident sign of his interest in acquiring cultural capital.

4   This campaign was launched in 1973 by the retrospectively named "Gang of Four" as an attempt to expose the political crimes of Lin Biao, who had been named as Mao's official successor in 1969 but then condemned following an alleged attempt to assassinate Mao in 1971. By 1975, the campaign had developed into a veiled challenge to the premier, Zhou Enlai.

5   At the time, private ownership of a TV was extremely unusual, particularly for poorer households. By 1985, with the onset of market reform, the number of households with a TV had risen considerably, to around 67 percent. Croll, *China's New Consumers*, 36–38.

Interlude 5

1   An online five-year review of the Dashilar Project described it as an organic redevelopment project launched in 2011, which, "over the past five years, relying on the power of design . . . has continuously injected fresh energy into this area . . . reflect[ing] the need of the community itself, and afford[ing] community residents the opportunity to criticize and consider their living environment as well." Beijing Guowenyan Cultural Heritage Conservation, "Dashilar Project."

2   Steinmüller, *Communities of Complicity*.

3   Wu Liangyong's blighted intention to use his design for the Ju'er neighborhood as a blueprint for "modernizing" the old dazayuan structure comes to mind here. Wu Liangyong, *Rehabilitating the Old City of Beijing*.

Chapter 7. Jia Yong

1 Thanks to Luo Pan for explaining these terms.
2 Both Susan Sontag and Roland Barthes give black-and-white photographs a status of authenticity judged in relation to past time "properly" captured. For Sontag, monochrome gives an image a sense of age, historical distance, and aura. Grainge, "TIME's Past."
3 This comment derives from Doreen Massey's conceptualization of place as an interwoven site of shifting individual and collective memories, not formed out of fixed cultural traditions and material forms that "freez[e] moments of the past of a place." Massey, *For Space*, 115.
4 This brings to mind Yomi Braester's comment about the "documentary impulse" of Chinese filmmakers since the 1990s, who are "tinged with a fear for the future of memory, an anxiety for the loss of identity, and an urge to preserve images of the city." Braester, *Painting the City Red*, 22, 225.
5 Massey, *For Space*, 5.
6 In Chinese cosmology, the dominant traditional calendrical framework for dating events derives from the sequence of the ten stems and the twelve branches. Some older people continue to use this system to date big events such as births and deaths.
7 Branigan, "China's National Day Parade."

Interlude 6

1 Steinmüller, *Communities of Complicity*.
2 Feuchtwang, *Making Place*.
3 Yan, *Flow of Gifts*.

Conclusion

1 Scott, *Weapons of the Weak*.
2 Mueggler, *Age of Wild Ghosts*, 18.
3 These arguments are inspired by Mueggler's discussion about the state as a constitutive force at the heart of the social world of his informants in *Age of Wild Ghosts*.
4 Evans, "Patriarchal Investments."
5 Evans, "Patriarchal Investments."
6 Sangren, "Masculine Domination."
7 This argument is wonderfully explored by the late Saba Mahmood in *The Politics of Piety*.
8 The main exception to this tendency is Karl, *Mao Zedong and China in the Twentieth Century*, which insists on locating Mao's revolutionary politics within its historical and global context.
9 Mahmood, *Politics of Piety*, 10.
10 Fraser, "Rethinking Recognition."

BIBLIOGRAPHY

Anagnost, Ann. "Making History Speak." In *National Past-Times: Narrative, Representation, and Power*, edited by Ann Anagnost, 17–44. Durham, NC: Duke University Press, 1997.

Barmé, Geremie R. "Spiritual Pollution Thirty Years On." Australian Centre on China in the World, *The China Story*, November 17, 2013. https://www.thechinastory.org/2013/11/spiritual-pollution-thirty-years-on/.

Beijing Annals Editorial Committee, ed. *Beijing zhi, shizheng juan, fangdichan zhi* [Beijing annals, volume on municipal administration, property annals]. Beijing: Beijing Publishing House, 2000.

Beijing Guowenyan Cultural Heritage Conservation Center Company. "Dashilar Project—5 Years Review and the Launch of Adaptive Guidelines." Dashilar.org. Accessed November 15, 2018. http://www.dashilar.org/en/#B!/en/ing/iBeijingDesignWeek.html!D!/en/D/bdw_2016_05.html.

Beijing shi Xuanwu qu Dashalar jiedaozhi bianshen weiyuan hui [Editorial Committee of the Dashalar Annals, Xuanwu District, Beijing Municipality], ed. *Dashalar jiedao zhi* [Annals of the Dashalar Street Committee]. Beijing: Beijing shi Xuanwu qu Dashalar jiedaozhi bianshen weiyuan hui, 1996.

Belsky, Richard. *Localities at the Center: Native Place, Space, and Power in Late Imperial Beijing*. Cambridge, MA: Harvard University Press, 2005.

Bourgois, Philippe. "Confronting Anthropological Ethics: Ethnographic Lessons from Central America." *Journal of Peace Research* 27, no. 1 (February 1990): 43–54.

Braester, Yomi. *Painting the City Red: Chinese Cinema and the Urban Contract*. Durham, NC: Duke University Press, 2010.

Branigan, Tania. "China's National Day Parade: Public Barred from Celebrations." *Guardian*, September 30, 2009. https://www.theguardian.com/world/2009/sep/30/china-national-day-parade-communism.

British Broadcasting Corporation (BBC). "On This Day: 1989, Massacre in Tian'anmen Square." Accessed January 19, 2018. http://news.bbc.co.uk/onthisday/hi/dates/stories/june/4/newsid_2496000/2496277.stm.

Broudehoux, Anne-Marie. "Civilizing Beijing: Social Beautification, Civility and Citizenship at the 2008 Olympics." In *Olympic Games, Mega-Events, and Civil Societies*, edited by Graeme Hayes and John Karamichas, 46–67. London: Palgrave Macmillan, 2012.

Broudehoux, Anne-Marie. *The Making and Selling of Post-Mao Beijing*. London: Routledge, 2004.

CCCCP. Communist Party of China, Central Committee. "Resolution on Certain Questions in the History of Our Party since the Founding of the People's Republic of China." Adopted by the Sixth Plenary Session of the Eleventh Central Committee of the Communist Party of China, June 27, 1981. USC US-China Institute, https://china.usc.edu/chinese-communist-party-central-committee-"resolution -certain-questions-history-our-party-founding.

CEIC (China Economic Information Center) Data. "China Average Income per Capita. Ytd: Urban: Beijing." Accessed January 28, 2018. https://www.ceicdata.com/en /indicator/china/data/average-income-per-capita-ytd-urban-beijing.

Chang, Jung. *Wild Swans: Three Daughters of China*. London: HarperCollins, 1991.

Chau, Adam Yuet. "An Awful Mark: Symbolic Violence and Urban Renewal in Reform-Era China." *Visual Studies* 23, no. 3 (2008): 195–210.

Chen, Janet. *Guilty of Indigence: The Urban Poor in China, 1900–1953*. Princeton, NJ: Princeton University Press, 2012.

Chuang. "Adding Insult to Injury: Beijing's Evictions and the Discourse of 'Low-End Population.'" Chuangcn.org, January 9, 2018. http://chuangcn.org/2018/01/low -end-population/.

Croll, Elisabeth. *China's New Consumers: Social Development and Domestic Demand*. London: Routledge. 2006.

Davies, Gloria. "The Problematic Modernity of Ah Q." *Chinese Literature: Essays, Articles, Reviews (CLEAR)* 13 (December 1991): 57–76.

Diamant, Neil J., et al., eds. *Engaging the Law in China: State, Society, and Possibilities for Justice*. Stanford, CA: Stanford University Press, 2005.

Dong, Madeleine Yue. *Republican Beijing: The City and Its Histories*. Berkeley: University of California Press, 2003.

Dutton, Michael, Hsiu-ju Stacy Lo, and Dong Dong Wu, eds. *Beijing Time*. Cambridge, MA: Harvard University Press, 2008.

Evans, Harriet. "Patriarchal Investments: Expectations of Male Authority and Support in a Poor Beijing Neighborhood." In *Transforming Patriarchy: Chinese Families in the Twenty-First Century*, edited by Gonçalo Santos and Stevan Harrell, 182–98. Seattle: University of Washington Press, 2017.

Evans, Harriet. *The Subject of Gender: Daughters and Mothers in Urban China*. Lanham, MD: Rowman and Littlefield, 2008.

Evans, Harriet. *Women and Sexuality in China: Dominant Discourses of Female Sexuality and Gender since 1949*. Oxford: Polity, 1997.

Feuchtwang, Stephan. *After the Event: The Transmission of Grievous Loss in Germany, China, and Taiwan*. New York: Berghahn, 2011.

Feuchtwang, Stephan. *Making Place: State Projects, Globalisation, and Local Responses to China*. London: University College London, 2004.

Fincher, Leta Hong. *Leftover Women: The Resurgence of Gender Inequality in China*. London: Zed, 2014.

Fraser, Nancy. "Rethinking Recognition." *New Left Review* 3 (May–June 2000): 107–20.

Frisch, Michael. *A Shared Authority: Essays on the Craft and Meaning of Oral and Public History*. Albany: State University of New York Press, 1990.

Gamble, Sidney D. *How Chinese Families Live in Peiping.* New York: Funk and Wagnalls, 1933.

Grainge, Paul. "TIME's Past in the Present: Nostalgia and the Black and White Image." *Journal of American Studies* 33, no. 3 (December 1999): 383–92.

Guo Yuhua. "Daiji guanxi zhong de gongping luoji jiqi bianqian: Dui Hebie nongcun yanglao shijian de fenxi" [The logic of fairness and its change in cross-generational relations: An analysis of cases of elderly support in rural Hebei]. *Zhongguo xueshu* [China scholarship], no. 4 (2001): 221–54.

Guo Yuhua and Sun Liping. "Su ku: Yizhong nongmin guojia guannian xingcheng de zhongjie jizhi" [Speaking bitterness: An intermediary mechanism for creating the concept of a peasant state]. *Zhongguo xueshu* [China Scholarship], no. 4 (2002): 130–57.

Hall, Stuart. "When Was 'the Post-Colonial'? Thinking at the Limit." In *The Post-Colonial Question: Common Skies, Divided Horizons,* edited by Iain Chambers and Lidia Curti, 242–60. London: Routledge, 1996.

Hershatter, Gail. "The Gender of Memory: Rural Chinese Women and the 1950s." *Signs: Journal of Women in Culture and Society* 28, no. 1 (autumn 2002): 43–72.

Hershatter, Gail. *The Gender of Memory: Rural Women and China's Collective Past.* Berkeley: University of California Press, 2011.

Hinton, William H. *Fanshen: A Documentary of Revolution in a Chinese Village.* 1966. Berkeley: University of California Press, 1997.

Hogg, Chris. "China Law to Limit Home Demolitions and Evictions." BBC News, July 1, 2011. http://www.bbc.co.uk/news/world-asia-pacific-13986456.

Honig, Emily. "Native Place and the Making of Chinese Ethnicity." In *Remapping China, Fissures in Historical Terrain,* edited by G. Hershatter, E. Honig, J. Lipman, and R. Stross, 143–55. Stanford, CA: Stanford University Press, 1996.

Hsing, You-tien. *The Great Urban Transformation: Politics of Land and Property in China.* Oxford: Oxford University Press, 2010.

Human Rights Watch. "China's Rights Defenders." Accessed November 22, 2018. http://china.hrw.org/chinas_rights_defenders/.

Human Rights Watch. "Demolished: Forced Evictions and the Tenants' Rights Movement in China." March 2004. https://www.hrw.org/reports/2004/china0304/1.htm.

Human Rights Watch Asia. "China: Stop Violent Assaults by 'Chengguan' Forces." July 22, 2013. http://www.hrw.org/news/2013/07/22/china-stop-violent-assaults -chengguan-forces.

Johnson, Ian, and Jason Leow. "Builder Soho China Stumbles in Beijing." *Wall Street Journal,* December 24, 2008. https://www.wsj.com/articles/SB123006399599230901.

Judd, Ellen R. *Gender and Power in Rural North China.* Stanford, CA: Stanford University Press, 1994.

Kandiyoti, Deniz. "Bargaining with Patriarchy." *Gender and Society* 2, no. 3 (1988): 274–90.

Karl, Rebecca E. *The Magic of Concepts: History and the Economic in Twentieth-Century China.* Durham, NC: Duke University Press, 2017.

Karl, Rebecca E. *Mao Zedong and China in the Twentieth-Century World: A Concise History.* Durham, NC: Duke University Press, 2010.

Kipnis, Andrew. "Suzhi: A Keywords Approach." *China Quarterly* 186 (June 2006): 295–313.

Kuruvilla, Sarosh, Ching Kwan Lee, and Mary E. Gallagher, eds. *From Iron Rice Bowl to Informalization: Markets, Works, and the State in a Changing China.* Ithaca, NY: Cornell University Press, 2011.

Laccino, Ludovica. "China: More Than 82 Million People Live below Poverty Line." *International Business Times,* October 16, 2014. http://www.ibtimes.co.uk/china-more -82-million-people-live-below-poverty-line-1470313.

Lambek, Michael, ed. *Ordinary Ethics: Anthropology, Language, and Action.* New York: Fordham University Press, 2010.

Lao She. *Rickshaw Boy: A Novel.* Translated by Howard Goldblatt. New York: Harper-Collins, 2010.

Layton, Kelly. "Qianmen, Gateway to a Beijing Heritage." *China Heritage Quarterly,* no. 12 (December 2007). http://www.chinaheritagequarterly.org/articles.php ?searchterm=012_qianmen.inc&issue=012.

Li, Jie. *Shanghai Homes: Palimpsests of Private Life.* New York: Columbia University Press, 2015.

Li, Jie. *Utopian Ruins: A Memorial Museum of the Mao Era.* Durham, NC: Duke University Press, 2020.

Li, Shi, and Terry Sicular. "The Distribution of Household Income in China: Inequality, Poverty and Policies." *China Quarterly* 217 (March 2014): 1–41.

Liu Yangshuo. "Lianlian lao Beijing" [For the love of old Beijing]. *Renwu zhoukan* [People weekly], no. 33 (October 7, 2013): 26–42.

Lu, Duanfang. *Remaking Chinese Urban Form: Modernity, Scarcity, and Space, 1949–2005.* London: Routledge, 2006.

Lu, Hanchao. *Beyond the Neon Lights: Everyday Shanghai in the Early Twentieth Century.* Berkeley: University of California Press, 1999.

Lu Hsun (Lu Xun). *The True Story of Ah Q.* Translated by Yang Hsien-yi and Gladys Yang. Beijing: Foreign Languages Press, 1972.

Ma, Zhao. *Runaway Wives, Urban Crimes, and Survival Tactics in Wartime Beijing, 1937–1949.* Cambridge, MA: Harvard University Press, 2015.

Mahmood, Saba. *Politics of Piety: The Islamic Revival and the Feminist Subject.* Princeton, NJ: Princeton University Press, 2005.

Mann, Susan. *The Talented Women of the Zhang Family.* Berkeley: University of California Press, 2007.

Massey, Doreen. *For Space.* London: Sage, 2005.

Massey, Doreen. *World City.* Oxford: Polity, 2007.

Meyer, Michael. *The Last Days of Old Beijing: Life in the Vanishing Backstreets of a City Transformed.* New York: Walker, 2008.

Millar, Kathleen. "The Informal Economy: Condition and Critique of Advanced Capitalism." In *Underground Economy: Issues and Approaches,* edited by Asha B. Joshi, 55–74. Hyderabad, India: ICFAI University Press, 2008.

Moore, Henrietta L. *A Passion for Difference: Essays in Anthropology and Gender.* Cambridge: Polity, 1994.

Mueggler, Erik. *The Age of Wild Ghosts: Memory, Violence, and Place in Southwest China.* Berkeley: University of California Press, 2001.

Mueggler, Erik. *Songs for Dead Parents: Corpse, Text, and World in Southwest China.* Chicago: University of Chicago Press, 2017.

Ou Ning. *Meishi jie* [Meishi Street]. Distributed by dGenerate Films, 2006. 85 minutes.

Ou Ning. "Poverty and Politics: A Case Study of Da Zha Lan, Beijing." June 2008. http://www.slideshare.net/ouning/poverty-and-politics.

Pan, Jeff. "Stabbing Leads to Conviction and Retrospection." Chinadaily.com.cn, April 16, 2007. http://www.chinadaily.com.cn/china/2007-04/16/content_851907.htm.

Patel, Vikram, and Arthur Kleinmann. "Poverty and Common Mental Disorders in Developing Countries." *Bulletin of the World Health Organization* 81, no. 8 (2003): 609–15.

Prakash, Gyan. "The Impossibility of Subaltern History." *Subaltern Studies* 1, no. 2 (2000): 287–94.

Prakash, Gyan, and K. M. Kruse, eds. *The Spaces of the Modern City: Imaginaries, Politics, and Everyday Life.* Princeton, NJ: Princeton University Press, 2005.

Ransmeier, Johanna S. *Traffickers and Family Life in North China.* Cambridge, MA: Harvard University Press, 2017.

Rofel, Lisa. *Other Modernities: Gendered Yearnings in China after Socialism.* Berkeley: University of California Press, 1999.

Roy, Ananya. "Slumdog Cities: Rethinking Subaltern Urbanism." *International Journal of Urban and Regional Research* 35, no. 2 (2011): 10–39.

Roy, Ananya, and Nezar Alsayyad, eds. *Urban Informality: Transnational Perspectives from the Middle East, Latin America, and South Asia.* Lanham, MD: Rowman and Littlefield, 2017.

Salaff, Janet Weitzner. "Urban Communities in the Wake of the Cultural Revolution." In *The City in Communist China*, edited by John Wilson Lewis, 289–323. Stanford, CA: Stanford University Press, 1971.

Sangren, P. Steven. "'Masculine Domination': Desire and Chinese Patriliny." *Critique of Anthropology* 29 (2009): 255–78.

Scott, James C. *Domination and the Arts of Resistance: Hidden Transcripts.* New Haven, CT: Yale University Press, 1992.

Scott, James C. *Seeing Like a State: How Certain Schemes to Improve the Human Condition Have Failed.* New Haven, CT: Yale University Press, 1998.

Scott, James C. *Weapons of the Weak: Everyday Forms of Resistance.* New Haven, CT: Yale University Press, 1985.

Shao, Qin. *Shanghai Gone: Domicide and Defiance in a Chinese Megacity.* Lanham, MD: Rowman and Littlefield, 2013.

Sicular, Terry. "The Challenge of High Inequality in China." *The World Bank: Inequality in Focus* 2, no. 2 (August 2013): 1–5.

Siu, Helen. "Grounding Displacement: Uncivil Urban Spaces in Postreform South China." *American Ethnologist* 34, no. 2 (May 2007): 329–50.

Smith, Arthur H. *Village Life in China: A Study in Sociology.* New York: Revell, 1899.

Spivak, Gayatri. "Can the Subaltern Speak?" In *Marxism and the Interpretation of Culture*, edited by Cary Nelson and Lawrence Grossberg, 271–316. Urbana: University of Illinois Press, 1988.

Stafford, Charles. "Actually Existing Chinese Matriarchy." In *Chinese Kinship: Contemporary Anthropological Perspectives*, edited by Susanne Brandtstädter and Gonçalo D. Santos, 137–53. Abingdon, UK: Routledge, Taylor and Francis, 2009.

Stafford, Charles. *Separation and Reunion in Modern China*. Cambridge: Cambridge University Press, 2000.

Steinmüller, Hans. *Communities of Complicity: Everyday Ethics in Rural China*. New York: Berghahn, 2015.

Strand, David. *Rickshaw Beijing: City People and Politics in the 1920s*. Berkeley: University of California Press, 1989.

Terkel, Studs. *Hard Times: An Oral History of the Great Depression*. New York: Pantheon, 1970.

Thompson, Paul. *The Voice of the Past: Oral History*. Oxford: Oxford University Press, 1978.

Tian Zhuangzhuang. *The Blue Kite*. Produced by Beijing Film Studio, 1993. 180 mins.

Wachtel Nathan. "Introduction." *History and Anthropology* 2, no. 2 (1986): 207–24.

Wang Jian. "Remembering Miyun Reservoir, Oral History Interview." Translated by Madeleine Ross and Fang Li. *China Heritage Quarterly*, no. 16 (December 2008). http://www.chinaheritagequarterly.org/features.php?searchterm=016_miyun .inc&issue=016.

Wang Jun. *Cheng ji* [Records of a city]. Beijing: Sanlian, 2003.

Wang Zheng. "Gender, Employment and Women's Resistance." In *Chinese Society: Change, Conflict and Resistance*, edited by Elizabeth J. Perry and Mark Selden, 62–82. London: Routledge, 2000.

Wang Zheng. "Gender and Maoist Urban Reorganization." In *Gender in Motion: Divisions of Labor and Cultural Change in Late Imperial and Modern China*, edited by Bryna Goodman and Wendy Larson, 189–209. Lanham, MD: Rowman and Littlefield, 2005.

Weller, Robert P. "Salvaging Silence: Exile, Death and the Anthropology of the Unknowable." *Anthropology of This Century*, no. 19 (May 2017). http://aotcpress.com /articles/salvaging-silence/.

Wolf, Margery. *Women and the Family in Rural Taiwan*. Stanford, CA: Stanford University Press, 1972.

The World Bank in China Overview. September 2017. http://www.worldbank.org/en /country/china/overview#3.

Wu Hung. *Remaking Beijing: Tiananmen Square and the Creation of a Political Space*. London: Reaktion, 2005.

Wu Hung. "Zhang Dali's Dialogue: Conversation with a City." *Public Culture* 12, no. 3 (fall 2000): 749–68.

Wu Liangyong. *Rehabilitating the Old City of Beijing: A Project on the Ju'er Hutong Neighbourhood*. Vancouver: University of British Columbia Press, 1999.

Xie Kailing. "Embodying the Exemplary Gender Ideal: The Lives of China's Privileged Daughters." PhD diss., University of Edinburgh, 2018.

Xie Kailing. *Embodying Middle Class Gender Aspirations: Perspectives from China's Privileged Young Women*. London: Palgrave Macmillan, forthcoming.

Yang Jisheng. *Mubei: Zhongguo liushiniandai da jihuang jishi* [Tombstone: A chronicle of the Great Famine in China in the sixties]. Hong Kong: Cosmos, 2008. Translated by Stacy Mosher and Jian Guo as *Tombstone: The Untold Story of Mao's Great Famine*. London: Lane, 2012.

Yan Yunxiang. *The Flow of Gifts: Reciprocity and Social Networks in a Chinese Village*. Stanford, CA: Stanford University Press, 1996.

Yan Yunxiang. *Private Life under Socialism: Love, Intimacy, and Family Change in a Chinese Village, 1949–1999*. Stanford, CA: Stanford University Press, 2003.

Ye Wa and Joseph W. Esherick. *Chinese Archives: An Introductory Guide*. Berkeley: Institute of East Asian Studies, University of California, 1996.

Yu Xia and Xiang Zhou. "Income Inequality in Today's China." *Proceedings of the National Academy of Sciences of the United States of America* III, no. 19 (2014): 6928–33.

Zhu Mingde, ed. *Beijing chengqu jiaoluo diaocha* [An investigation of urban corners of Beijing]. Beijing: Social Sciences Academic, 2005.

Zou, John. "Cross-Dressed Nation: Mei Lanfang and the Clothing of Modern Chinese Men." In *Embodied Modernities: Corporeality, Representation, and Chinese Cultures*, edited by Fran Martin and Larissa Heinrich, 79–97. Honolulu: University of Hawai'i Press, 2006.

administrative detention system, 107–8, 243n2

agency: conservative orientations of, 71; definition of, 71; as dignity claim, 222; Huiming's, 180; Jia Yong's, 201–2; Li Fuying's, 154, 158–59, 201–2; Meiling's, 125, 127, 129; Old Mrs. Gao's, 67–72, 102; Wang Wenli's, 180; Xiao Hua's, 125–26; Young Gao's, 71–72; Zhao Yong's, 102

Ah Q, 101

Anagnost, Ann, 237n9

Beijing: future visions of, 190; 1950s, 228n5; post-Mao transformations, 1, 227nn1–2; socioeconomic differences in, 3; Ten Great Buildings, 2, 37; wages in, 56, 239n18. *See also* Dashalar; "old Beijing"; Qianmen dajie; Tian'anmen Square

Beijing Capital Museum, 190

The Blue Kite (Tian Zhuangzhuang), 243n6

book overviews, 3–4, 18–20

Braester, Yomi, 247n4

Brave Li, 59, 105, 112–14, 120–21

Buddhism, 90, 242n8

car ownership, 239n21

chaiqian (demolition and relocation): criticisms of, 13; and human rights, 195, 227n1, 232n4; legal responses to, 245n3; mark of, 31, 234n22; media coverage, 13; resident relocation, 37; resistance to, 232n4; socio-economic contexts, 99

chaiqian in Dashalar, 5; beginnings of, 39–40; changes brought, 22; compensation maximizing strategies, 195; difficulties faced, 13, 36, 230n39; discussing, difficulties with, 15; enforcement methods, 14–15; evacuation notices, 31–32, 39; impacts of, 40, 208; mark of, 31, *32*; media coverage, 230n40; *Meishi jie* film, 14; and Olympics preparation, 39–40; protests, lack of, 15, 231n46; relocation of residents, 65–66, 123; residents staying, 123, 244n2; resistance attempts, 15; results of, 213; uncertainties produced by, 64–65

chapter summaries, 18–20

Chen, Janet, 227n3

chengguan (local patrol officers): abuse and violence of, 131, 140, 144, 156, 216; attacks on, 245n9; income, 245n8; and pedicab drivers, 86, 141–42, 144

China: eviction laws, 230n40; and global economy, 74; income inequality in, 241n1; inequality in, 232n1; legal system, 154; market reform era, 209–10; National Day (1999), 235n43; poverty rates, 240n6; single child policy, 242n7; 60th anniversary, 194, 247n6

Ci Xi, 242n8

commercial success factors, 202

corruption: campaigns against, 8, 229n21, 234n28; in Dashalar, 142–43, 153–54, 156–57, 234n28; in detention centers, 135; factors enabling, 156–57; Li Fuying on, 145–46

Cui Yingjie, 245n9

face: in Jia Yong's narrative, 205; in local narratives, 223; in Meiling's narrative, 116–17, 128; and recognition, 103; Zhao Yong's concern with, 91–94, 102–3, 223

famine years, 8, 42, 48–50, 209, 234n26

fangsheng (releasing life), 90, 242n8

Feuchtwang, Stephan, 73, 204

filial piety and patriliny, 158

Five Antis, 8, 229n21

Fraser, Nancy, 223

Frisch, Michael, 6

Gamble, Sidney D., 235n31

gender: changing relations, 126; equality, 50, 210, 238n10; and market commercialization, 218; and recognition-seeking, 222–23; and *renqing* ethics, 205; roles, 181–82, 217–18; stereotypes, 242n8. *See also* men; women

generational differences: child-parent relationships, 159; in Dashalar, 217; and gender roles, 217–18; individualism, 160; opportunities, 217

global economy, neoliberal, 99–100

Great Leap Forward, 8–9, 21, 37, 39, 168, 209

Guo Yuhua, 237n9

Hall, Stuart, 12

healthcare costs, 55, 238n15

Hershatter, Gail, 4, 7

historiography, 207

history, 6, 207–10

Honig, Emily, 157

household registration system, 37

Hua Meiling. *See* Meiling

Huang Mingfang, 44, 62, 69, 105, 117–18, 183

Huiming: agency of, 180; on apartment blocks, 169; author's visits, 166, 169, 180; biography, 167–72; Communist Youth League ban, 170; courtship and marriage, 171–72; cultural capital of, 176, 179; and Cultural Revolution,

168–70; *dazayuan*, childhood, 167–68; *dazayuan* life, 161, 169, 174, 179, 182; disability allowance, 177–78, 180; disability of, 163–64, 167–68; employment, 161; employment history, 164; gender roles performed, 181–82; grandparents, 161, 167–68, 170, 172–73; household income, 164–65; husband, deference to, 175–76; husband, praise for, 166; living arrangements, 161–63, 168–69; on marriage, 173–76, 181; marriage of, 171–72, 174–76, 179–81; material welfare of, 178–80; nostalgia of, 179; optimism of, 169; parents, 167, 174; political and social interests, 176–77; son, 161, 168, 172–74; the state, view of, 177, 180; on women and gender roles, 175–76. *See also* Wang Wenli

human rights: and agency, 71; assertions of, 17; and *chaiqian*, 195, 227n1, 232n4; detention center violations of, 135, 243n2; the law defending, 154, 245n3; in local narratives, 220–21; migrants lacking, 156; and property confiscations, 119; state violations of, 227n1, 230n40, 232n4; Zhao Yong on, 74, 81, 86, 222

hutong (lanes and alleys): of Dashalar, 34, 40; and Dashilar Project, 40, 178; and *dazayuan*, 40; definition of, 1; in Jia Yong's photographs, 185, 192; life in, 40, 194, 212; loss of, 1, 163, 178, 182, 190; and Olympics preparation, 22; and tourism, 165, 190, 212; transformation of, 178

individualism, 126, 159–60

inequality, 21–22, 99–100, 241n1

infanticide, 236n2

informal economy, 241n2

Jia Yong: adolescence, 188; adoption, 186–87; agency of, 201–2; arrest of, 197; bar owned by, 184–85, 196; biography,

daughter-in-law, 149–51, 159–60, 220; fracturing of, 150–51; grandson, 150, 220; son, Young Li, 130, 147–51. *See also* Zhang Yuanchen

Li Fuying and Young Li: concerns regarding, 147–49; estrangement from, 149–52, 158–59, 220; filial support expectations, 153, 158–59; financing of, 147–48, 153, 156; and Li's detainment, 139–40, 158; relationship, nature of, 147, 150, 158

Lin Zexu, 166, 246n3

local narratives: agency in, 222; and the archive, 7, 12; and class backgrounds, 221; commonalities, 215; Cultural Revolution in, 209, 220–21; Dashalar in, 210–14; differences between, 17; employment in, 217–18; face, interest in, 223; family in, 216; gender differences in, 217–18; human rights in, 220–21; *versus* official discourses, 12–13; *versus* official histories, 207–10, 221; and "old Beijing," 212; the past, uses of, 214; place, meanings of, 213–14; police in, 12; PRC founding, 208–9; precarity and exclusion in, 214–15; recognition, desire for, 222–24; recognition claiming in, 218; redemptive aspects, 224; sharing of, reasons for, 221–22; the state in, 12, 208–10, 216–17; temporalities of, 210; and truth, 13; uses of, 69; and victimhood claims, 220; violence in, 8, 209, 220–21

Lu, Hanchao, 227n3

Lu Xun, 101

Ma, Zhao, 227n3, 234n25, 236nn2–3, 237n5

Mahmood, Saba, 71, 222

Mann, Susan, 17, 19, 231n49

Mao era: Cultural Revolution conflations, 220; dominant narratives of, 220; food scarcity, 50; Great Leap Forward, 8–9, 21, 37, 39, 168, 209; in local narratives, 208–9; native-place lodges, 235n40; official evaluations of, 232n2; urban underclass during, 1–2. *See also* Cultural Revolution

market economy, 21, 159–60, 209

market reform era, 99, 209–10

martial arts: Old Mrs. Zhao, 75, 79; *Yi Jing*, 241n4; Zhao Yong, 74, 92–93, 96, 103

masculinity: of Jia Yong, 183–84, 205; and Jia Yong's authority, 199, 202, 205; "old Beijing" values, 202; thick, 181, 200–201; Wang Wenli's, 181–82; Zhao Yong's, 102–3, 181, 219

Massey, Doreen, 243n5, 247n3

matriarchy, 42, 52–53, 70, 124, 238n14

Mei Lanfang, 232n7

Meiling: abortion, 107; adolescence, 105–6; agency of, 125, 127, 129; appearance, 104–5; arrest and imprisonment, 105, 107–8; and the author, 117–18, 121–22, 128; "bad crowd" period, 106–7, 111; biography, 105–11; birth, 106; and Brave Li, 59, 105, 112–14, 120–21; childhood, 105–6; credit card debt, 114–15, 117–18; Dashalar, relationship to, 122–23; *dazayuan* life, 110–11, 113, 119–20, 122–24; desire to leave, 118–19, 122, 211; dog, 104; employment, 105, 122; exchange, ideas of, 128; face-saving, 116–17, 128; as filial daughter, 121, 129; "good person" concept, 118, 128–29; home of, 104, 118; household income, 105; independence of, 106, 126, 219; labor of, 124–25; loan-seeking, 105–6, 116–18, 121, 128; marriage, 109–10; as matriarchal, 124; morality and virtue of, 111, 118, 128–29, 222; narratives of, 125–27, 129; and Old Mrs. Gao, 52–53, 60, 116, 128; pastry factory employment, 109; and patriarchy, 127, 129; personality, 105, 116, 118, 122–23; prostitution, 107, 111; and Qingmei, 111; self-identification, 129; self-isolation, 113, 211; as source of

Cultural Revolution, 43, 50–51; May 7 Company, 51, 238n11; old age, 42–43, 45, 52–53, 236n1, 238n15; hospitalizations, 45, 61–62; Tianqiao move, 42, 65–66, 71–72, 211; death of, 66, 71

Old Mrs. Gao's family: daughter, elder, 45, 48, 51, 53, 62; daughter, younger, 48, 62; father, 45–46; granddaughter, 56–58; husband, 48–49, 63; mother, 45–47; mother-in-law, 48; siblings, 46–48, 51; son, elder, 43, 48, 53, 60, 62, 64. *See also* Xiao Xi; Young Gao

Old Mrs. Zhao: and the author, 75, 92, 94–95; character of, 75; childhood, 79–80; countryside, return to, 80–81; deterioration of, 81; and gender equality policies, 210; as homebound, 77; martial arts ability, 75, 79; and police, 76; and PRC founding, 208; psychological issues, 74–75, 77, 80, 92, 97; and Qian, 84; reading ability, 79; Zhao's caring for, 75, 86, 91; Zhao's frustrations with, 75, 91–92. *See also* Zhao Yong

Old Wei, 144

Olympics preparation: beautification programs, 56, 239n17; Dashalar, effects on, 21–22, 26, 39–40, 211; debarment, 215; impact on *hutong*, 22; *versus* National Day (1999), 236n43; pedicab regulation, 140, 145; police violence, 141–42; Qianmen dajie refurbishment, 35

oral history, 3, 6, 11–12, 223–24

Ou Ning, 14, 35, 39, 123

outsiders, 156, 213, 245n7. *See also* migrants

patriarchy, 127, 219

patriliny, 158–59, 219–20

pedicabs: bans on, 140–41; and *chengguan*, 86, 141–42, 144; clients, 142; confiscations of, 144–45; in Dashalar, 141; Li Fuying and, 134, 138, 140–45; Old Wei,

144; origins of, 140–41; regulation of, 140, 141, 145; in Tian'anmen Square, 141; and tourism, 163, 165, 246n2; Wang Wenli's business, 163–65, 167

police: abuse and violence of, 135, 138, 216, 221; corruption, 131, 143; detention centers, 134–39, 244n3; and evictions, 15; income, 245n8; Jia Yong and, 197; Li Fuying and, 133–35, 222; in local narratives, 12; Meiling and, 108, 110, 113, 116; Old Mrs. Gao's husband, 49; pedicab confiscations, 144–45; Zhao Yong and, 222; and Zhao Yong's mother, 76. *See also chengguan*

Prakash, Gyan, 6

PRC founding, 208–9

Qian: and the author, 95; birth, 83; character of, 75; childhood, 83–84; daughter, 75, 84, 94–96; family caretaking, 75, 84; financial challenges, 85; flat of, 77; income sources, 85; marriage, first, 84; marriage to Zhao, 84; travel desires, 88, 94; Zhao, relationship with, 88, 102, 218–19. *See also* Zhao Yong

Qian, Sima, 17–18, 231n49

Qianmen dajie, 27; gentrification of, 29, 190, 215; location of, 22; opening of, 195, 211; refurbishment of, 29, 34, 233nn18–19; regulations, 27, 28; tourism, 195

Ransmeier, Johanna S., 227n3, 237n4

recognition, 103, 124, 218, 222–24

red dates, 237n8

renqing ethics, 103, 205

Rickshaw Boy (Lao She), 69, 240n2

rights. *See* human rights

Rofel, Lisa, 237n9

Roy, Ananya, 236n46

Salaff, Janet Weitzner, 1–2, 238n12

Sangren, P. Steven, 158–59, 219